SOUTH AMERICAN
ARCHÆOLOGY

PLATE I

PERU

POTTERY FROM NASCA

SOUTH AMERICAN ARCHÆOLOGY

AN INTRODUCTION TO THE ARCHÆ-
OLOGY OF THE SOUTH AMERICAN
CONTINENT WITH SPECIAL REFERENCE
TO THE EARLY HISTORY OF PERU. BY
THOMAS A. JOYCE, M.A. WITH NUMEROUS
ILLUSTRATIONS AND A MAP

Reprinted by

HACKER ART BOOKS

NEW YORK

1969

First Published

G. P. Putnam's Sons

New York 1912

———

Reprinted Hacker Art Books

1969

Library of Congress Catalog Card Number 70-78361

PREFACE

I T is not without great diffidence that I have ventured to compile the following chapters on the archæology of South America. The subject is one of great magnitude, and the literature dealing with it is vast. Besides this, there exist so many gaps in our knowledge, gaps which can only be filled by years of patient excavation, that the formation of theories is still a precarious task. At the same time it is useful to pass in review the work which has already been completed, with the object both of pointing out the missing links in the chain of evidence, and of stimulating further research by calling attention to the results already achieved. Again, much of the literature is scattered broadcast in the pages of scientific journals, and therefore escapes the notice of the general reader ; while the fact that a large proportion of it is in German, Spanish or Portuguese, renders it inaccessible to many would-be students. Thanks to the labours of Sir Clements Markham, backed by the Hakluyt Society, many of the early chroniclers have now been translated into English, but there exist numbers of more recent treatises, all of great value, written by investigators in South America, which are not likely to find a translator. This country has taken little part, in recent years, in the scientific exploration of the South American continent. Expeditions from Germany, France, Sweden and the United States have been productive of the most valuable results, but this rich field for archæological enterprise has been strangely neglected by England. The national collection contains a fairly representative series of objects illustrating the archæology of South America, including many specimens of great value ; but the collection is small, and some regions, such as the Argentine Republic and Brazil, are poorly represented, while certain classes of Peruvian pottery are entirely lacking.   If this book can in the smallest degree help to stimulate interest in the early remains of South America, some of which are among the most remarkable in the world, the purpose of the author will be achieved.   As for the book itself, no claim for completeness can be put forward ; I have conscientiously tried to neglect no important source of information, and if I have omitted any such I apologize, not so much to the reader, as to the worker whose re- searches have thus passed unnoticed by me.

To Dr. Uhle, the Director of the Museum at Lima, I owe a great debt of gratitude, not only for permission to publish certain of the illustrations, notably the frontispiece, but also for his kindness in discussing by correspondence a number of questions relative to the early period in Peru, and in generously contributing some essential information.   To Miss Breton I must also express my thanks, for permitting me to select from her sketches the fine water-colour which appears as Plate I ; and again to Col. F. H. Ward, for placing at my disposal his collection of South American photographs. To Dr. C. H. Read, P.S.A., of the British Museum I owe much, not only for his permission to photograph many of the objects in the national collection, but for his advice and instruction on innumerable points connected with this subject ; and to Mr. Henry Balfour, Curator of the Pitt-Rivers Museum at Oxford, I am indebted for the photograph of Peruvian skulls on Plate IX.   I wish also to thank Dr. E. A. Wallis Budge of the British Museum for the interest which he has taken in the book, which, in fact, owes its inception to him.   My acknowledgments are due also to the Editor of *The Times* for permission to republish part of an article which appeared in the South American supplement of September 27th, 1910. Finally I would thank Messrs. C. J. Praetorius and Norman H. Hardy, and also my wife, for the care they have expended on the pen-and-ink drawings which constitute not the least attractive feature of the volume.

T. A. JOYCE.

LONDON,
   March, 1912

CONTENTS

ILLUSTRATIONS

xiii

ILLUSTRATIONS

ILLUSTRATIONS IN THE TEXT

ILLUSTRATIONS

MAPS

South American Archæology

INTRODUCTION

CERTAIN of the early chroniclers who wrote of South America, when they did not take the Flood as their starting-point, prefaced their remarks with a disquisition on the existence of the antipodes. Though, at the present date, either of these topics would hardly be regarded as relevant to the subject, a short summary of the physical history and geographical features of the continent is necessary for a proper understanding of its archæology. Shaped rather like an inverted pear, South America lies with the great bulk of its territory within the tropics, but with its southern extremity within measurable distance of the antarctic circle. Though it forms at the present time a single land-mass, it must, at an early period of geological history, have been a group of large islands, separated by a wide inland sea. The greatest of these in extent lay to the east, and is represented to-day by the Andes, stretching in an unbroken line from Panama to the Straits of Magellan, and sending an off-shoot eastward along the north coast of Venezuela. Greater in area than this, but occupying fewer degrees of latitude, was another island, which constitutes at the present time the highlands of Brazil, and bore a striking resemblance in outline to the entire continent of which it was destined later to form a part. A third island, smaller than the other two, lay to the north of the last, where the highlands of the Guianas

B

attain their greatest elevation. The great sea which they enclosed, a sort of American Mediterranean, was thus separated from the Pacific by the long Andean chain, but communicated with the Atlantic by channels represented to-day by the basins of the Orinoco, the Amazon, and the Rio de la Plata. As time went on, through the gradual elevation of the Andes and the deposits of alluvial soil washed down from the great islands, this inland sea gradually disappeared, leaving as its only traces the mighty river systems above mentioned, and the swamps about their water-sheds. Even at the present time these river systems are connected at their sources, the Orinoco with the Amazon, and the Amazon with the Parana ; and at the divide between the two latter, the so-called lake Mojos, at certain seasons of the year the country becomes inundated to such an extent that it presents in miniature a picture of the primeval inland sea. As the ground appeared above the surface of the waters, it became covered with vegetation, still existing in the great forest of the Amazon basin. Even the Patagonian plateau, now desert, or covered only with grass and low scrub, must have been wooded, since the remains of great sloths have been found there, animals which are forest-dwellers. But here, as the land continued to rise, a process of desiccation set in, which, combined with the more southerly latitude, proved fatal to the larger forms of vegetation and the fauna which sought their shelter.

But Patagonia is not the only region where this has occurred. The narrow west coast of South America, between the Andes and the Pacific, is for the most part a waterless region. Here rain is exceptional, and beyond the range of the few short rivers which empty themselves into the Ocean on this side, the country is desert. The cause of this lies in the fact that the easterly trade-winds, after supplying with rain the eastern portion of the continent, deposit their remaining moisture upon the Andes, which thus rob the coast of its rainfall. But there is reason to believe that at one time the Andes were several thousand feet lower, and did not offer an insurmountable barrier to the rains. At this period the coast must have been wooded, and a forest must have stood where now is the waterless desert of Tarapaca, a forest of which the only traces are the numerous skeletons of anteaters which once it harboured. Further evidence of the gradual elevation of the country is afforded by the presence of beaches now raised many feet above the sea-level and some miles from the coast ; while it is evident that this elevation has been proceeding since the advent of man, since traces of his settlements have been discovered in these raised beaches. At points along the coast, however, a good deal of erosion has taken place and the victory has sometimes rested with the sea.

The history of the Brazilian highlands has been in the main the converse of the Andean region, since they seem to be the remains of mountain country which once attained a far more imposing elevation than at present, but which has been greatly reduced by atmospheric agencies. The coast, too, seems to have sunk in places, so that the Tocantins, which was once a tributary of the Amazon, now communicates direct with the Atlantic. But along the more southern coast of Brazil the land has encroached locally upon the sea, a fact to which the presence of great shell-heaps at some distance from the coast bears witness. Where such variety of physical features prevails, a similar variety of climate must necessarily follow. Within the tropics, on the low-lying coast and in the forested plains, the temperature is extreme, and aggravated in the latter region by the excessive moisture ; but in the uplands, especially the valleys of the Andes, conditions more akin to those of the temperate zone prevail ; while on the loftier plateaux the cold is often intense and cereals cannot ripen there. The open plains of the extra-tropical region are in the main extremely healthy, but the country, as we proceed south, is more suited for grazing than agriculture.

Such, very briefly, is the environment, and the question of man now arises. The earliest traces of man are found in the southern portion of the continent, in Buenos Aires and Patagonia, and certain of these date back to quaternary times. Along the coasts of Peru, Chile, and Brazil are found the remains of a very early population, who lived chiefly on shellfish, and who were probably related to, and even contemporary with, the early inhabitants of the country further south. All these tribes were long-headed, and had no knowledge of metals, but used rough implements of shell, bone, and stone. Later there came another wave of people, distinguished by round heads, who, with the Andes as their principal home, gradually drove the early population from the eastern half of the continent, until the inhospitable regions of Tierra del Fuego and the dense forests of the Amazon alone afforded them shelter. Whence the two types of man came is a question which cannot be discussed with profit until geologists are agreed as to the relation of America to the other continents ; but it is possible that the long-headed race travelled *viâ* Greenland from Europe, and that the round-heads crossed the Behring Straits from Asia. But both these immigrations must have occurred at a time so remote that the invaders brought with them no implements, customs, or even language, that was characteristically " European " or " Asiatic," in the cultural senses of the words. The evolution of the various forms of culture characteristic of the different regions of South America was, as always, in accordance with environment. In the stifling forests but little progress was made, and some of the tribes remained at the lowest ebb of culture, without knowledge of weaving or pottery.

Here agriculture was impossible, and hunting the only means of subsistence. The inhabitants of the open plains were more advanced, though they were compelled to lead a nomadic existence in search of the game on which they lived ; and the conditions of a nomadic life preclude the formation of organized communities in which alone a high state of culture can be evolved. In fact, the only environment suitable to be the birthplace of a civilization are the fertile valleys of the Andes, where the temperature of the tropics is tempered by the elevation, the soil is fertile, and water-supply constant. Here man can provide himself with means of subsistence, not indeed with the fatal facility of the tropics elsewhere, which seems to discourage all enterprise, but without having to expend the whole of his energies on providing the necessary food-supply, and so being left with no leisure to apply to the perfection of arts and crafts. And, in fact, it is just in this region that South American culture reached its zenith, culminating in the organized empire of the Inca, which the Spaniards found upon their arrival. The exact position of the Inca class, the people originally dominant in the valley of Cuzco, has often been misapprehended. There is a tendency to regard this people as the *fons et origo* of all advanced culture ; as the creators of an elaborate and thoroughly efficient form of imperial government and the inaugurators of a communistic social system admirably suited to the needs and characters of their subjects. As the rulers of the empire they have been viewed as in some way antithetically opposed to the tribes which they conquered, and the fact that they were originally merely one of a large number of similar tribes has been often overlooked. Neither the form of government, nor the social system, nor the religion of the empire were invented by them, but were common to all the Andean tribes from Colombia to the Argentine highlands, and the rapidity of the Inca conquest was due chiefly to the fact that a general homogeneity of culture and beliefs underlay all the local differences which might be expected to exist between tribe and tribe. The picture afforded by the Colombian tribes who lived in the highland valleys of Cundinamarca is remarkably illustrative of this fact, and it is well known that the Inca never penetrated so far north ; and, to the south, the Inca empire stopped short where the nomadic tribes began, that is to say, where the common Andean culture ceased. The genius of the Inca states-man lay not in the creation of new forms of govern-ment, but in the adaptation of a constitution devised for small states to the needs of an extended empire.

From the cultural point of view, therefore, the peoples of South America may be divided into three—the dwellers in the Andes, the nomads of the plains, and the inhabitants of the forests ; and the order in which they are named is their order in the scale of culture.

In the use of the term " Archæology " as applied to America far greater latitude must be allowed than when the Old World is under discussion. Though Ameri-can archæology goes back to quaternary times, and deals with many remains which are prehistoric in the sense that they have no history, yet it is usually allowed to include within its sphere all those manifestations of higher forms of culture which the European discov-erers found flourishing in the sixteenth century, and which in so short a time became obsolete. This being so, it is obvious that a work such as this must deal principally with the inhabitants of the Andean region. Here alone we find an advanced form of culture, and here alone was preserved any traditional history of the times prior to the discovery. For the rest the archæ-ologist must gather what evidence he can from pottery fragments and stone implements. As will be seen in the later chapters, this evidence does not amount to very much, partly owing to the fact that scientific exploration of vast areas has not yet been effected, and partly because so many of the finds do not from their position afford any indication of their date. A great deal, however, remains to be done in the way of investigating the traces left by the tribes of lower culture, but it is not surprising that archæologists should have turned their attention principally to those regions where the arts and crafts had reached a higher stage of development, and where historical evidence could be applied to the elucidation of the remains and *vice versâ*.

The present book deals only with the archæology, as defined above, of the actual continent of South America. From one point of view it should also include that of the Isthmus of Panama and of the Antilles. The tribes of the Isthmus seem to be connected culturally with those of Colombia, a connection which appears especially in the pottery and gold-work of the Chiriqui. But Antioquia and Chiriqui are separated by forests which probably at no time sheltered a population of any numbers, and when we reach the Chiriqui Lagoon we come in contact with another influence, that of the Nahua tribes of Mexico. In the Antilles are found traces of an early population who seem to have been a branch of the South American Arawak, and who were exterminated, as far as the Lesser Antilles are concerned, by later Carib immigrants, also coming from South America. But for reasons of space it has been considered desirable to confine attention to what is geographically the continent of South America.

CHAPTER I—COLOMBIA

THE north-western corner of the South American continent, known to-day as Colombia, affords a picture of great geographical diversity. The twin chain of the Andes, shortly after entering Colombian territory from Ecuador, divides into three branches. Of these, the eastern branch continues for some distance unbroken, but later splits up into several chains which extend through Venezuelan territory to the sea. The western branch runs parallel with the coast until it reaches the gulf of Darien; while the central branch dies away in the marshy plains of the two northernmost provinces of Colombia, Bolivar and Magdalena. These three chains or *cordilleras* confine, not, as throughout the greater part of Peru, a series of tablelands, but two deep valleys along which run two important rivers northwards, to the west the Cauca, to the east the Magdalena. The courses of the two are approximately parallel, until, after the disappearance of the central cordillera, the Cauca joins the Magdalena, which is the larger of the two, being, indeed, the fourth longest river in South America. East of the eastern cordillera is a vast series of plains sloping gradually to the Orinoco and Amazon.

Corresponding to this geographical diversity, Colombia possesses an equal diversity of climate. In spite of the tropical latitude the temperature of the tablelands is extremely pleasant and uniform ; in the valleys and the eastern plains the heat is excessive, with a mean of 86 or 88 Fahr. ; on the coasts, the temperature, though lower, is still very high, and is aggravated by the dampness attendant on a tremendous rainfall. Amid this variety we may safely seek for the remains of such culture as existed among the early inhabitants, not in the torrid regions of the coast and eastern plains, where the conditions are more favourable to vegetable than human development, but on the elevated slopes and tablelands of the cordilleras.

The Spaniards on their arrival found the country peopled by a large number of tribes differing considerably in language, and representing various stages of cultural development. Of the vast majority of these little or nothing is known save the name alone, and as no systematic attempt has yet been made to explore the country from an archæological point of view, it is impossible to speak with certainty as to the inter-relation of the more advanced sections of the population. From the scanty materials at hand in museums and from the indications given by early Spanish writers, four culture centres may be distinguished, all situated on the higher ground bordering the valleys of the Cauca and Magdalena rivers. The first and most northerly of these lies in Antioquia, where the Tamahi and Nutabi tribes had developed agriculture and attained some proficiency in the weaving and dyeing of cotton ; the second is found to the south, in the country around Cartago, where lived the Quimbaya, the most skilled of all the gold-working tribes ; the third, around Popayan, of which the Coconuco may be taken as the representative tribe ; and fourthly, the highland region on either side of the modern provinces of Boyaca and Cundinamarca to the east of the Magdalena, where the Chibcha or Muisca people had attained a political development far in advance of the rest of the Colombians.

Though the respective cultures of these tribes differed in detail, yet underlying the differences was a very strong similarity, a similarity which extended also to the culture of the Peruvian highlands. In fact, when due allowance is made for the difference in environment, we may take it that the more advanced Colombians afford a good illustration of the condition of the various tribes of Peru before the Inca welded them into a single empire.

Surrounding the peoples of higher culture were many tribes, some possibly as advanced as they, but the majority more primitive, some even in the lowest stages of savagery. A long list might be given of the names of these, but it would be of little interest to the general reader, especially as it would, for the most part, be unaccompanied by any details concerning their manners and customs ; it will be better to concentrate attention on the more civilized peoples concerning whom most information can be gathered from the accounts of early historians and from the remains in musems.

Little can be said of the respective origins of the Colombian tribes ; the gold-work of the Cauca valley and some of the pottery show considerable similarity to the corresponding manufactures from the Chiriqui people of the Isthmus (see Pl. IV) ; it is stated also that a language akin to that of the Chibcha was spoken by the early inhabitants of the high ground on the sea-coast, east of the mouth of the Magdalena river ; but the Chibcha, to judge from their traditions as recorded, seem to have regarded themselves as indigenous. Certain tribes, such as the Quimbaya, and the Muzo and Colima, western neighbours and enemies of the Chibcha, claimed definitely to be immigrants from the north,[1] and it is said that a certain tribe called Achagua settled near Popayan after wandering all the way from Venezuela. Further evidence of the westerly and southerly

[1] Further evidence of this is contained in the fact that two hills, sacred in the eyes of the Chibcha, were situated in Muzo territory ; thither the Chibcha would make secret pilgrimages by night to perform certain rites, even at the risk of being killed by the hostile Muzo. The explanation would seem to be that this tract of country belonged originally to the Chibcha, but was seized by Muzo invaders.

drift of tribes is contained in the native tradition, preserved by Oliva, that the early inhabitants of South America landed first at Caracas in Venezuela and spread thence along the coast to Ecuador. All that can be said is that while there are traditions of a southerly and south-westerly movement of peoples, there is no single account of a movement in the reverse direction ; but at the same time, to speak generally, there is no definite break in the continuity of culture between Colombia and Ecuador.

Of the origin of the world and themselves the Chibcha gave the following account. In the beginning all was darkness, until a Being, named Chiminigagua, created light and a number of great birds; these birds, acting under his instructions, seized the light in their beaks and distributed it over the earth. Subsequently Chiminigagua created the sun and moon. Like many creators in primitive mythology, no actual worship was paid him, his work was done and he was not regarded as a force to be reckoned with; but the sun and moon, his handiwork, were the centre of an elaborate cult. Shortly after this a woman emerged from a lake, called Iguaque, north-east of Tunja, bearing in her arms an infant boy ; this woman, called variously Bachue and Furachogue, came down to the plain, where she lived until the boy grew up. She then married him and bore innumerable children, changing her abode from time to time until the land was peopled. Finally she returned to the lake with her husband, and the pair disappeared beneath the waters in the form of snakes. Bachue, afterwards worshipped as one of the gods, is believed to have given men their first laws and form of worship. A different creation legend was current locally at Tunja. Two chiefs named respectively Iraca and Ramiriqui, uncle and nephew, lived in the primeval darkness. Feeling lonely they made men from yellow earth and women from a certain plant; Iraca then bade Ramiriqui ascend to heaven and become the sun, while he himself became the moon. It is possible that the first part of the story may have been introduced from the Muzo, who maintained the tradition that a ghost or shadow named Aré formed faces of sand and sprinkled them with water, whereupon they became men and women ; the latter part of the Tunja myth may be based upon local pride, since Ramiriqui was the name of the early capital of the district of which Tunja became the later centre, and Iraca was the site of one of the holiest temples of the Chibcha country.

The next feature of Chibcha mythological history is one common to all the cultured peoples of Central and South America, namely the arrival of a white culture-hero who gave the people laws and instructed them in arts and industries. Such is the Quetzalcoatl of the Nahua, the Uiracocha of the Peruvians, and the Tsuma of Venezuela. This personage, known variously as Bochica, Nemterequeteba, and Xue, is said to have come from the east and to have entered the territory of Bogota at Pasca on its southern border, and finally to have disappeared at Sogamoso or at Iza, east of Tunja, where his footprint was shown on a rock. His worship was universal in Chibcha territory and many temples were raised to him. The Tamahi of Antioquia had a culture-heroine named Dabeciba. The preaching of Bochica enjoined a serious mode of life, and his laws were severe, but it is related that shortly after his disappearance a woman appeared, none knew whence, named Huitaca or Chie, whose teaching bore a very different complexion ; she bade the people rejoice and indulge to the utmost in dances and revelry, but her rather frivolous turn of mind was displeasing to the creator, who is said on this occasion to have interfered with the affairs of men and to have turned her into an owl. In anger at this treatment, Huitaca is related to have aided Chibchachum, the special god of the Bogota section of Chibcha, to cause a great flood. The inhabitants took refuge in the mountains, and in their distress called upon Bochica, who appeared in the rainbow and, with a golden rod, opened a passage for the waters in the mountains. Bochica further punished Chibchachum by compelling him to bear the earth, Atlas-like, upon his shoulders, but the god often grows weary and shifts his burden from one shoulder to the other, causing an earthquake. A deluge myth was also current in Antioquia among the Tamahi, and indeed such stories are found all over America.

The Chibcha alone of the Colombian tribes have left a history ; meagre as the details are, they are nevertheless of great interest in so far as they show the first steps in the creation of what might, but for the arrival of the Spaniards, have become an empire. At the moment of the conquest there were five centres of power in the Chibcha country. In the extreme north was Guanenta, ruled by a chief of that title ; to the south-east was Tundama, also ruled by an eponymous chieftain ; south of Tundama lay Sogamoso, the smallest principality, again ruled by a chief who took his title from his territory ; south and west was the important district of Tunja, the ruler of which bore the title of Zaque ; and finally in the extreme south lay the most powerful state, that of Bogota, under the leadership of a chief entitled Zipa. All these chieftains were emperors on a small scale, exercising suzerainty over a number of petty chiefs who were supreme in their own districts, and succeeded to power in accordance with their ancient laws, but whose accession required ratification at the hands of their respective overlords. But the country was not always divided after this fashion ; the history of Chibcha territory as it has come down to us is largely the story of the rise of the formerly insignificant and dependent chief of Bogota, and the incorporation in his sphere of influence of several independent chiefs and their respective territories. Iraca and Ramiriqui, as has been seen from the early mythology, seem to have been important states in early days ; indeed the earliest Chibcha chief known to history is Nompanem of Iraca, who codified the laws of Bochica immediately after his disappearance. As Nompanem had no male heirs he was followed by his sister Bumanguay and her husband, a man of Firavitoba. The next, or a later, chief, named Idacansas, claimed supernatural power over the elements and diseases ; his fame waxed great, and his kingdom and the temple of Iraca acquired a reputation for holiness and attracted many pilgrims. After the death of Idacansas a rather remarkable event occurred; it is possible that the combination of civil and religious authority acquired by him appeared dangerous to the surrounding chiefs, and they took measures to prevent such authority from falling into the hands of a man who might use it against them. Whatever the reason, the fact remains that the normal succession was interrupted, and four chiefs were appointed hereditary electors, their choice being limited to the inhabitants (presumably the ruling families or prominent men) of Firavitoba and Tobaza alternately. So carefully was the rule observed that on one occasion when a man of the former town usurped the power out of turn, the electors made war upon him and killed him. If the electors were unable to agree on the candidate, the chief of Tundama was called in to settle the question.

Ramiriqui, however, soon lost its important position at the hands of a chief named Garanchacha, the reputed son of the Sun and a daughter of the chief of Guacheta in the south-west of the Chibcha country. This Garanchacha killed the chief of Ramiriqui in revenge for the death of one of his attendants, and usurped his kingdom, later removing the seat of government to Tunja. This legend is recounted only by Simon, who says that Garanchacha was still ruling when the Spaniards entered the country, a statement which, from other evidence, is contrary to fact. Elsewhere we hear of other Zaque of Tunja : Hunsahua, who married his sister and thus inaugurated a custom which was observed by his successors, a custom which was also found among the Inca ; Tomangata, who is said to have possessed a tail and four ears, and to have been granted power by the Sun to change men into beasts ; Tutasua his nephew ; and lastly Michua and Quemuenchatocha mentioned below in connection with the history of Bogota. So powerful was the Zaque of Tunja that it has been said that at one time he was the overlord of the whole of the Chibcha country ; this, however, does not seem to be likely. Another point of importance was Guatabita, which, even more than Iraca, may be regarded as the religious centre of the whole of the Chibcha country ; here were held periodical religious ceremonies, to which came pilgrims from all the Chibcha tribes, and during which all hostilities were suspended. In early times Guatabita had probably been an independent principality, but later it seems to have fallen under the influence of Tunja, later still of Bogota. In fact the whole of the struggle between the Zaque of Tunja and the Zipa of Bogota appears to have resulted from the determination of the latter to secure control of Guatabita and Iraca, which, from a religious point of view, were the two most important villages of the southern Chibcha country.

The exact position of Bogota at the time of its rise towards the end of the fifteenth century is not quite clear ; one account seems to make its ruler the vassal of Guatabita, the other, of Tunja. In either case the inhabitants were well qualified to make a bid for power ; for years they had been engaged in hostilities with the warlike Panche and Muzo to the west and north-west respectively, and they had thus developed into better fighters than the rest of the Chibcha. Their ruler at this moment, Saguanmachica, was a bold and able general, as ambitious as he was capable. While his pre-decessors had been content to extend their power slowly, absorbing the weaker chiefs on their borders, he boldly attacked and reduced most of the more powerful rulers of the southern part of Chibcha territory. Finally Guatabita took alarm and sent a force against the Zipa, but the latter prevailed and carried the war into the territory of Guatabita. The latter then appealed to the Zaque of Tunja, Michua, but even this powerful ruler was unable to lend material assistance. According to one story the Zipa conquered Guatabita by treacherously breaking the truce imposed at the season of the great festival, but however this may be, an incursion of the Panche, and the revolt of certain lately-conquered chiefs in the neighbourhood of Bogota, forced Saguanmachica to divide his forces, and for the moment Guatabita and the Zaque were able to resume the offensive. After some years' struggle the Zipa was again free to resume his attempt on Guatabita, but only to fall in a pitched battle, in which the Zaque Michua also lost his life. But though the inaugurator of the scheme of conquest was dead, the Bogotans found a worthy successor in Nemequene, who speedily suppressed all attempts at revolt on the part of his immediate neighbours, and compelled the Panche to keep within their border. Finally Guatabita fell to him by a stratagem. The inhabitants of that region were famed for their gold-work, and their services were in request in many parts of Chibcha territory. To prevent serious de-population the ruler had made a regulation that every chief who obtained a goldsmith from his country must replace him by two of his own men, and the Zipa took advantage of this ordinance to fill the court of the chief of Guatabita with his own retainers. He made a forced march upon Guatabita; his men rose to his assistance, and the territory of Guatabita fell into his hands, the chief and all his relations being killed. Following up his success Nemequene next proceeded against the Zaque Quemuenchatocha and the chief of Iraca; a fierce battle was fought, but while fortune was still in the balance he received a severe wound and was obliged to retire, dying shortly afterwards. His nephew Tisquesusa, however, resumed the campaign, sending an army against Tunja under the command of an able general named Saque-saxigua, but the arrival of the Spanish interrupted operations, and Tisquesusa himself fell in an engagement with the white invaders.

Whether the rulers of Bogota would have succeeded ultimately in extending their rule over the whole of the Chibcha it is difficult to say ; so far they had been hampered by continual incursions on the part of a war-like and unsubdued foe on their borders, as well as by the continual revolt of neighbouring chiefs. From the former danger the Inca were free, from the latter they suffered much in the early days of conquest ; but the Inca possessed one advantage which the Zipa never had, their claim to divine origin ; and the religious character which this claim gave to their wars of conquest, was of inestimable value to them in dealing with tribes so susceptible to supernatural influences as the Andean races of South America. It is possible that the possession of Guatabita and Iraca, the two chief religious centres, might have given the Zipa the prestige they lacked, and it is certain that the conquest of Tunja, which appeared probable as matters stood, would have increased their temporal power enormously. Whether fate would have granted to Bogota, as to the Peruvians, the rulers capable of consolidating its power remains of course an unsolved question ; but at least the first steps towards empire had been taken with a courage and determination worthy of ultimate success.

Politically speaking, the Colombians were in a low stage of evolution. With the exception of the Chibcha

c

they were ruled by independent petty chiefs, and history shows that even the Chibcha had not advanced very far in the science of government. The Quimbaya, among whom the arts and crafts had attained a higher level than among the Chibcha, were still living, it is stated, under the rule of sixty petty chieftains at the time of the conquest ; these chieftains would usually unite under the leadership of one of their number in order to repel a common foe, but they were perfectly ready to fight among themselves when peace reigned along their borders.

The chiefs of the Chibcha were all absolute monarchs ; they made their own laws, carried on the civil government, and directed warlike operations, as far as is known, with entire irresponsibility. In matters of religion too they exercised considerable control, since the appointment of the priests lay in their hands ; in fact, no small portion of their power was derived from the semi-divine state with which they encircled themselves. No subject dared look his ruler in the face, but when in his presence turned aside or assumed a stooping attitude ; no messenger might appear before him without bearing in his hand some gift as a ceremonial acknowledgment of his high rank. Regulations somewhat similar were observed in the Inca court. The Zipa of Bogota, perhaps for the very reason that he was a *parvenu* among the overlords, maintained a state which in a small way resembled that of the divine rulers of Peru ; his garments were of the finest cotton, his throne was of gold studded with emeralds, and he travelled in a litter hung with golden plates, preceded by officials who removed all obstacles, spread textiles and scattered flowers in his path. His head-dress was of gold and a golden crescent ornamented his brow ; nose- and ear-ornaments were of the same metal, and also the breastplate he bore upon his chest (Pl. IV). Though the power of a chief was absolute in his territory, and no detail was beneath his cognizance,[1] it is probable that no ruler would have ventured directly to contravene the traditional customary laws handed down from the legendary legislators, though he might modify these or make new ordinances.

All the great chiefs, of Bogota, Tunja, Guatabita, Iraca, and elsewhere, possessed pleasure palaces, like those of the Inca, a little removed from their respective capitals, whither they retired to refresh themselves after the cares of State, to bathe in hot or cold springs, and to enjoy the society of their numerous wives.

But if the position of a chief in power might be regarded as enviable, he was forced to undergo a very severe probation before he could enter upon a life of despotic ease. Office was hereditary in the female line, that is to say, a chief was succeeded normally by his sister's son, his own sons receiving only a portion of his personal property. In default of nephews on the sister's side, the power devolved upon the brother next in age; if there were no heir, an independent chief would designate his successor before his death, but in the case of a dependent chief, the successor was chosen by the overlord. In any case the succession of a dependent had to be ratified by his superior. In the territory of Bogota the chieftainship of Chia, due north of Bogota, was always conferred upon the heir of the Zipa, just as the title "Prince of Wales" is borne by the heir to the British throne. The origin of this practice is explained in the following legend. The brother of an early chief of Chia had an intrigue with one of the royal women; his guilt was discovered and he was sentenced to impalement, a fate which he escaped by flight. He took refuge at the court of the Zipa and eventually became a successful general in

---

[1] It is said that if a subject of the Guatabita wished to wear a dress of a pattern different from that which was customary, he was obliged to obtain his lord's approval and receive the new garment from his hands.

his service. As the Zipa had no heirs, he designated the warrior as his successor, and at his death the former fugitive became lord of Bogota and overlord of his brother who had condemned him. The brother in fear sent his mother and sister to intercede, and it was finally arranged that the son of the sister should be heir to the chiefdom of Chia, and subsequently to that of Bogota. From that time the chief of Chia has always succeeded to the throne of Bogota. As said above, the heir to a chiefdom was obliged to submit to a severe probation. For five years or more he was secluded in a temple, whence he issued only by night; he mortified the flesh with frequent scourgings and fasts, and abstained from meat, salt, and *aji* (red pepper, a very favourite condiment); he was bound by oath to confess any breach of the stringent regulations with which his life was hedged, and severe penances were imposed on him. At the end of this trying period his nose and ears were pierced for the ornaments which his rank entitled him to bear, and he made an offering of golden figures of animals to the gods.

The ceremonies attending the installation of a chief were conducted with great state; and in this connection special allusion must be made to the rites performed when the chief of Guatabita ascended to power. Not only was the ceremonial particularly elaborate, but it gave rise to the stories of *el Dorado* which so fired the imagination of the early conquerors and gave such impetus to the exploration of the interior. According to Fresle the population of the neighbourhood repaired to the sacred lake of Guatabita clad in their finest ornaments of gold and feathers. Innumerable sacrificial fires were kindled on the banks, and the lake was encircled with a cloud of incense. The ruler-elect was divested of his garments, anointed with an adhesive earth, and powdered with gold-dust. Attended by his four principal sub-chiefs he embarked upon a reed raft orna-

mented with gold and furnished with four braziers for
incense ; at his feet was piled a mound of gold and
emeralds, and amidst the shouts of the multitude, and
the sound of whistles (Pl. IV, 6) and other instruments,
he proceeded to the middle of the lake. There he
plunged into the waters and washed off the offering of
gold-dust, and the gold and emeralds were thrown in at
the same time, the four chiefs making offerings on their
own account. The raft then returned and the proceedings terminated with the revelry and *chicha*-drinking so
dear to the heart of the Colombians.

Tribute in gold and textiles was exacted by the chiefs
from their subjects, and the method of dealing with
defaulters was decidedly original ; when a man failed to
send his due contribution, a court attendant together
with a bear or puma was quartered upon him, and he
was further forced to give a cloth garment for each day
that he was in arrears; it is probable that he made
great efforts to rid himself of such undesirable "men in
possession." In some places less severe measures were
taken, the defaulter's fire was extinguished and he was
not permitted to rekindle it until the debt was paid.
The customary law, which was preserved by oral tradition, was on the whole severe ; in Guatabita the punishment for most crimes was death; the code of Nompanem imposed the capital penalty in cases of homicide,
but lesser crimes were punished with flogging the first
time, infamy the second, and infamy extending to the
relations of the culprit the third. Cowards were compelled to assume female dress and perform the work
of women. Women suspected of infidelity were usually
forced to eat red pepper until they confessed the
name of their lover, after which their agony was alle-
viated with a draught of water and they were killed,
unless they were ransomed by the man named. Theft
was punished with stripes on the first two occasions, but
on the third the offender was compelled to look the chief

in the face, a proceeding which branded him with perpetual infamy. The mutilation of hands, noses and
ears was also practised occasionally as a punishment.
In the case of offenders of higher rank the punishments
were lighter, and consisted in tearing the garments or
cutting the hair, but the disgrace attending the penalty
was greater in proportion to the rank of the culprit.

As may be gathered, high rank and purity of blood
were held in great estimation, and a wide gulf separated the nobles from the commoners ; the upper classes
possessed many privileges, mostly connected with the
wearing of certain ornaments, which they held in virtue
of their station; others, such as the right to be carried
in a litter, could only be granted by one of the great
chiefs.

Slavery existed as an institution, at least among the
Quimbaya and Chibcha, but, as among most primitive
peoples, the slaves appear to have been well treated.
Among the Chibcha the slaves seem to have been native-
born prisoners of war, the subjects of some hostile chief
captured in fight. As a rule, at any rate in the Bogota
region, men so taken were sent to fight the national
enemy, the Panche and Colima, serving as archers.

A plurality of wives appears to have been permitted
throughout Colombia, but the "table of prohibited degrees" varied from one locality to another. In the
neighbourhood of Cartago a man's first cousin seems
to have been regarded as his natural mate, but in the
Zipa's territory no marriages were permitted within the
second degree of consanguinity. In the Tunja district,
however, even marriage with a sister was not forbidden.
The Panche were the most particular of all, since the
man was compelled to seek a wife outside his sub-tribe.
The intending husband was obliged by custom to hand
over a price to his prospective father-in-law, and the
bride brought no dowry save her ornaments and a quantity of chicha.

The Chibcha wife seems to have enjoyed rather unusual privileges ; on the authority of Jimenez de Que-
sada, Piedrahita relates that she was permitted to beat
her husband, though the number of lashes she could in-
flict was limited to six. The chief wife, moreover, that
is to say the first married, had even greater power. If
she so willed she might on her death-bed condemn her
husband to chastity for a certain period, even up to five
years. Children, except, apparently, among the Quimbaya, were regarded as belonging to the mother's family;
this fact is seen in the custom by which a man inherited
from his maternal uncle (except in the case of sons of
free men and slave women), and also in the ordinance which compelled a man, who lost a wife and child
at birth, to pay one-half of his property as compensation to the woman's relatives. When a child was born
a ceremony was often performed which was supposed
to give an indication of the fortune which might pur-
sue him throughout life. A tuft of cotton, moistened
with the mother's milk, was wrapped in grass and
thrown into a stream; six chosen swimmers immediately
plunged into the water and tried to seize it before the
bundle became unrolled. If they were successful, the
omen was good, and the parents rejoiced in the certainty that the infant would be lucky. Twins were
regarded as a proof of inconstancy and were killed.

The various peoples of Colombia appear to have had
but little intercourse with their respective neighbours,
and that chiefly of a warlike nature ; our knowledge
of friendly relations between tribes is confined mainly
to the facts that the Quimbaya obtained gold from their
neighbours in exchange for salt, and that the southern
Chibcha procured the same metal from tribes on the
Magdalena, below Neiva, in barter for salt, textiles, and
emeralds. Within the borders of their own territory,
however, the Chibcha at least were energetic traders ;
periodical markets were established at many of the

larger villages, and even a kind of currency was in vogue. The existence of this currency, the only thing of the kind in South America, is attested by several of the early chroniclers. It consisted of gold discs, of which the value was estimated by measuring against the first joint of the thumb ; besides being employed in commerce it was also used by the chiefs subordinate to the Zipa and Zaque in the payment of their tribute.

Even the military operations of the more civilized peoples seem to have been confined within their own borders. Certainly the Quimbaya at one period undertook a war of conquest when they exterminated the aborigines of the country where they were found by the Spaniards ; but in historical times they had sadly degenerated, and confined their energies to guarding against the attacks of their fiercer and more savage neighbours, always avoiding a combat when possible. The Chibcha, too, were content to keep at bay the Panche and Colima on their south-western and southern border, and, so far as can be gathered, never attempted reprisals, nor even made an effort to reconquer the territory from which they had been driven by the Muzo. But the continual strife with the Panche had the effect of inuring the southern tribes to war and was the cause of the rise of Bogota; it had, moreover, a more surprising effect in producing the only democratic institution in this land where hereditary rank counted for so much. Upon men who showed unusual bravery in war was conferred the title of Guecha, and certain privileged ornaments. The Guecha wore his hair short and bore in his lips and ears a number of gold rods, said to correspond with the number of foes slain by him in fight, as well as the nose-ornament which was in other cases the sign of high birth. To such proved warriors was entrusted the guardianship of the villages on the Panche frontier. War was declared formally by messengers sent to the enemy, who were entertained unharmed by the latter as long as hostilities lasted. Certain religious ceremonies were performed, including the sacrifice of a child to the Sun and Moon; and the petty chiefs of most distinguished lineage, who bore the military title of Usaque, summoned their retainers. The fighting-men grouped themselves round their feudal lords, whose tents were dyed each some distinguishing colour, and many women followed in the train with a generous supply of *chicha* for the thirsty warriors. An army in the field afforded a fine spectacle. The nobles glittered with gold : gold forehead-ornaments in the shape of crescents, gold nose- and ear-ornaments, gold collars, gold bracelets, gold breast-plates (Pl. IV) and shields, and over all a feather crest set in gold and emeralds. The rank and file, though less richly clad, made a brave show adorned in the many-hued feathers of tropical birds. They were armed with spears of palmwood with the points hardened in the fire, with long and heavy two-handed swords of hard wood, with slings and spear-throwers. The last-mentioned appliance is found widely distributed throughout America, and again in Australia, and consists of a rod with a hook at the end which fits into a socket in the butt of the javelin,[1] by this means the arm of the thrower is artificially lengthened and he is enabled to hurl his weapon with far greater force than with the unaided hand. This appliance was also used in Peru (see Fig. 8). Some of the fighters carried bows, but this weapon was not used nearly to the same extent as by the wild forest tribes to the east, who, again unlike the Chibcha, were accustomed to anoint their arrows with poison. The battle-array of the Quimbaya was similar, though in this district a chief was always to be distinguished

---

[1] In parts of America, though not in the Andes, the end of the spear-thrower is furnished with a socket in which the spear-butt rests instead of the hook mentioned above.

by a hemispherical casque of gold bearing designs in relief (Pl. V. 1). Among the Chibcha, as among certain Peruvian tribes, the mummies of famous warriors were carried into battle in the hope that the spirit of the brave departed might animate their compatriots. Head-hunting was practised to some extent in Colombia, especially by the less civilized tribes, such as those of the Cartagena coast, the Muzo, the Colima, and the Panche; and even the Chibcha decorated their sanctuaries with the heads of Panche enemies.

In the arts of pleasure the Colombians were more expert than in war, but they were much addicted to drunkenness ; large stores of the intoxicating *chicha* figured prominently on all occasions of rejoicing and religious ceremonial, and the carousals, especially among the Quimbaya, frequently ended in a fight. A more strenuous form of amusement consisted of the foot-races so dear to the heart of the Chibcha, in which the winner received a prize of textiles and was accorded the privilege of wearing his garment so as to touch the ground, while the Lache people to the north-east of the Chibcha indulged in general *mêlées* in which fists were the only weapons. Feasts and games were a great feature of religious worship, and this subject requires a short consideration.

CHAPTER II—COLOMBIA (*continued*)

VERY little is known of the religion of the Quimbaya ; it is stated that they had no idols nor temples, and practised no cult of animals nor plants. Mention is made of a creator, Abira, an evil deity, Canicuba, and a culture-heroine, Dabeciba, in Antioquia, but nothing is related of the worship paid to them. About the Chibcha more information exists ; at the head of the pantheon stood the creator, Chiminigagua, and the culture-hero and god of chiefs, Bochica. Bachue, mentioned before, was the patron of agriculture ; Chaquen, of races and boundaries ; Nencatacoa, the bear-shaped god, of *chicha*-drinking, weaving and dyeing ; and Chibchachum, the peculiar god of the Bogotans, of commerce. It is more than probable that definite gods of this nature were only found among the more highly-organized Chibcha, and that elsewhere prevailed the cult of natural features, the heavenly bodies, mountains, rocks, lakes, and streams. Such seems to have been the primitive religion of all the Andean tribes, surviving among the Chibcha and also locally among the Peruvians, and based on the desire to propitiate the hidden powers of nature, or on the idea that the object of the cult was in some way connected with the ancestry of the worshippers. The Sun, Sua, and the Moon, Chia, were important deities among the Chibcha and the more primitive tribes on their south-eastern border, and the Moon was also worshipped by the Panche on the west. The cult of water was very important in the Chibcha country, and this is not surprising, since the inhabitants were agriculturists and droughts were not uncommon. There were five sacred lakes, of which the most important was that of Guatabita. Mountains also were considered sacred, and offerings were deposited on them, but chiefly because of their association with some god, principally the Sun. A snake-cult was found among two tribes to the west of Chibcha territory, and traces of similar worship were found also among the Chibcha themselves, in so far as a large snake was supposed to issue from the lake of Guatabita and receive the offerings of gold and emeralds placed on its banks. Two tribes conterminous with the snake-worshippers paid reverence to two stones said once to have been men, and stone worship was found among the neighbouring Lache, who believed, moreover, that the dead became stones, and were later reincarnated. A similar idea is seen at the root of the legend of the former chief of Tunja who married his sister and, with her, was subsequently turned to stone.

It is only of the cults practised by the Chibcha that any detailed accounts have come down to us, and most of these relate to the worship of the Sun. To Bochica and the Rainbow offerings were made of gold and emeralds; to Chibchachum, of gold; Bachue received certain agricultural produce, and Nencatacoa libations of *chicha*; to Chaquen were dedicated the feather ornaments worn by the competitors in races and by the warriors in war. The Sun was more exacting. Besides offerings of gold, emeralds and incense,[1] of which the two former were often buried on mountains, human sacrifices were made to him. Not far from Bogota, to the south-east, was a temple to the Sun, in which was reared a large number of children, purchased in infancy by traders in distant provinces. These children were regarded with the utmost

---

[1] The invading Spaniards were received at first with offerings of fire and incense, since, as in Peru, they were thought to be the children of the Sun.

PLATE II

COLOMBIA

1. STONE PENDANT : CHIBCHA	6, 8. POTTERY STAMPS : N.E. CAUCA
2. COPPER FISH : SANTANDER	7. STONE PLATE : ANTIOQUIA
3, 4, 5. POTTERY SPINDLE-WHORLS :	9. POTTERY VASE : BOGOTA
N.E. CAUCA AND TOLIMA	10, 11. POTTERY VASE : ANTIOQUIA

(Scale : 1-8, 1/4TH ; 9-11, 1/8TH)

veneration, and acted as mediators between penitents and the offended deity ; they were not permitted to touch the ground with their feet, and their chief occupation was as singers in the temple. At the age of puberty they were sold to chiefs for sacrifice ; the victim's blood and heart being offered to the Sun amidst music and song somewhat after the fashion of the Nahua people of Central America. If one of these Moja, as they were called, were found to be guilty of unchastity, he escaped the fate destined for him, but lost his sacred character, and was thenceforward regarded as an ordinary individual. Children were also sacrificed in time of war or drought. In the latter case the victim was taken on a fine day to the summit of a mountain and beheaded with a cane knife, his blood being smeared on the rocks where the first rays of the sun would fall ; the body was sometimes hidden in a cave, and sometimes left on the mountain for the sun to " devour." Another common form of human sacrifice was the following : a slave was conducted in procession to a lofty pole supporting a small platform which stood in the corner of the chief's enclosure ; on this he was set, and arrows and darts were hurled at him until he died of his wounds ; meanwhile priests collected in bowls the blood which constituted the offering ; the body was buried on a hill-top. In some cases parrots, brought from the hot plains and trained to talk, were substituted for human victims, as many as two hundred being offered at a time. The practice of human sacrifice was not confined to the Chibcha country ; in Tolima the custom was also found, and in certain features the ceremony closely resembled that of the Aztecs in so far as the victim was himself supposed to be the god. Prisoners of war were sacrificed in Antioquia and by the Quimbaya. Of other celestial phenomena the Rainbow was personified under the name of Cuchabiba ; it was regarded as the protector of women in childbirth and of the fever-stricken, and offerings of emeralds were made to it.   Its appearance, however, was supposed to portend death.

Closely connected with the cult of the Sun was the cult of idols, at any rate in the Chibcha territory. These idols were made of various materials—wood, clay, cotton, wax, copper, and even gold. One of the most celebrated of those in the precious metal was a solid image of the son of Bachue in a temple at Iguaque. There were many idols in a single temple, and offerings were made to them through the priests, in the hope that they might intercede with the Sun and Moon to grant the prayer of the petitioner. Offerings consisted of textiles, emeralds, and gold figures of men, beasts, birds, reptiles, and insects, as well as tiaras and other ornaments also of gold ; and were deposited in vases shaped like a human figure (Pl. II, Fig. 9), sunk in the ground up to the neck, and furnished with a cover of clay or feathers. When the vase was full it was removed and buried with its contents in a secret place.   Besides the temple idols, which were usually arranged in pairs, male and female, were the private idols, approximating more in character to fetishes, which individuals kept in their huts and carried with them in small baskets. These served a variety of purposes, such as to guard the possessor against sickness and the like. Idols of wood, pottery, and gold were also found in Antioquia, Southern Cauca, and among the Sutagao, neighbours of the Chibcha on the south ; but it is said that neither the Quimbaya nor the inhabitants of Tolima made use of them. If this statement is true the two small figures shown on Pl. III, Figs. 6 and 7, one of which still retains the gold nose-ring which usually adorns these figurines, must be of a votive character.

A few words must be said about the cult of the sacred lakes in the Chibcha country. Connected with this cult was the ceremony of investiture of the chief of Guatabita, which has been described above, but more important from the national point of view were the ceremonial pilgrimages which were made periodically to the chief lakes of the country. The lake of Guatabita was thus honoured by the northern Chibcha, while the lake of Ubaque, south of Bogota, was rendered similar homage by the southern tribes. During the period of the pilgrimage hostilities were suspended, and the assembled tribes held foot-races and indulged in prolonged drinking-bouts. With such zeal were these amusements pursued that deaths from exhaustion or over-drinking were not unknown, and the victims were buried in holy caves on the spot and honoured as martyrs to religion. In conclusion was celebrated a great sacrifice to the lake. At Guatabita the populace thronged the holy shores, which twinkled with the flames of their incense-fires ; long cords were stretched from bank to bank, and to the sound of drums and whistles the offerings were made. Chiefs and nobles cast their gold and ornaments into the lake, but the commoners buried their contributions on the shores, standing with their backs turned towards the holy waters. Some of these offerings have been discovered; one lucky explorer securing gold to the amount of no less than 12,000 pesos.[1] On the banks of Ubaque pottery figures have been disinterred, their faces turned away from the lake, probably the offerings of the poorer class. Apart from the sanctity which seems to have attached to large sheets of water, Guatabita seems to have possessed additional holiness from the fact that its waters were supposed to be inhabited by the wife of a former Zaque of Tunja, of whom a legend was told.

An important ceremony took place in Bogota on the occasion of the harvest, which occurred in September. The people in all their finery, accompanied by the priests wearing golden tiaras, assembled in the broad street leading to the chief's house; many were clad in the skins of wild beasts, a custom which is also found in Peru. Prayers were made to the Sun and to Bochica, and an appeal was

[1] The value of the *peso de oro* is about £2 12s. 6d.

made to their pity by the use of masks on which were painted tears. The priests were followed in procession by a troop of worshippers manifesting every sign of joy and announcing that the Sun had granted their supplications; next came a number of men wearing gold masks, spreading textiles before a richly adorned band of musicians who escorted the Zipa and his dependent chiefs. At the end of the street offerings were made to idols, and the proceedings terminated in dancing and chichadrinking. At Tunja a ceremony was performed in memory of the two mythical chiefs who became respectively the Sun and Moon. This took place at the end of the year, when twelve men clad in red formed a circle round a thirteenth in blue and sang songs mainly concerned with death. The performers were considered to represent respectively the months and the sun. An interesting piece of symbolism was manifested in some of the drinking-bouts which occurred after sacrifices; two men sat at the gate of the enclosure where the revelries were taking place and played mournful airs on flutes. These men, who neither ate nor drank during the proceedings, were supposed to represent death.

The ceremonial which the Chibcha religion had developed required the services of a priesthood. The priesthood was hereditary in the female line, but the chiefs seem to have had some control over the disposal of the more important offices. After a period of twelve years' probation, during which the candidate received both religious and medical instruction, and practised various austerities in the seclusion of an isolated hut, he was inducted into his office, his ears and nose were pierced, and he was allowed to assume ornaments of gold. The life of a priest involved much self-denial; he lived abstemiously and in celibacy, performed many penances, and slept but little, spending the greater part of the night in chewing coca. His position in general was that of intercessor between man and the supernatural powers; for instance, in

PLATE III

COLOMBIA

1, 2, 5-7, 9-14. POTTERY: CAUCA VALLEY, ANTIOQUIA

3. VASE: TOLIMA

4. VASE: GUATABITA

8. FIGURE: BOGOTA

(Scale: 1-8, 1/6TH; 9-12, 1/8TH)

time of drought a number of priests, after fasting, proceeded to the top of a mountain and there burnt various offerings, including hair soaked in resin, scattering the ashes to the winds. In times of sickness, the invalid, after fasting, brought some offering, such as a gold figure wrapped in cotton, to the priest, who had meanwhile prepared himself also by a fast. The latter would then divest himself of his clothing, declaim the circumstances of the illness in a loud voice, and cast the offering into a lake, deposit it in a cave, or bury it in the earth. Next morning he announced the divine will to the suppliant. Such were the offices of the regular priesthood, in the ranks of which there was no hierarchy, all being, at least nominally, equal. But there existed in addition a number of itinerant diviners, whose methods included some such proceeding as the following. If a man lost an object of value he would call in the services of a diviner; the latter would trace in the dust ten lines radiating from the spot where he stood, and associate each of these with one of his fingers. After taking an intoxicating drug he awaited the twitching of one of his fingers, by which he was supposed to discover the direction in which the robber might be found. The popular magic was extremely varied; omens were taken from dreams, the cries of foxes and owls, and the twitching of various parts of the body; and no one would undertake a project of importance without ensuring success by the consumption of certain herbs. The Quimbaya possessed prophetic priests who interpreted the supernatural will from the observation of natural phenomena, and similar diviners were found among the Colima and Muzo. In the plains south-east of the Chibcha, candidates for the priesthood were educated for their future profession in the temples.

The Chibcha temples were ordinary huts, such as are described later, furnished with small stools on which were set the idols; the floor was usually covered with grass and the walls with mats. In the case of the im-

D

portant temples, such as that of Iraca, the main posts were planted each on the body of a living slave. The houses of chiefs were similarly " established in blood." Each temple was dedicated to some particular god, and small shrines were scattered over the country, on the hills, on the shores of lakes, and by the roadside.

The Chibcha believed that the souls of the dead travelled to another land in the centre of the earth, crossing a river in a boat made of spider's web, for which reason spiders were never killed. There they entered upon another life, similar to that in this world, but the position they occupied depended to some extent upon the death by which they had perished. Men who had fallen in battle, and women who had died in childbirth, were supposed to be particularly fortunate in the other world. When a chief came to power the priests prepared him a grave in a secret place, in a wood, on a hill, or in the bed of a stream; at his death his body was embalmed with resin, and a public mourning was accorded him, at which his various exploits were recounted, a practice which obtained also in Peru. The priests then buried him in secret, placing with the body bags of coca and maize and jars of chicha. In the grave, or in the earth above, as at Tunja, they placed much gold and jewels, and over his body they buried his favourite wives and slaves so that they might serve him in the other world. The ruler of Bogota was buried seated on a gold-plated stool, and the Zaque of Tunja was enfolded in many wrappings and placed on a couch in the temple, jewels and gold having been placed in his body at the embalming. In the palace at Tunja the Spaniards found an urn of gold, set with emeralds and weighing thirty libras[1] which contained the bones of a former chief. Caves, as in Peru, were often used as mausolea, and the mummies of chiefs have been found in them surrounded by

[1] 437½ oz. troy, the value of the gold, if pure, being about £1700, exclusive of that of the jewels.

the bodies of their retainers. Like the Chibcha, the Quimbaya buried maize with the dead and, in the case of a man of importance, deposited his favourite wives and slaves in the earth above his body. But the latter was usually burnt and the ashes placed in an urn of gold or clay. The graves too were much more elaborate and of considerable variety. They consisted in the main of one or more vaults, lined with stone slabs or plastered with clay ornamented with painted and engraved designs, and access was gained to them by a vertical or inclined shaft, sometimes furnished with stairs. The body was laid from east to west, the grave filled in with earth of a different colour from that of the locality, and a mound, the proportions of which corresponded with the importance of the deceased, reared above it. The graves were grouped in regular cemeteries, connected by roads, on the upper slopes of the cordillera, and individuals of the same class were buried together. The practice of mummification was known also, it is said, to the Panche tribes.

The practice of moulding the heads of infants in accordance with certain preconceived ideals of beauty, a custom which was common among other Andean races, was found also in Colombia. Among the tribes which practised it were those of the Cauca valley and the province of Tolima. The usual method practised by the Quimbaya was to apply two boards, by means of which the forehead and the back of the child's head were flattened, and a corresponding bulge on either side of the skull was produced. The square heads of the clay figurines from the neighbourhood of Cartago and Manizales (Pl. III, Figs. 6 and 7) give some idea of the shape which the process was designed to produce. Occasionally pressure was applied at the sides so that the head became elongated in a backward direction, but this was less common. The right of wearing nose- and ear-ornaments, especially in the Chibcha country, was only allowed to men of the highest rank, the chiefs, Usaque, Guecha, and priests; and, as in Peru, the piercing of the ears was a jealously guarded privilege. Such ornaments were invariably of gold, in the shape of rings or plates (Fig. 1, *c*, *e* and *f*) for the nose, and rings, plates, cylinders and spirals (Fig. 1, *d*) of thick wire for the ears. The ornaments of greatest variety and perfection of workmanship were found among the Quimbaya, including

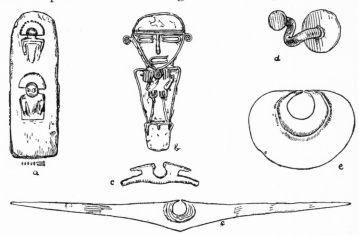

FIG. 1.—Colombia—*a*, Stone die for gold reliefs; *b*, gold figure, Chibcha; *c*, *e*, *f*, gold nose-ornaments; *d*, gold ear-ornament.

necklaces of gold, stone and quartz beads, pendants of various materials, some in the form of animals (Pl. II, 1) or small rattles and circlets for the arm and leg. Other ornaments have been mentioned in the course of the preceding pages. Among most of the Colombians, clothing was reduced to a minimum; in fact the Chibcha alone wore anything worthy of the name. Men wore a short cotton skirt and a shoulder-cloth knotted on each shoulder, women a long skirt and a shoulder-cloth fastened with a pin of gold or copper. In general the garments of the ordinary man were white, those of the nobles were ornamented with red or black designs, but the women of the north-eastern boundary tribes wore clothes woven of variously coloured cotton. The hair was worn long, but was usually concealed by the head-dress, a narrow fillet of cotton, a net, or a cloth or skin cap with a high crown and sometimes with ear-flaps, as seen in Peru. The rank of an individual was indicated by the pattern of his head-covering. Men plucked out their scanty beards with small tweezers of gold. Neither shoes nor sandals were worn. The rest of the tribes were content with a girdle and their ornaments, but the Quimbaya chiefs wore cotton garments ornamented with gold plate. Painting the body was a recognized method of increasing beauty, at feasts and in war, and for this purpose stamps or cylinders of pottery with geometrical designs in high relief (Pl. II, Figs. 6 and 8) were frequently employed by the Chibcha and Quimbaya. These appliances were also used in the decoration of textiles.

The dwellings of the Colombians were constructed of canes supported by wooden posts, the walls, in the Chibcha country, being sometimes plastered with clay ; the roofs were of thatch, and the more important buildings were usually enclosed in one or more palisades, the doors and windows were small. Though constructed of primitive materials, the huts of the Quimbaya and Chibcha were often large enough to be imposing, and contained several apartments. The walls of the Zipa's palace were ornamented with reed-grass, interwoven with thread of different colours, and a broad corridor encircled the building, sheltered by an awning of coarse cotton cloth. The palisade-doors of the chiefs of Tunja and Sogamoso were hung with plates of gold, which gleamed in the sun and clashed melodiously when the wind blew. It is stated that the value of the gold from the door of the Sogamoso palace amounted to eighty thousand ducados.[1] The Quimbaya huts contained separate rooms for the

---

[1] The value of the ducado is nearly £2.

men and women, and were invariably constructed on the banks of a stream.

Stone implements were used by the Colombians for various agricultural and other purposes, and polished axe- or adze-blades are often found. They are usually more or less trapezoid and regular in outline, but some are grooved at the butt to facilitate attachment to a haft.

Though at the time of the Spanish conquest the only people who used stone for structural purposes were the Quimbaya (who lined their graves with stone slabs), yet remains of stone-working are not absent in the Chibcha area. Not far from Tunja, in a north-westerly direction, are a number of well-dressed stone columns, measuring seven to eight feet in length. When first discovered, many were still standing ; others again had fallen. Most of them were cylindrical or elliptical in shape, and a few were faceted. In some cases one end was encircled by a groove, possibly for the attachment of the cords by which they were dragged into position ; in other cases the masons had not yet completed the task of shaping them. Their purpose is still a mystery, unless indeed it can be explained by the story related by Simon. He says that the Zaque Garanchacha, who, according to him, ruled from the time of Bochica to the Spanish conquest, projected building a stone temple to the Sun, his father, and for that purpose had a large number of rough columns brought to Tunja secretly and by night ; but the arrival of the Spaniards interrupted his plans. Unfortunately the later inhabitants of the neighbouring villages have used this site as a quarry, and many of the columns have disappeared.

But the most extraordinary ruins of this region are found in the neighbourhood of a small village called San Agustin, on the right bank of the upper Magdalena, just outside the boundary of Chibcha territory. Here, at some time unknown, was built a series of small chambers, the walls composed of large slabs of stone, roofed with a slab of still greater proportions. Pillars, sculptured with the figures of men or gods, stood at the entrances, and carved slabs formed part of the interior decoration. The figures are armed with clubs, and above their heads the conventionalized representation of some animal, probably a puma, is shown. But the most striking feature, according to the accounts of travellers, is constituted by the large tusks which are shown projecting from their mouths. This characteristic, which is also seen on the early pottery of the Peruvian coast, we shall meet again, when we come to consider the early stone remains of Peru. Sculptured slabs, again, are found on the Ecuadorian coast. There seems little in common between these remains and the Chibcha civilization, and it is probable that they date from an earlier period. It is in the highest degree desirable that the site should be properly investigated, since there is every reason to believe that additional light would thereby be thrown on the earliest remains of the Ecuadorian and Peruvian coasts and the pre-Inca culture of the Peruvian highlands.

The Colombian tribes lived by hunting and agriculture ; they possessed no domestic animals and no beasts of burden, since the range of the llama, the only animal in South America which was ever put to such a use, did not extend so far north. Of the agriculturists the Chibcha were the most adept ; game was not plentiful in the high ground, and was carefully protected by the chiefs. The chief produce was maize and potatoes, the former of which yielded two hundred to three hundred-fold and the latter twenty to thirty-fold. In the valleys, yuca, sweet potato, cotton and leguminous plants were grown. The ground was prepared with wooden spades or digging-sticks, hardened in the fire ; but irrigation was probably not practised before the conquest, though droughts were not infrequent. The Chibcha harvest took place in September ; but the Panche, who inhabited a far moister district, gathered their crops three times in the year. The Quimbaya were hunters rather than husbandmen, though among them also maize was the principal food. Coca and tobacco were much prized throughout the country, and the latter was both used as snuff and smoked in stone pipes. The coca-leaves were carefully dried in pots over the fire and reserved for chewing. Maize was prepared for eating in various ways, principally by grinding on stones ; the meal was then wrapped in leaves and boiled or roasted. Salt was a valuable article of trade and was exported from those districts, such as Cartago, where salt-springs existed. It was obtained by evaporation in large vessels constructed, among the Quimbaya, of copper, among the Chibcha, of pottery. In the latter case the pots could be used but once, since they had to be broken to extract the salt. Cannibalism was practised by many of the more savage tribes of Colombia, particularly in the north of the province of Antioquia and the northern part of the Cauca valley, though it was less prevalent in the south. Even the comparatively civilized Quimbaya were not innocent of the custom, although they only partook of human flesh ceremonially.

Of the various industries practised in Colombia most interesting is the working of gold, owing both to the great quantities of gold ornaments which have been, and are still, found throughout the country, and to the ability which certain of the tribes, notably the Quimbaya, showed in the treatment of the metal. Most of the tribes except those on the lowest plane of culture worked gold to some extent, but the principal centres of manufacture were the Cauca valley, Antioquia, and the Chibcha district, named in order according to the quality of their respective products. Neither the Quimbaya nor the Chibcha obtained the raw metal locally, but were supplied by their neighbours ; both, however, were adepts in casting and soldering. The Quimbaya seem to have performed the former operation by the *cire perdue* process; a model of the required object was made in wax on a core of clay, and over this more clay was plastered to form a mould; the mould was then baked, the wax run out through a hole left for the purpose, and the molten metal poured in. The core and mould were kept apart by small pieces of wood set in the wax, and the holes which appeared in the finished cast were carefully concealed by small plates soldered on. The mask on Plate IV, 5, has been cast on a pottery core, of which traces remain in the nose. The gold figures of the Chibcha, which were far inferior to the work of the Quimbaya, consist apparently of plates of metal cut to the desired outline, with the edges and details emphasized by gold wire soldered to the surface (Fig. 1, *b*). It is improbable that the *cire perdue* process was extensively employed by this people, if indeed at all; but it is evident that some of the figures belonging to this type were produced by a process of casting. In some cases the metal background is incomplete, and the "wire" details project unsupported. Here a model, probably of copper, must have been prepared, by soldering wire on a plate, and a mould taken from this; small irregularities show where the mould crumbled when removed from the model, a mishap which the "undercut" details formed of round wire rendered inevitable. Where the plate was thin the molten metal might well fail to make its way between the walls of the mould, but would run readily along the broader channels formed by the wire. Gold was also worked by hammering, and designs obtained by beating out the metal on stones carved in relief with the design required. Such stones (Fig. 1, *a*) have often been found in the Chibcha country, and at first gave rise to the supposition that a system of hieroglyphic writing existed in Colombia, a supposition which is entirely without foundation. Gold was alloyed with silver and copper, the former giving a greenish, the latter a reddish tinge to the finished article; sometimes both were used, with the result that a pale yellow was obtained. The fine surface on some of the Quimbaya objects was probably obtained by polishing with stone burnishers. The graceful shapes of the Quimbaya vessels and whistles (Plate IV, 4 and 6) bear ample evidence to the skill of their goldsmiths, who were also capable of producing minute beads, of which thirty-five go to the gramme. Some of the figures found are of a base alloy with a surface of pure gold, and from this it would appear that the art of gilding was known.

The best emerald mines were situated in the territory of the hostile Muzo, but others existed at Somondoco, which were worked by the Chibcha. The earth was dug out with pointed stakes and washed with pond water. Mining took place in the rainy season, and was preceded by religious ceremonies.

In the making of pottery the Chibcha were surpassed by the Quimbaya and the other Antioquians, the ware of the two latter being superior both in design and finish. A considerable amount of Colombian pottery exists in various museums, but no systematic study has been made of it, and the number of specimens which are accompanied by exact details as to the locality where they were found is comparatively small. At the same time it is possible to assign certain types to certain definite areas. Two kinds of clay appear to have been used generally, one reddish in colour, the other a greyish buff; ware of a dark grey is sometimes found locally, especially in the neighbourhoods of Manizales and Anzerma. In the Quimbaya and Antioquian pottery the clay is better worked and more homogeneous; it is to a large extent micaceous, and a small percentage of sand seems to have been added. The Colombian potter built up his vases solely by hand, for the use of the wheel was entirely unknown to him; the larger vases appear to have been made in several pieces, which were allowed to harden before they were put together. After firing, which was

PLATE IV

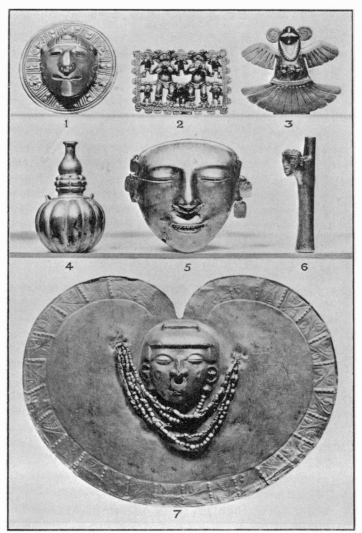

COLOMBIA AND ECUADOR

1. GOLD REPOUSSÉ MASK : ECUADOR   5. GOLD MASK : QUIMBAYA
2, 3. GOLD PENDANTS   6. GOLD WHISTLE : QUIMBAYA
4. GOLD VASE : QUIMBAYA   7. GOLD BREAST-PLATE : QUIMBAYA

(Scale : about 1/4TH)

done in the open air, the pots were decorated with a
coloured slip, red, black, or buff; usually a single
colour was employed, but vases with painted designs
in two or more colours are by no means uncommon,
especially from Manizales and the neighbourhood
(Pl. III, Figs. 9, 11 and 13). Painted patterns are purely
geometrical, and not of high artistic merit. Engraved
ornament is far more common, and in this case again
the deeply incised, bold decoration characteristic of the
buff and grey ware of the last-mentioned district (Pl. III,

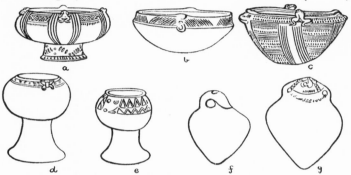

FIG. 2.—Colombian Pottery—*a*, Anzerma ; *b*, Neiva ; *c*, Tunja ;
d-g, Popayan.

Fig. 3) is superior to the more minute and less effective
patterns of the red Chibcha ware (Fig. 2, *c*). Many of the
vases from all parts are in the form of human figures, or
are furnished with a human head or features in relief
(Pls. II and III). Such specimens show the Colombian
artist at his worst; a naturalistic treatment of the human
form seems to have been beyond his powers, and some
of the faces are so conventionalized as to be barely
recognizable.

Characteristic of the Bogota region are the figures
in buff ware covered with a cream-coloured slip (Pl.
III, Fig. 8), and the large vases in human form, greyish
buff in colour, which were used as receptacles for the
offerings to the gods (Pl. II, Fig. 9) ; while figures with

exaggerated legs (such as Pl. III, Fig. 14) are generally to be attributed to Manizales and the surrounding country. Small moulded ornaments, other than the features of the human form, applied after the formation of the body of a vase, are rare, and consist chiefly of figures of frogs (Fig. 2, *a* and *c*). Characteristic again of the Cauca-Antioquia boundary are graceful vases and shallow bowls of grey ware with carefully moulded bodies (Pl. III, Fig. 2), but stemmed vessels are not usually found so far north. Such shapes are far more common in the Popayan district, where vases with pointed bases are also found (Fig. 2, *d–g*). This pottery, which is almost always red, relies far more on the beauty of its outline for artistic effect than on applied or engraved ornament. Vases with pointed bases are not unknown further north, but were usually large in size and used for cooking.

The spinning and weaving of cotton were practised by many of the Colombian tribes, and the engraved spindle-whorls of pottery are common in museums (Pl. II, 3–5), as well as the pottery stamps with which dyed patterns were applied to the textiles (Pl. II, Figs. 6 and 8). The latter were also employed for ornamenting the body.

Such was the state of culture which prevailed in Colombia when the Spaniards arrived ; at one end of the scale naked and savage cannibals ; at the other, a people with a feudal form of government, whose political system was not decadent but progressive, who possessed indeed no form of writing, or any substitute for such (as the *quipu* of Peru), but who had a system of measures and a calendar, and who had made considerable progress in craftsmanship.

A few words may be said here about Venezuela, though this country has been so little investigated from an archæological point of view that no connected picture can be given of it. At the same time the northern portion of it is, geographically, a continuation of Colombia, and certain of the remains suggest a relationship with the Colombian tribes. Geographically Venezuela can be divided into three distinct zones: in the north is a strip of agricultural land; south of this, a zone of steppe affording good pasturage; and south of this again are plains covered with thick forest. The high ground was inhabited by a number of distinct tribes, the very names of whom are doubtful, but who offered the most determined resistance to the Spaniards, a resistance which resulted in their ultimate extinction. They were ruled by petty chiefs, who exercised a patriarchal authority, and were quite independent one of the other until they combined against their common foe, the white man. They lived in small huts with low doors, wore very little clothing, and gained their livelihood by agriculture and the chase. Maize and the sweet potato were the principal food-plants, the former being ground in stone mortars with large stone pestles, some of which are too heavy for a single person to manipulate. Like the Colombians, they worshipped the powers of nature, as personified in certain mountains, trees and animals, and made their offerings in special huts, or deposited them on rocks, on river-banks, or in the forks of trees. Their arms consisted of arrows and darts pointed with bone, and sword-shaped clubs of hard wood. Their implements were of stone, and axe-blades of rectangular, or triangular, shape have been found in some numbers. Their pottery is rude and thick, but is interesting owing to the variety of moulded ornament with which it is decorated. Vases in form of tortoises or birds are common, and most of the pots, bottles and bowls were adorned with human faces or the figures of monkeys, frogs and other animals in relief, or with incised geometrical patterns. Plain bottles and bowls are also found, always with rounded bases, as well as the pottery stands upon which they rested. Gold was the only metal known in the northern valleys, and was used entirely for ornament. Other forms of adornment were necklaces of shell, clay and stone beads, and stone pendants in form of animals. Burial customs were various; in places the dead were buried in the house, but some form of urn-burial was more usual. In this respect the Venezuelan tribes differed from those of Colombia, and show an affinity with the Carib and Arawak peoples (see Ch. XII). The most interesting burials are found in the neighbourhood of Lake Valencia, the ancient Tacarigua, the seat of a primitive hunting population. Here a large mound has been discovered, within an enclosure of rough stones, in which had been deposited a number of urns, most of which contained bones. Round the mound were traces of the funeral feasts which had accompanied the obsequies. Other similar burial mounds occur in the neighbourhood, as well as sites where the urns have been deposited in simple trenches. In the latter case remains of as many as eight skeletons have been extracted from a single urn. Like the burials of the Arawak and Carib, the bodies were evidently dismembered before burial, or more probably had been buried for a season and the bones collected and deposited in the urn as their final resting-place. Many of the skulls show that artificial deformation was practised, the foreheads being flattened, probably by the application of a board. Other remains are pottery ocarinas, shell trumpets, bone flutes and pottery figurines, many of which have pierced ears. Numbers of pictographs are found on the rocks, which show great similarity to those of Colombia, and a further link with the region to the south-west is constituted by the stone statues which are found especially in the Sierra de Merida.

CHAPTER III—ECUADOR

SOUTH of the river Ancasmayu, roughly as far as the boundary between the modern states of Ecuador and Peru, existed, some century before the arrival of the Spaniards, a state which was more advanced politically than that of the Chibcha, but still considerably inferior to that of the Inca, by whom it was conquered. If the Chibcha may be regarded as illustrating in broad outline the condition of the Peruvian tribes before the people of Cuzco had established their hegemony, the small empire of Quito may equally be taken to represent the Inca empire in its infancy. The comparison must not, of course, be pressed too closely ; the Cara, the dominating tribe in Ecuador, did not possess that genius for organization which distinguished the Inca, and their power rested on far less stable foundations. In fact the relations existing between them and the powerful Cañari in the south of Ecuador were rather those between allies, than between a suzerain state and its subjects, and the bond soon broke under the stress of the Inca invasion. From the geographical point of view the country exhibits the same main features as Colombia, with the exception that the central mountain chain disappears, and the two remaining cordilleras enclose, not a single unbroken valley, but a high table-land intersected by small valleys and transverse chains of hills. The coast in northern Ecuador is still well wooded and possesses a heavy rainfall, but moisture and vegetation decrease towards the south, and here commences the succession of arid coastal deserts which extends through Peru far into Chile. The general aspect of the country between Quito and the river Maule has been so well summarized by Cieza de Leon that it will be as well to give his description in his own words.[1]

" In this land there are three desert ranges where men can in no wise exist. One of these comprises the *montana* (forests) of the Andes, full of dense wildernesses, where men cannot, nor ever have lived. The second is the mountainous region, extending the whole length of the Cordillera of the Andes, which is intensely cold and its summits are covered with eternal snow, so that, in no way, can people live in this region, owing to the snow and the cold, and also because there are no provisions, all things being destroyed by the snow and the wind, which never ceases to blow. The third range comprises the sandy deserts from Tumbez to the other side of Tarapaca, in which there is nothing to be seen but sandhills and the fierce sun which dries them up, without water nor herb nor tree nor created thing, except birds, which, by the gift of their wings, wander wherever they list. This kingdom, being so vast, has great deserts, for the reasons I have now given. The inhabited region is after this fashion. In parts of the mountains of the Andes there are ravines and dales, which open out into valleys of such width as often to form great plains between the mountains, and, although the snow falls, it all remains on the higher part. As these valleys are closed in, they are not molested by the winds, nor does the snow reach them, and the land is so fruitful that all things which are sown yield abundantly, and there are trees and many birds and animals. The land, being so fertile, is well peopled by the natives. They make their villages with rows of stones roofed with straw, and live healthily and in comfort. Thus the mountains of the Andes form these dales and rav-

[1] From the translation by Sir Clements Markham, published by the Hakluyt Society.

ines, in which there are populous villages, and rivers of excellent water flow near them."

The inhabitants of this area, with one important exception, differed in no very marked degree from the southern tribes of Colombia on the one hand, and from the northern tribes of Peru on the other, at any rate before the coming of the Inca. Practically the same culture persisted as we have described in the last chapters, modified indeed by local influences, but showing no indications of abrupt transition. In the north were the Quillacinga and Pasto tribes, in and around Quito were a people compounded of the Quitu and Cara, of whom more will be said immediately, Riobamba was the centre of a tribe called Puruha, and, to the south of them, were the powerful and turbulent Cañari and the Palta. Along the coast was a series of tribes, varying slightly in culture among themselves, but differing in a more marked degree from the inhabitants of the highlands than from each other. In this region the coastal strip is of particular interest ; the early inhabitants were artistically far more advanced than the tribes of the Colombian coast, and from this point we begin to find that peculiar antithesis between the culture of the coast and the culture of the highlands, neither of them being of a low order, which exists throughout the whole of the Inca Empire. The question is intricate and complicated, since sporadically in the highlands exist traces of a very early culture, which, as will be seen, seems to be connected by certain similarities with that of the coast. Another point, of even greater interest, connected with the maritime district of Ecuador lies in the fact that several legends have come down to us which afford definite indications of immigration from the sea ; traditional evidence on this point is almost entirely lacking for the rest of the South American coast with the exception of the neighbouring Peruvian province of Lambayeque ; and for the sake of completeness the myth which has

E

been preserved concerning intrusive culture at this point will be related in this chapter. In Guayaquil a story prevailed that once upon a time a number of men of great stature arrived from the sea in large *balsas* (reed rafts of peculiar construction which are described below). They were a fierce people who wore little clothing, and they perpetrated many cruelties upon the original inhabitants. Nothing is known of their culture, except that certain remarkable well-like excavations in the neighbourhood were attributed to them, and that they lived by fishing with nets and other gear. Owing to the remoteness of their arrival and the fear with which they were regarded by the aborigines, an atmosphere of myth had gathered around their persons and their ultimate fate. Their large stature had been magnified until it attained gigantic proportions, and the fossil bones of huge mammals were pointed out as their bodily remains ; while their disappearance was assigned to supernatural means. It was said that their crimes incurred the wrath of the unseen powers, and a youth, gleaming like the sun, came down from the sky and drove them to a valley, where he slew them with flames of fire.

The Lambayeque story is more rational ; a number of balsas arrived from the sea under the command of a chief named Naymlap. The company seem to have been a complete tribe or clan rather than a marauding party, since it included many women, and the chief himself was surrounded by a whole suite of personal attendants. The legend details the names and functions of these attendants in the most circumstantial manner ; there were a conch-blower, a guardian of the royal throne, a cup-bearer, an official to scatter shell-dust in the path of the chief, another to prepare his bath, another to supervise the preparation of his body-paint, and a maker of feather garments. With them these travellers brought an idol of green stone, which they called Llampallec, and their first act on landing was to build a temple for it, to which they gave the name Chot. The chiefs of these immigrants seem to have laid claim to divine attributes ; at the death of Naymlap a report was spread that he had ascended to heaven with wings, and his successor Cium, after a long reign, shut himself in a secret chamber underground, and starved himself to death, so that his decease should not be witnessed and the fictitious immortality of the sovereign might be preserved. Ten more chiefs followed, all of whom reigned but a short time, and the last of these, Tempellec, was guilty of an act of sacrilege which put an end to the dynasty. He wished to move the idol Llampallec from its shrine, and thus apparently incurred the anger of the god ; a deluge of rain, rare on this part of the coast, fell without intermission for thirty days, and was followed by a year of famine. This misfortune was attributed by the priests and nobles to the wickedness of the chief, and the unfortunate ruler was seized, bound hand and foot, and cast into the sea. By this time the immigrants had increased in numbers ; most of the chiefs had been blessed with a numerous progeny, and the younger sons had moved off and founded other villages. After the death of the ill-fated Tempellec, a republic was established which lasted until the country was annexed by the powerful chieftain of Chimu, whose seat of government lay in the neighbourhood of Truxillo farther south. The conqueror established a line of tributary chiefs, nine of whom had succeeded in order by the time the Spaniards arrived. We are told that the reigns of all the rulers were short, and the fact is explained by the statement that the prolonged fasts which a chief had to observe at his succession invariably proved prejudicial to his health. But the true explanation may be that the Lambayeque chieftains were divine kings, in whom was incorporate the collective soul of the community ; as long as the chief retained the vigour of youth, this vital principle flourished, but when he began to show signs of age, it was necessary to remove him lest the general prosperity might become impaired.   At his death the communal soul was automatically transferred to his successor, who continued to reign until he, in his turn, showed signs of waning powers.   Chiefs of this nature are known in several parts of the world, as may be seen in Dr. Frazer's monumental work the *Golden Bough*.   If this explanation be accepted the peculiar circumstances surrounding the deaths of the first two chiefs become much more intelligible, and the fact that Tempellec was held responsible for the misfortunes of his people follows as a matter of course.

Yet a third immigration remains to be related, which had a more enduring effect upon the district with which we are immediately concerned.   At an early date a descent was made upon the coast north of Manta by a people who, like the giants, came from the sea in balsas. Their chief, or Scyri, was named Caran, and their first settlement was called after him Cara.   After some stay they turned northward along the coast, and, upon reaching the river Esmeraldas, ascended the stream until they arrived at the territory of the Quitu on the slopes of Pichincha.   The Quitu were then ruled by a chief of the same name, and were surrounded by a number of tribes of similar culture who lived under petty independent chieftains.   The immigrants, called Cara after their first leader, seized a number of villages, and, being better armed and more warlike than the aborigines, succeeded in establishing themselves firmly in the country.   The reason which led them to migrate from the coast to the highlands is obscure ; it is said that they moved inland to escape from the proximity of the giants, but it is more probable that the climate of the coast proved too unhealthy for them, and it is equally likely that this same climate proved fatal to the giants.   Once established in the country, the Cara soon succeeded in annexing the territory of the Quitu, and amalgamated with the former inhabitants, forming a single nation.   As time went on, a policy of expansion was inaugurated, and the land to the north fell under their influence. The conquest of the south followed, at least as far as the territory of the Puruha ; here, however, the Cara received a check, and it was not until the reign of the eleventh Scyri after the conquest of Quito that the province of Puruha was included in their empire. Even then the annexation was effected by diplomatic means and not by force of arms. The course of events was as follows: With the eleventh Scyri the male line of the ruling house became extinct ; all his sons died young, and he had no nephews. One daughter, however, was left to him, and, though women were by law excluded from power, it was agreed that a husband should be found for her, who should rule in her name. The Scyri, ambitious of further extending his dominions, suggested to the chief of Puruha that a marriage should be arranged between the latter's son Ducilela and the girl, whose name was Toa. At this time the state of Puruha was engaged in war with the Huancavillca of Guayaquil and the Cañari on the southern border, and no doubt the chief was glad to avail himself of an arrangement which promised not only to relieve him from fear of attack on the north, but also to yield him assistance against his other foes. The marriage took place, and it was agreed that the two provinces should be united, that of Puruha being included in the empire of Quito. The subsequent course of events, however, was little to the taste of the chief of Puruha ; the Scyri died, and Ducilela succeeded to his position. To be vassal to his own son was more than the haughty chieftain of the Puruha could brook ; he retired from the country into the mountains farther inland and was never heard of again. The hostilities with the Cañari were soon replaced by an alliance, which was later extended to include the Palta chiefs, and the influence of the new Scyri thus included practically the whole of the Ecuadorian highlands.

How far these three immigrations, of the "Giants," the people of Naymlap, and the Cara, were connected it is almost impossible to say. Information concerning the "Giants" is almost entirely lacking ; the remains of the Cara empire show such similarity with the regions to the north and south that it is evident their original culture became absolutely merged in that of the aborigines as soon as they migrated inland ; while the archæology of Lambayeque does not differ in any important degree from that of the coast as far as and beyond Truxillo. The remains of the Ecuadorian coast, though possessing an individuality entirely their own, show, nevertheless, certain similarities with those of the Peruvian coast, as will be seen later. It is conceivable that the whole of the coast culture, from Esmeraldas to Yca, may owe its origin to a series of migrations from a common centre, the divergencies being explained by local development. No traditions have been preserved from the maritime population further south which shed any light on the question ; but this is not surprising, since the people were practically extinct before their folklore was regarded as aught but the direct fabrication of the devil. The question of origin is best reserved until the remarkable culture of the Peruvian coast has been discussed.

To return to the history of the Cara empire, after the union of Quito and Puruha, a short period of peace prevailed ; Ducilela was followed by his son, Antachi Ducilela, and he again by his son Hualcopo. The succession of the latter prince was marked by circumstances which indicate that the system of government was constitutional rather than autocratic. Hualcopo was not the eldest son, and his brother Guallca should normally have become Scyri, but the latter was cruel and unpopular, and the assembly exercised their right of selection and passed him over in favour of his younger brother. In this reign trouble fell upon the country ;

the Inca had been extending their power northward, and the great conqueror Tupac Yupanqui arrived with a large army at the southern borders of the empire. After an attempt at resistance the country of the Palta fell into his hands, and Hualcopo, rejecting the overtures of the Inca, determined to entrench himself in Puruha, sacrificing the country of the Cañari to the invader. In this he was wise, the Cañari were allies rather than subjects, and no doubt the Scyri did not feel sure of their fidelity; besides this we are told that there were no fortresses in the country, and communication was difficult owing to the absence of regular roads and bridges. The Inca advance was slow as it was sure ; it was part of Tupac Yupanqui's military policy to ensure control over every foot of newly conquered ground, and he spent two years in the country of the Cañari building large fortresses and otherwise making his position secure. Meanwhile the Scyri prepared for an energetic resistance, and in this he was aided by his brother Epiclachima, who was a general of no mean ability. Fortifications were raised in Puruha, as well as in the country farther north, in order to provide a retreat in case the first line of defence fell. At length, all being ready, the Inca advanced, and after three months made himself master of Puruha. No doubt the death of Epiclachima, which occurred early in the course of hostilities, did much to discourage the defenders, and ultimately proved a greater disaster than the loss of the province itself. Whether the city of Quito fell into the hands of the invader at this time is doubtful, but at any rate the Inca was obliged to return to Cuzco before he had made his footing absolutely secure. In his absence Hualcopo died, and was succeeded by his son Cacha, who, though infirm in health, possessed the indomitable spirit of his father. Aided by Calicuchima, the worthy son of Epiclachima, the new Scyri succeeded in reconquering Puruha, but spent his energies in vain against the Cañari. In this province the Inca had established too firm a hold, many of the inhabitants had been deported and their places filled with colonists well-disposed to the Inca, and those who remained had grown accustomed to the new rule. Finally, another Inca host appeared, under the command of Huayna Ccapac the son of Tupac Yupanqui, and gradually forced the Scyri back to the northern provinces of his empire, until Quito definitely fell into the hands of the invader. In these operations the Cañari were of much assistance to the Inca troops, and the forces of the Scyri were continually diminished by desertion. The last act was played in the plain of Hatuntaqui, not far from Cayambe, where a desperate battle took place. Fortune at first inclined in favour of the defenders, but the death of Cacha spread dismay among his troops and the Inca achieved a signal victory. The body of the ill-fated prince was taken to Quito for burial, and his daughter Ccacha was installed as regent under the suzerainty of the Inca. One last effort was made by the northern provinces, but the revolt was soon subdued; many of the rebels were captured and all were executed, their bodies being thrown into a lake which afterwards bore the name Yahuarcocha, or "Lake of Blood." Finally Inca rule was placed on a constitutional foundation by the marriage of Huayna Ccapac, now himself Inca, with Ccacha, by which union the imperial emerald of Quito was added to the *llautu* (fringe), which was the *insigne* of the rulers of Peru. The country was organized on the lines usually adopted by the Inca; great buildings were erected in the important towns, especially at Quito, which soon rose to be the capital of the northern part of the Peruvian empire, almost rivalling Cuzco in importance; large sections of the population were deported and replaced by colonists from elsewhere; roads were made; a hierarchy of officials introduced; and the river Ancasmayu was established as the northern frontier of the Peruvian empire. So complete, in fact, was the conquest, with the exception, perhaps, of the provinces in the extreme north, that, in spite of the short time which elapsed before the arrival of the Spaniards, the archæology of the Ecuadorian highlands is represented in museums by almost as many Inca remains as aboriginal.

Along the coast different conditions prevail ; though in part conquered by the Peruvians, the hold of the latter upon this region was comparatively slight, and their progress was marked by several notable reverses. It is said that Tupac Yupanqui first journeyed to the coast at the invitation of the people of Tumbez, and proceeded thence to Guayaquil, where he prepared a fleet of balsas in which he sent an expedition to certain islands far off in the Atlantic. If the latter part of this account is true it would seem as if he reached the Galapagos islands, but the evidence is very doubtful. At any rate, the Inca troops made a reconnaissance in the maritime district, and Huayna Ccapac subdued the district. At the time that the latter leader arrived, the people on the island of Puna, under the leadership of their chief Tumbala, were engaged in a war with the people of Tumbez. The Inca, after settling the strip of mainland, including the region of the Huancavillca in Guayaquil, sent for Tumbala and demanded his submission. The chief complied, though with an ill grace, a body of Inca troops with leaders of royal blood was established on the island together with officials to organize the district, and the Inca departed. Then followed the tragedy. Tumbala conspired with the Huancavillca to murder the intruders, and a cunning plan was arranged. The Inca had left instructions that the main portion of the garrison was to be conveyed by the islanders to a certain spot on the coast where they were to rejoin him. The convoy started, but when at some distance from the land, the treacherous islanders cut the ropes which held the rafts together and precipitated the unfortunate Peruvians into the water. "If any that knew how to swim," writes Cieza de Leon, "tried to save their lives, they were killed by fierce and cruel blows, and if they dived, and thus tried to fly from their enemies by seeking favour of the fishes that dwell in the depths of the sea, it was of no avail, for the islanders, who live much in the sea employed in their fisheries, swim as well as the fishes, and easily overtook the fugitives and strangled them." A second convoy fell victims to a similar fate, and the rest of the garrison, together with the troops and officials on the mainland, were overpowered by a sudden rising. Those that were not killed outright were reserved for sacrifice, and their hearts were offered up at the temple on the island. The Inca exacted a terrible vengeance ; large numbers of the islanders and Huancavillca were put to death in a cruel fashion, and the survivors on the mainland were compelled, as a mark of disgrace, to extract four teeth in addition to the two which each individual removed in accordance with local custom. The imposed ordinance was still observed at the time of the Spanish conquest. But in spite of these drastic measures the Inca seem to have paid little subsequent attention to the coastal districts, and the result is that few of their remains are found in that region (an exception being the island of La Plata, where remains of Inca type, including the vase shown in Fig. 6, c, have been discovered).

In the general sketch of Ecuadorian culture which follows, attention will be confined as far as possible to those features which appear to be independent of Inca influence. As might be expected, our knowledge of the people from literary sources is far less complete than in the case of the Chibcha, since the country had been reorganized by the Inca before the white man arrived upon the scene. Still many of the old customs had survived, and some of the gaps can be filled by deduction from the archæological remains. What literary evidence is available is practically confined to the inland parts and is found principally in the writings of Velasco. Some features of

the social system of the Cara have already appeared in
the sketch of their history; the government was mon-
archic, and hereditary in the male line; if the deceased
chief left no sons, the succession passed to the sons of his
sisters, but not, in the ordinary course of events, to a
woman. The throne was supported by a feudal nobility,
who exercised considerable control; the ordinances of
the chief required ratification at their hands, and they
even had the power of diverting the succession, within
the limits mentioned above, if the natural heir was unfit
for the position of Scyri. As before stated, the *insigne* of
the Scyri was a large emerald; it is possible that the use
of this stone as a royal emblem was a pure Cara practice,
since we are told that the coast people of Manta worshipped an emerald as a god, and it may be that the "idol"
of green stone of the Lambayeque immigrants was also
an emerald. At the same time, as we have seen, emeralds
were held in high estimation as ornaments by the Chibcha.

The people of the highlands were agriculturists, growing maize, *quinoa* (a small grain similar to buckwheat)
and potatoes; the first and last of these were also cultivated on the coast, together with other plants, such
as pepper, which were suited by the warmer climate.
The llama was not found in the maritime provinces,
and at the present time its northern limit inland is Riobamba, but it existed in the northern provinces of Ecuador as late as the time of the Spanish conquest, as we
know from the following amusing story. The news of
the white strangers, and their audacity in seizing the
sacred person of Atahualpa, had filled the empire with dismay; the stories of their invincible power, the terrible
monsters which they bestrode, and their lust for gold—
stories which, we may be sure, lost nothing in the telling
—had increased the general apprehension. In particular the chief of Cayambe, near Otovalo, was filled with
anxiety, since he had a large treasure stored at the village
of Caranqui. The chief of Otovalo, taking advantage

of his fears, concocted the following ingenious plan. He mounted a number of his men on llamas, placed wands in their hands, and told them to show themselves on the mountain slopes above Caranqui. He then with the rest of his retainers rushed in disorder to that village, crying out that the Spaniards were coming, and pointing out the strange troop which was descending the mountain-side. The ruse was successful, the inhabitants of Caranqui sought safety in immediate flight, and the chief of Otovalo possessed himself of the treasure at his leisure.

On the coast, and especially in the islands, the inhabitants were expert fishers, and the peculiar craft in which they plied their trade merit a word of description. These rafts, or *balsas* as they were called by the Spaniards, were made of an odd number of poles or bundles of rushes fastened together, the longest in the centre ; on these the passengers sat or knelt, and plied a single paddle of wood or bamboo first on one side, then on the other (see Pls. XIII, 1, and XXI, 2, and Fig. 9). In fishing, when the Indian got fast in a large fish, he clasped his small craft with his legs and allowed the quarry to tow him hither and thither until worn out. The balsas were mostly small, but some were seen by the Spaniards which could carry fifty men and three horses. This type of boat, which in this neighbourhood seems occasionally to have been used with sails in the pre-Spanish days, was found all down the Peruvian coast, as well as on lake Titicaca.

The clothing of the peoples of Ecuador differed from that of the Colombians, and was based on two garments, a girdle with a strip passing between the legs and a short tunic. In the highlands a robe was worn also and the women wore a short skirt. Here the tunics reached to the knees, but on the coast they were cut short at the lower part of the chest or at the waist. The clothing was woven of cotton, and also, in the highlands, of llama-wool. Methods of hairdressing and types of head-covering differed considerably, since it was the custom among the Andean peoples for different tribes to observe different fashions in this respect. With regard to the inland tribes of Ecuador, it is difficult to say how far the local fashions were of Inca introduction, since the Inca were accustomed to regulate the hair- and head-dresses of their vassals by law, so that a man's tribe could at once be known from his costume. Thus the Cañari wore their hair long, but fastened up on the head and confined by a cane hoop, from which depended a fringe, or by a calabash; the Puruha plaited their hair into numerous little tresses. On the coast the centre of the head was shaved, and the hair at the sides brushed up so as to add breadth to the head and exaggerate the form of artificial deformation which was common in the district. Here the heads of infants were confined between two boards, fastened along the forehead and at the back of the head, so that these parts were flattened, while free expansion was allowed at the sides (compare Pl. X, 1 and 2); a like practice was common among the Palta, neighbours of the Cañari. From a study of the many figurines which have been found on the coast, we know that close-fitting caps, sometimes with flaps for the ears, were worn, and that the inhabitants pierced their earlobes, nostrils, and lower lips for the reception of ornaments. Gold and emeralds were worn in this way. Other ornaments were beads of gold, pottery, and stone, finger-rings, breast-plates, and pendants. Similar ornaments were worn in the highlands; here the semilunar nose-plates of the Quillacinga were particularly characteristic, and probably gave this tribe their name, which is said to mean "Men of the crescent." Sandals were also worn in the upland districts. It seems probable that some form of tattooing was practised locally on the coast; Garcilasso speaks of people who "punctured their faces with sharp-pointed stones," and Cieza de Leon of men who were "marked in the face, and the mark begins at the root of the ear and descends to the chin." The coast people of Peru certainly tattooed themselves, and also, as will be seen, practised the same form of head-deformation.

But the most interesting form of mutilation concerns the teeth ; some individuals, presumably the more prominent men, had small holes drilled in the outer face of the incisors, and small plugs of gold hammered in. This was done solely for ornament, and the practice does not correspond in any way to the dentist's "filling" of civilized countries. The enamel of the teeth is an extremely hard substance, and it is difficult to imagine by what means these holes were made. It is possible that the implement used was armed with one of the small flakes of transparent quartz-crystal which are found only on the coast (and which may also have been used for cutting emeralds, an operation in which the coast-people were very adept). In any case it is interesting to note with what skill the operator has avoided the nerve. The holes are sunk about half-way through the tooth, the base is flat, and the sides quite perpendicular. Of ornaments expressing rank the great emerald worn on the forehead by the Scyri has already been mentioned ; the Cara nobles were entitled to bear on their heads a crest consisting of a double row of feathers, while the warriors bore a similar crest, but with only a single row of plumes.

The habitations of the Ecuadorian tribes fall roughly into two types, corresponding to the coastal and inland regions. Inland were found small dwellings, built of rough stones and roofed with thatch, and it is probable that such buildings were in use before the coming of the Inca. But of more important buildings, even in the sixteenth century, traces of two alone remained which could with certainty be assigned to the aborigines. One of these was of rough stone, the other of mud. On the

PLATE V

British Museum

COLOMBIA
GOLD HELMET : QUIMBAYA
(Scale : 2/5THS)

British Museum

ECUADOR
STONE SEAT : MANABI

coast mud was regularly employed, fashioned into
large bricks called *adobes*, and a roof of mats was added;
huts of cane were also constructed. But in Manabi,
just that region where, as we have seen, tradition relates
that immigration occurred, remains of stone dwellings
have been discovered, with which are associated remains
of a peculiar character. Many of these buildings are
large, as much as 190 feet long; some are divided into
several chambers, and some are on terraced slopes approached by graded ways.
The walls consist of a double
facing of rough stones filled
with smaller stones and earth.
Associated with these buildings are certain remarkable
chairs, cut from solid stone,
consisting of a seat with arms
but no back, supported on the
back of a crouching man or
puma (Pl. V, Fig. 2). A comparatively large number of
these seats has been discovered, but all within a small
area, and it is of interest that
no mention either of them or
of the buildings is made by
the early chroniclers. Large
stone slabs carved with fig-

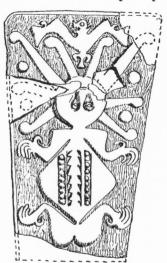

FIG. 3.—Stone slab carved in relief;
Manabi (after Saville).

ures of men and animals in relief also occur in the
neighbourhood and are quite peculiar to the district
(Fig. 3). In some of the figures the face is represented
upside-down, as if to imply, by a peculiar convention,
that the creature is gazing sky-ward, a convention also
found occasionally in Peru, both in the inland and maritime districts.

Other peculiar objects are stone pillars, some with
animal supporters, the object of which is unknown,

but which bear a certain resemblance to the carved wooden tables made by the prehistoric inhabitants of the Greater Antilles, and used by them as altars on which to deposit offerings. The wells mentioned above, which were attributed to the " giants," are found in this locality ; they are deep circular excavations cut in the solid rock or lined with rough stones.   One of the former class is 42 feet deep, exclusive of the earth which has been washed into it ; many of them are now filled up, but the water reappears as soon as they are cleared.

Several forms of burial were practised ; of which that indigenous to the highlands seems to have been simple inhumation, which is recorded of northern Ecuador, Puruha and the original inhabitants of Quito. Velasco states that the Cara introduced another custom ; the body was laid on the ground, or seated on a stool, and the nearest relation placed a stone at its side ; more stones were brought until a wall was built enclosing the corpse. A vault was then added, and the whole, by the further addition of stones and earth, transformed into a mound, the height of which was proportionate to the rank of the deceased. Such mounds or *tolas* are said to be characteristic of a definite region, extending roughly from Quito northwards, and the attribution may be correct. These tolas are of various shapes, circular, oval or cruciform, and sometimes contain more than one body. In some places rude stone statues have been found in them. The finding of stone statuary appears to link this type of burial with the Manabi district of the coast, where so many stone sculptures have been found, and where mound-burial was also practised. The tomb of the Scyri was a more elaborate construction, rectangular in plan and pyramidal in outline, built of large stones.   The bodies were arranged round the walls, and above each was a niche in the wall with a figurine of pottery or metal representing the deceased ; over all a mound was heaped. Velasco says that the bodies of the Scyri were embalmed, and that the small figurines were encrusted with stones of various colours which indicated the age of the dead Scyri and the length of their reigns. The Ecuadorians had no form of writing, and the Peruvian method of recording events and keeping accounts by means of knotted cords was also unknown to them; but it is stated that small pebbles of various sizes, shapes and colours were used for a similar purpose.

Of the coast little can be said on this subject except of Manabi and Esmeraldas, where Saville's excavations have produced interesting results. Here, as said above, the dead were buried in large mounds; these are low flat structures, larger than the inland tolas, reared in some cases on a floor of baked clay. The upper surface measures at times as much as 50 by 30 feet, and there is usually a short monolith at each end. An important feature of the mound is a clay platform at one end, where pots with ashes have been found. Such platforms may have been placed where offerings were made. It is said that the Cara performed ceremonies on the tola, both at the funeral and on the subsequent anniversaries, and possibly these coast people did the same. The bodies are generally found dotted here and there in the mound, and various fragments of pottery, implements, and stone statues are found associated with them. Mortuary chambers and pits were also cut in the rock, for the reception of the dead. Of the inland peoples it is said that, in the case of an important individual, his favourite wife was interred with him, but no trace of any form of human sacrifice on the occasion of a funeral has been found on the coast, though Cieza de Leon attributes the practice to the inhabitants of Porto Viejo. It is interesting to note that urn-burial, which seems in general not to have been practised by the Andean peoples, has been reported of one of the northern provinces, and, further, that the Puruha are said to have sacrificed their first-

F

born and preserved the bodies in vessels of stone or metal. It will be seen later that in the territory of the Diaguite tribes of the mountainous districts of north-west Argentina cemeteries have been discovered in which the bodies of new-born children were deposited, enclosed in well-painted pottery vases, while in parts of Peru the bodies of twins are said to have been similarly preserved.

With regard to religion, the beliefs and practices throughout Ecuador seem to have been much the same, to speak generally, as in Colombia. In the highlands, the "official" cult was that of the Sun and Moon, and Moon-worship was found also among the Cañari. In Quito were two chief temples on opposite hills; one of these was dedicated to the Sun, a square building of stone with a pyramidal roof and a door facing the east. On either side of this door was a monolithic pillar, said to have been used as a gnomon for calculating the calendar, and round the building were twelve shorter pillars repre-senting the months. The other temple was that of the Moon, a circular construction with windows of similar shape. These temples were erected by the early Scyri, but the cult seems to have existed in the country before they arrived, since Sun-worship, probably, was not prac-tised on the coast before the Inca conquest. At Liri-bamba was a temple to the god of war, whose image was a pottery vase in the shape of a human head into which the blood of prisoners was poured before the Scyri abol-ished the practice. But the popular religion consisted in the worship of certain animals; for instance, the Cañari believed themselves to be descended from a huge snake, which had its home in a lake above Sigsig, and to which offerings of gold in the form of figures were thrown, just as in the Chibcha country. A similar snake-cult was found in the northern provinces, and the local worship of pumas, trees, and stones was common throughout the country. This more primitive form of religion was also typical of the coast. Trees, stones, snakes, beasts, and fishes were worshipped. According to Zarate, writing of Manabi, the doors of the temple faced east, and were covered with cotton hangings, inside the door were two figures of black goats to which incense was offered. These " goats " were probably pumas, such as that seen by Benzoni. But, besides the local cults, there existed a general worship of the sea, the element from which the inhabitants drew their supplies, and which here took the place accorded to the Sun by the inlanders. At Manta in Manabi was a celebrated temple to the god of healing, named Umiña, whose image was cut from an enormous emerald. On the island of Puna was another, equally famous, to Tumbal, the god of war, where the hearts of prisoners were offered up ; and the island of La Plata was also regarded as sacred. Human sacrifice seems to have been fairly common on the coast, the blood and heart of the victim constituting the offering. In Manabi the victims were flayed, the skins filled with ashes, and preserved ; and omens were taken from the condition of the entrails. At Guayaquil human sacrifices were made at the season of sowing, and the same occasion was marked by sacrifices of children among the Cañari inland.

With regard to the arts and crafts of the Ecuadorians some details have already transpired in the foregoing passages. It has been seen that the coast people, at any rate in the district of Manabi, worked stone with considerable facility. Indeed, they were far more expert in this particular than the inland peoples, among whom nothing comparable to the sculptured slabs, seats, and pillars of the coast are to be found. It is a little surprising, therefore, to note that, in the area where such sculptures are relatively common, implements of stone are extremely rare, and that in the highlands they have been found in considerable abundance. These consist in the main of club-heads and axes, all of pol-

ished stone, of various patterns, none of which are peculiar to a given district. The variety of type is best
expressed by means of illustration, and can be seen in
Fig. 4. The most common form of club-head is that in
the form of a star (Fig. 4, *g*), somewhat similar to the
type found in New Guinea, and this is furnished with a

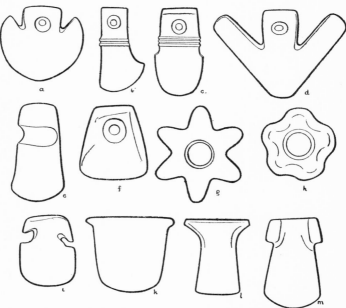

FIG. 4.—Stone axe-blades and club-heads from the Ecuadorian highlands. *a*, Riobamba; *b*, *c*, and *g*, Quito; *d*, Cuenca; *e* and *i*,
near Riobamba; *f*, *k*, and *l*, Otovalo; *h* and *m*, Cayambe.

hole in which the handle was inserted. Some bi-conical
stones, however, have been found, encircled by a shallow
groove, and these must have been attached to the haft
with a lashing. The axe-heads are more varied; some
are pierced, others notched, others again are furnished
with "ears." The latter type has been found on the
coast, and of such a size as to be of no practical use. It
has been suggested that these enormous specimens, one

of which, found on the island of Puna, is no less than
19½ inches in length, were used as gongs, but it seems
more likely that they had a ceremonial significance.
Stone mortars and grindstones for preparing grain are
not uncommon, especially on the coast, while miniature
mortars, probably for grinding pigment, and models

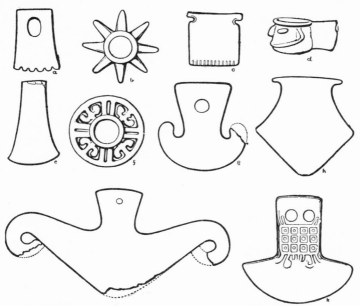

FIG. 5.—Copper axe-blades and mace-heads from Ecuador ; all from
Pindilie, Cuenca, except *k*, which was found at Chordeleg.

of maize-heads (like Fig. 27, *d*), most likely charms,
have been found inland. We know that slings were
used almost everywhere, the Cañari slingers being
especially adept and proving of great value in the
service of the Inca, and many of the indeterminate
spheroid stones discovered may be sling-stones. Spear-
throwers, similar in type to those of the Chibcha,
were used for hurling darts, and the hooks of these
seem in many cases to have been made of stone. The

coast-people were very adept at cutting precious stones, especially emeralds. Gold was known and worked with some facility, though it is not common. The metal was both beaten and cast, such specimens as Pl. IV, Fig. 1, a thin disc with a face in high relief, being masterpieces of hammered work. In the northernmost provinces of the highlands the work is very similar to that of the Quimbaya, but on the coast the technique is different. Here gold seems to have been less rare, and we are told by Zarate that the people of Puna used axes, spear-heads and vessels of this material. However, the weapons at least may have been of plated copper ; the Cañari and the coast people were skilled in covering copper objects with thin gold leaf, and most of the axes shown in Fig. 5 are specimens of this art. The exact method employed is not known, but the leaf may have been hammered on, or the mould may have been lined with leaf before the molten copper was poured in. Copper is much more common, and most of the stone axe-heads have their copper counterparts. The gold-plated specimens from Cuenca are thin, and seem to have been intended rather for ceremonial than practical use; no doubt they were carried by chiefs. Of the more " business-like " examples the type shown in Fig. 5, *k* is characteristic of the Chordeleg and Sigsig district of Cuenca, though examples have made their way to the coast (Guayaquil). Copper club-heads with ornamental open-work have also been found in the Cañari district (Fig. 5, *f*), and copper bowls, bells, and small tweezers for plucking out hair, are common in most localities. But the most curious objects are large discs, similar to the gold specimen mentioned above, but of greater size, which are characteristic of Manabi (Pl. VII, 2). These were probably used as breast-ornaments, though the suggestion has been made that they were gongs. At Manabi a mound has been found, containing an excavation lined

PLATE VI

ECUADOR

1, 4-11. HIGHLAND POTTERY

2. POTTERY GRATER SET WITH STONE: ESMERALDAS

3. POTTERY WHISTLE: ESMERALDAS

(Scale: 1-3, 3/10THS; 4-11, 1/7TH)

with clay, which has been calcined by heat; at the bottom was a quantity of vitrified slag, and it is possible that this was a furnace for metal-casting. But, as no trace of metal was discovered there, it may equally well have been a pottery kiln. A few words must be said of the pottery, which constitutes so large a proportion of the archæological remains. In this respect also the inhabitants of the maritime districts surpassed the inlanders ; not only is the quality of the paste better, but the forms are more varied and graceful, the modelling more skilful (Pl. VI and Fig. 6, *b*), and polychrome decoration, rare in the highlands, is frequently applied. Of the inland districts (see Pls. VI, 4–11, and VIII, 1 and 2), those in the north appear to furnish the best pottery, and the vases of the region near the boundary bear a resemblance to those of Colombia. The Quillacinga graves have yielded vases of good paste mixed with sand, moulded in a variety of shapes, human and animal, and sometimes ornamented with painted designs. Ornament in relief, in the form of monkeys, frogs, snakes, birds, and lizards, is common, the first of these animals predominating, and pottery trumpets, in the form of conch-shells, are often found. Much of the ornament in relief appears to have been formed by the aid of moulds. Elsewhere in the highlands both red and black ware is found, but the former is far more common ; the forms are sufficiently varied, bowls with or without feet (Pl. VI, 5, 6, 9, 11), cups (Pl. VI, 4), and anthropomorphic vases (Pl. VIII, 1 and 2) are all found. The latter, however, seem to be more common in the Puruha district, and are usually rude and conventional. In the north a subdued decoration in red, buff or black slip is often added, as may be seen in Pl. VI, 7–9. Of these the first was found in the Puruha country, but was probably imported thither from further north. Standard bowls of the type seen in Pl. VI, 5, 6 and 9, usually have most of

the decoration on the interior surface, but incised ornament seems again to be characteristic of the Puruha.
Some of the anthropomorphic vases from this neighbourhood (Pl. VIII, 1 and 2) represent a figure
holding a cup ; this design, as we have seen, is found
in Colombia, and it will be met again in Peru (Pl. VIII, 3),
and even as far south as the north-west Argentine.
Moulded ornament, apart from the latter type of vase,
is not common.   On the coast some of the most interesting pottery remains are the numerous figurines
(Pls. VI, 3, VII, 1), which shed considerable light upon

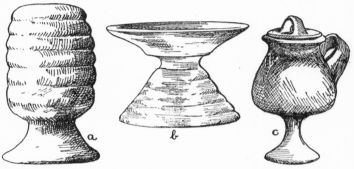

FIG. 6.—Pottery from the Ecuadorian coast.   a and b, Manabi (after
        Saville) ;   c, La Plata I. Inca type (after Dorsey).

the dress, ornaments and appearance of the inhabitants.   Most of these, especially in Manabi, are modelled
with considerable skill and exhibit no little character.
The majority were painted with red and green slip.
As regards vases, those of Manabi, again, are the
best, and the moulded cups and standing bowls of this
district are admirable specimens of pottery made solely
by hand without the use of the wheel (Fig. 6, a and b).
Such vases are usually without painted ornament, relying for their general effect solely on the quality of
their modelling and their burnish, but painted decoration is found, in black, brown, yellow, and blue.   Pottery of a coarser type also occurs, large urns with

rude human features on the necks. The paste varies greatly in quality ; in the majority of specimens it is reddish, but the moulded cups are usually black. Pottery of a pale grey, much mixed with sand, is also found, and is quite characteristic of Esmeraldas as well as of Manabi; and of this grey pottery were made the objects which are perhaps the most typical of the coast district, flat pottery graters (Pl. VI, 2), which are often set with minute chips of stone. Some of the ornament in relief was formed by means of stamps and moulds, both of which are found in some quantities. The former are very similar to those of Colombia, and the latter to those of the Peruvian coast ; many of the figurines were evidently mould-made. Whistles, or ocarinas, often in human form, with two or more notes, are found all over Ecuador. Two of these, each with two finger-holes at the back, are figured in Pl. VI, Figs. 1 and 3, and illustrate well the difference in skill shown in modelling the human figure by the inland and coastal tribes respectively. Pottery braziers, such as Pl. VII, Fig. 1, appear to be confined to the coast-land. Of other pottery objects, mention must be made of the spindle whorls which are found in numbers especially in Manabi, engraved with more or less conventional figures of animals. The pottery of La Plata Island resembles rather that of the highlands.

This sketch of Ecuadorian culture is necessarily incomplete, since the archæology of a large part of the interior is very little known. Much requires to be done in the way of research, especially in the southern districts, and the remains in museums need careful classification before it can be said that this or that type is definitely characteristic of a given region. As far as the coast is concerned, much useful work has been, and is being, done by the George G. Heye expedition, which has shown that in spite of certain similarities, great differences exist between the respective cultures of

Manabi and Esmeraldas ; of which the most important are as follows : stone implements are rare in Manabi, but relatively common in Esmeraldas ; but on the other hand stone sculpture, which is highly developed in the former, is hardly found in the latter province ; and the remains of stone buildings are confined to Manabi.

CHAPTER IV—THE GROWTH OF THE PERUVIAN EMPIRE

IN the last chapter some account was given of the final victories in that series of conquests by which the Inca people became masters of an empire extending, at the time of the Spanish conquest, from the river Ancasmayu in the north, to the river Maule in Chile, and including the modern states of Ecuador, Peru, Bolivia and part of Chile and north-west Argentina. The country included within these limits, as far as its physical aspect is concerned, has already been described in the words of that admirable observer Cieza de Leon ; all that need be added is that he has perhaps not laid sufficient stress upon the extreme beauty and fertility of the valleys, especially in the neighbourhood of Cuzco, and the almost breathless grandeur of the mountain scenery in the same region. The heroes of the following short historical sketch are the tribes who peopled the valley of Cuzco ; and the most important of their neighbours were the following. To the south-west, south, and south-east were the Cotabamba, Chumpivilca and Ayamarca. Beyond these were the Cana and Canchi of the upper Vilcomayu, and southward of them the Colla[1] tribes. To the west were the Quichua and the Chanca of Andahuaylas, the latter of whom extended to the

[1] Prof. Uhle objects to the term Colla on the grounds that it is merely geographical and not ethnographical ; but even so it seems preferable to " Aymara," as a general term for the tribes south of Cuzco. Sir Clements Markham has shown that the term Aymara, as applied to the language of this district, rests on a misapprehension of the early Jesuit missionaries, who learnt the tongue from certain *mitimaes* (colonists), coming originally from a small place of that name within the Quichua-speaking region. The region inhabited by the Colla is termed generally the Collao.

north-west ; beyond the Chanca, around Xauxa, were the Huanca, and beyond the Quichua the Lucana. To the east and north-east, beyond the Paucartambo, were many savage forest tribes known collectively as Anti, the Chuncho, Moxo, etc. ; while along the coast the valleys were peopled by a people of high culture to whom was asssigned the general name Yunca. To the four quarters of the empire as it grew the four following names were given : to the south and south-east, Colla-suyu ; to the east and north-east, Anti-suyu; to the north and north-west, Chinchay-suyu ; and to the west and south-west, Conde-suyu.

At the time when Pizarro entered the Peruvian Empire, the Inca had evolved, if not a civilization, at least a very magnificent barbarism ; their empire was well organized and governed according to a traditional code of laws, the various provinces were administered by a hierarchy of officials who collected tribute and administered justice, and large armies could quickly be raised and maintained on lengthy campaigns in any part of the dominion. It is not surprising, therefore, in spite of the fact that no form of writing was known, that the people capable of such political organization had preserved in traditional form much of their early history. Feats of memory which seem almost miraculous to civilized races, who have become dependent upon written records, have been chronicled of several peoples below the Peruvians in the scale of culture. The nobility among the Polynesians received regular instruction in their past history, and the chiefs could repeat long genealogies which had been faithfully handed down from generation to generation. Even among African races traditional records are not unknown, and in one case a list of over one hundred chiefs, together with many historical details, has been recently obtained from a tribe in the heart of the southern Belgian Congo. The Peruvians were aided in this respect by an elaborate

PLATE VII

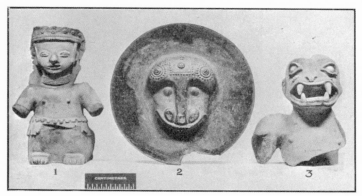

British Museum

ECUADOR

1. POTTERY BRAZIER : ESMERALDAS
2. EMBOSSED COPPER DISC : MANABI
3. POTTERY FIGURE : ESMERALDAS

PERU

ANCIENT POLYGONAL MASONRY : CUZCO

(From Wright's "Old and New Peru," by permission of Messrs. Barry & Sons)

system of knotted cords, which to some extent took the place of writing, and many details of past history were collected by the early travellers and explorers from natives of high standing who were acquainted with the traditions of their race. These accounts have been so ably collated and so graphically set forth in a recent work by Sir Clements Markham, whose knowledge of the literary sources of Peruvian history is unrivalled, that it is almost an impertinence on the part of the writer of this book to attempt a similar task. However, for the sake of completeness some sketch of the growth of the Inca Empire is necessary, and those who desire a more detailed account more graphically told will find it in the book above mentioned.

Our view of the history of Peru must inevitably be coloured by the degree of authenticity which we assign to the writings of Montesinos. While nearly all of the early writers give a list of twelve or thirteen sovereigns, Montesinos records about one hundred. For a long time it was believed that his account was of no value, and it was attributed to an indiscriminating credulity or a fertile imagination. But quite recently evidence has been brought to show that his list may have been copied from the work of Blas Valera, a chronicler, quoted extensively by Garcilasso, whose writings, believed to have been lost, were universally recognized as evidence of the greatest value. As will be seen, the archæology of Peru supports the theory that an extensive empire existed in days long prior to the first Inca of the shorter list, but it seems strange that Garcilasso, who had access to the manuscript of Valera, should have made no allusion to the earlier rulers. Most of the chroniclers, including Montesinos, start their history with the same myth, which will be related immediately, and nearly all of them give the last twelve sovereigns in the same order. It seems possible that these later rulers alone bore the title of

Inca, and that the earlier kings of Montesinos, if his list be accepted, were known by other titles. The Inca proper were as follows :—

1. Sinchi Rocca.	7. Uiracocha.
2. Lloque Yupanqui.	8. Pachacuti.
3. Mayta Ccapac.	9. Tupac Yupanqui.
4. Ccapac Yupanqui.	10. Huayna Ccapac.
5. Rocca.	11. Huascar.
6. Yahuarhuaccac.	12. Atahualpa (usurped).

Garcilasso (and also Betanzos and Velasco) gives one more, inserting a ruler named Yupanqui between Pachacuti (8) and Tupac Yupanqui (9), but it is believed that this Yupanqui was the ruler who appears both in his list and elsewhere as Pachacuti (the word Pachacuti itself not being a name, but a title meaning "Reformer"), and that the deeds attributed to him must be shared between the two Inca mentioned.

The myth, with which most authors preface their accounts of the history, deals with the settlement in the Cuzco valley of a group of people destined eventually to become the rulers of the whole of Peru. There are several versions of the myth, all differing slightly in details, according to the section of the people from whom they were respectively obtained, but the most extended account is as follows. Southward of Cuzco is a place called Paccari-tampu ("House of the Dawn"), where rises a hill, called Tampu-tocco ("House of Windows "), which contains certain caves. From these caves issued a number of people led by four brothers all bearing the title of Ayar, and named respectively Manco, Cachi (Salt), Uchu (Pepper), and Auca (Pleasure). They were accompanied by four sisters, all entitled Mama (Mother), and named Occlo, Huaco, Cura, and Raua. Of these, the eldest brother Manco was the ruler, his power being based on the possession of a fetish in the form of a bird called Inti (Sun), which was kept in a basket and which was supposed to act as his supernatural adviser. This group of eight individuals, by laying claim to divine descent (from the Sun) obtained the leadership over ten tribes who dwelt in the neighbourhood, and, finding the country comparatively sterile, started with their followers on a migration farther north. Manco, the leader, carried a golden staff which, it was prophesied, would sink into the earth at the spot destined by fate for their future home. This staff was probably merely an implement for testing the depth of the soil, and thereby affording an indication of its agricultural quality. The journey proceeded by slow degrees, the travellers making frequent halts to sow and reap the harvest ; but it was not without incident. Apparently Manco became jealous of his brothers, and took means to remove them, but the account of their fate has become invested with the glamour of the supernatural. Ayar Cachi was persuaded to return for certain golden vases and the figure of a llama, the latter being a kind of sacred standard, which he was told had been left in a cave. As soon as he entered the cave to search, his faithless companion rolled a great rock up to the entrance, and Cachi perished, the traitor himself being turned to stone. Uchu, in the course of their wanderings, was told to seize a stone figure which was found upon a hill ; to do this he leaped upon its back, but was himself turned to stone. The place where this occurred, called Huanacauri, was thenceforward regarded as one of the most sacred in Peru, and was the scene of the Huarachicu ceremony, to be described later, at which the young knights were initiated. Ayar Auca was the last to perish ; he had developed wings, and when the travellers came in sight of their promised land, his brother bade him fly to the top of the hill, where afterwards stood the great Sun-temple, and take possession. This he did, but the action was fatal to him, for he forthwith became a stone. The others followed ; the test of the golden staff was applied and found satisfactory, and Cuzco was founded.

The account is particularly interesting as giving many indications of the worship of stones which, though to some extent eclipsed by the official Sun-cult of the Inca, prevailed generally throughout Peru and was of the greatest local importance. It appears that the Cuzco valley at this time was not without inhabitants, but the immigrants no doubt mustered a company sufficiently large to make their settlement good. The tribes which they found in the neighbourhood were gradually incorporated, partly by diplomacy (and in this respect the claim of the leader to divine descenl must have stood him in good stead), partly by actua warfare, and at the death of Manco the immigrants were paramount in the district. As stated above, nearly all the accounts commence with some version of this story, but while the majority proceed immediately to the reign of Sinchi Rocca, representing him to be the son of Manco, that of Montesinos furnishes a list of some ninety rulers before that prince is reached. It is impossible, in view of the recent attempt to prove the authenticity of this author's account, to neglect it entirely ; no doubt many of the incidents belong more properly to the later history, and it seems in some cases as if Montesinos had duplicated certain events, assigning them in modified form both to the early period and what may be called the Inca period proper ; but a short sketch of the events as chronicled by him will be useful as throwing a little light upon the archæology which will be discussed later. The first few reigns were dedicated to the expansion of Cuzco domination within the valley ; the city was built in stone, and a number of immigrants from the south were incorporated in the tribe. Hostilities with neighbours resulted in the capture of the third ruler's heir, but the child was afterwards restored,[1] and the new settlement

---

[1] This story is related by certain authors in connection with the sixth ruler of the later list when a child (see p. 90).

was threatened by no actual danger until two powerful chiefs of Andahuaylas, to the west of the Cuzco
valley, attacked Cuzco and nearly succeeded in captur-
ing it. This episode is the important Chanca rebellion attributed by other authors, and again by Montesinos himself, to later times. The conquest of
Andahuaylas opened a wide sphere to the new-comers ;
the foundation of provincial government was laid, the
building of great roads commenced, and we are even
told of an expedition to Tucuman, though the conquest of the intervening country was not an accom-
plished fact until somewhat later. In the reign of the
twelfth ruler we have an echo of the coming of the
giants and the people of Lambayeque, related in the
last chapter ; many tribes, coming by sea, arrived upon
the coast, from Manabi to Pachacamac, where they
built the famous temple ; and we are told of a projected
expedition against the people of Truxillo.

About the nineteenth ruler a change of dynasty appears
to have taken place; from henceforward a new title,
Amauta, frequently appears, and many of the chiefs are
distinguished as skilful astrologers and reformers of the
calendar. It would seem almost as if a priestly dynasty,
similar to that of the Magi, had succeeded in seizing the
throne, and the worship of Uiracocha, hitherto the state
religion, was eclipsed by the cult of the heavenly bodies.
About this time the first indications of religious wars
appear, in the shape of a projected invasion of the coast,
where doctrines subversive of the Cuzco cult prevailed.
The first signs, too, of the cataclysm, which was destined
to overwhelm the old empire, may be seen in attacks
made by the peoples of Tucuman and Chile ; but the
time was not yet, the invasions were successfully re-
pulsed, and the bounds of empire were extended as far
north as Huanuco, where a fortress was built. The
extent of this early empire, according to Montesinos, is
shown in Fig. 7, *a* ; in a later passage he implies that

G

it extended as far as Quito. However, the end came at last, in the sixty-fourth reign. A general invasion was made by the peoples on the east, south and west, and the subject tribes rose in revolt. The invaders ultimately retired, but the power of Cuzco was broken, and the ruler slain ; the city was left to the priests, and the inhabitants under a new sovereign took refuge at Tampu-tocco, the place of their origin. So complete an overthrow of the empire seems almost inexplicable unless it be imagined that the general uprising was the result of too drastic action on the part of the Amauta dynasty in forcing an unwelcome cult upon their subjects. Possibly they had tried to eradicate the various local forms of worship, and had instituted a religious persecution to which the empire could not submit. Hence the general exodus to Tampu-tocco under a new leader. Indications of some such religious persecution are not wanting in the account of Montesinos. It is interesting to note in passing that according to this author a form of writing on banana-leaves and stones had long been practised, but became obsolete under the rulers of Tampu-tocco, and the system of *quipus*, or knotted cords, as a means of re-cording figures and facts, was invented under the thirteenth of these chiefs. Twenty-four princes ruled in succession over the small state of Tampu-tocco, and their reigns were marked by very few events of importance. It is said that the seventh desired to rebuild Cuzco, but his religious advisers dissuaded him. The first indications of recuperation made their appearance in the reign of the tenth chieftain, who collected a large army, but died before he could make any use of it, and it was not until the thirteenth that a few of the provinces of the old empire were again reduced to submission. But at length, in the reign of the twenty-fourth ruler, occurred events which brought about a change of dynasty and marked the commencement of the rise of the later Inca empire.

By this time the provinces once under the sway of the

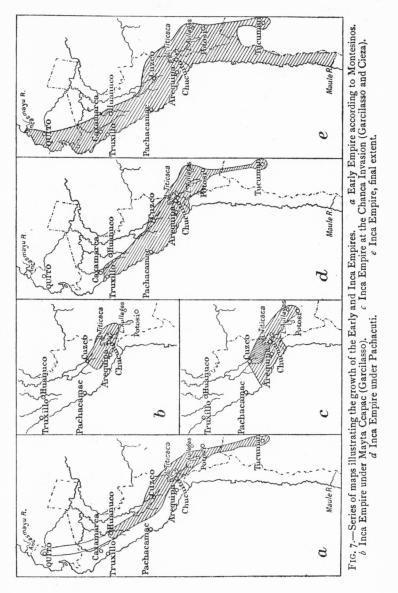

FIG. 7.—Series of maps illustrating the growth of the Early and Inca Empires. *a* Early Empire according to Montesinos. *b* Inca Empire under Mayta Ccapac (Garcilasso). *c* Inca Empire at the Chanca Invasion (Garcilasso and Cieza). *d* Inca Empire under Pachacuti. *e* Inca Empire, final extent.

princes of Cuzco had relapsed into barbarism, the early religion had been overgrown and stifled by local cults, and vice was rampant. But the memory of their early glories was cherished by a number of the members of the former ruling family. One of these, a woman of high birth named Siyu-Yacu, with the assistance of her son and sister, contrived a plot to subvert the present dynasty and to place on the throne one who would initiate a bold attempt to recover the power once possessed by their forefathers. The individual selected was Siyu-Yacu's own son, Rocca, who, as events showed, was a man of singular capacity. A long garment, covered with plates of gold, was prepared for him, and he was secreted in a cavern, known as Chingana, in the Sacsahuaman hill overlooking Cuzco. The persons privy to the plot then spread the report that the youth had been carried off by the Sun in order to receive supernatural instruction, but would return ere long to rule as a divine king over the people. On the fourth day at noon a glittering figure appeared in full view of the populace at the mouth of the cave ; it vanished again, but the vision was sufficient to arouse the greatest excitement and to win full credence for the story told by the plotters. A few days afterwards the vision again appeared, and the crowd rushing up the hill-side discovered Rocca in his golden garb, who told them that he bore a message from the Sun. Conducted to the temple he explained to the assembled people that all their misfortunes had fallen upon them owing to the wrath of the Sun at the corruption of their religion. Let them reform, and under his leadership, the adopted son of the Sun himself, their old power should be restored to them and peace and prosperity return. Full of enthusiasm the people shouted their assent, and Rocca was proclaimed ruler.

From this point the history of Montesinos is more or less in accord with that of the other chroniclers, but, before proceeding, attention may be called to a few points raised by the account given in outline above. It is said that the chief deity worshipped by the immigrants was a god of the name of Uiracocha, at once an elemental nature-god and a culture hero. He was the god of the people as a whole, revered by all alike, but there were many other minor deities reverenced by different tribes, by sections of the tribe, and even by separate families; these were usually various natural objects, stones, lakes, animals, and the like, called by the general name of *huaca*, from which in many cases the worshippers claimed common descent. In this way the members of the ruling family appear to have practised a cult of the Sun, averring that they were his children, and it was only natural that the cult of the ruling house should, as time went on, acquire considerable importance. Its importance would be increased by the construction of a large Sun-temple in the capital city, and the establishment of a special priesthood, until finally it came to be the official religion and began to eclipse the original worship of Uiracocha. Whether the Sun-priesthood acquired such an ascendancy that it was actually able to place one of its members on the throne is uncertain, but at any rate it became sufficiently powerful to inaugurate a religious persecution of the huaca and their worshippers, especially of the cults of a like nature which had begun to spread inland from the coast. But the empire was yet too young, and the bonds which held it too loose, to stand the strain of bitter religious dissension, and the result was fatal. The transference of the civil power to Tampu-tocco hints at a revival of Uiracocha worship, and a temporary eclipse of the Sun-cult, which, however, still continued to be practised at Cuzco. Though Montesinos says nothing of the early steps by which this city began to regain its former importance, yet it is evident that it was in a fairly flourishing condition by the time that Siyu-Yacu made her great *coup d'état*, for the scene of action was the city itself, and the population was evidently strong enough in numbers to support the new ruler, in spite of the fact that the country to the south refused to recognize him.

To turn now to the history of Rocca and his successors, it has been said above that Montesinos alone tells the story of the plot by which he obtained the throne ; the other chroniclers regard him as the son of Manco and imply that his claim to power was based on hereditary right, but they do not agree in the accounts which they give of his reign. In fact, though nearly all the authorities are in agreement respecting the course of events which go to the making of Inca history, they are by no means unanimous respecting the reigns in which these events occurred ; furthermore the accounts of many of the writers are strongly coloured by the individual prejudices of the respective authors. Thus the half-caste historian Garcilasso de la Vega is actuated throughout by the desire, praiseworthy in itself, to depict his mother's people in the most favourable colours. According to him, the Inca were influenced by the noblest motives in their work of empire-building, each war is shown in the light of a crusade to spread good government and a spiritual religion among less enlightened tribes ; forcible measures were only employed in the last resort when long and patient negotiation had failed ; the people loved and trusted the Inca whose rule was wise and beneficent, and who lived blameless lives in the full recognition of the responsibilities of their position. Sarmiento de Gamboa, on the other hand, whose history bears the stamp of authority, in so far as it was collected from a council of high dignitaries, all of whom deposed to the correctness of the information which they contributed, gives quite a different picture. In his work the Inca appear as greedy beyond all else of power, and unscrupulous in the methods by which they obtained it ; their wars were wars of aggression pure and simple, and they welcomed any pretext, no matter how flimsy, for extending their sway by forcible

PLATE VIII

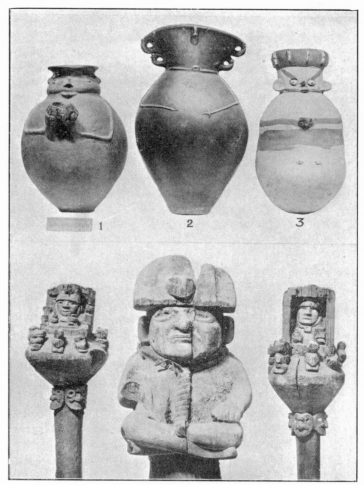

British Museum

ECUADOR AND PERU

1, 2. VASES : THE HIGHLANDS, ECUADOR
3. VASE : PERU
4, 5, 6. WOODEN CARVINGS : MACABI ISLANDS
(Scale : 1-3, 1/9TH ; 4-6, 1/5TH)

means ; towards their subjects they were cruel and unmerciful, holding them fettered in the bonds of a miserable oppression. Sarmiento's aim was to prove that the Inca were cruel tyrants who abused the power which they had unjustly usurped, and thereby to invest the conquering Spaniard with the halo of a liberator, an attempt which, viewed from the standpoint of the present day, is not without a certain humour of a rather grim nature. Between these two extremes the truth must lie, and to judge from the ac ounts of other historians and witnesses, some of whom even, to their subsequent repentance, had taken part in the oppression which followed the overthrow of the Inca kingdom, it lies in this respect nearer to Garcilasso than to Sarmiento. No doubt the Inca, as the Spaniards themselves, used the name of religion as a pretext for extending their power, but the power once gained was not abused, and the laws by which they governed, though strict, were not unnecessarily harsh, and were well suited to the psychology of their subjects.

One of the first acts of Rocca was to enlarge the temple of the Sun, the famous Curicancha, and to inaugurate certain improvements in the city, notably the filling up of a swamp. As to the question whether he attempted to extend his sway by external conquest, historians differ. The majority represent this Inca, and also his two successors, as confining themselves more or less to the Cuzco valley, and gradually, by diplomatic means, extending their influence over the surrounding inhabitants.

Garcilasso, however, makes the expansion of Inca power far more rapid. Sinchi Rocca, indeed, according to him, employed peaceful rather than warlike methods (a fact which is rather surprising, since the title *Sinchi* was that given to war-chiefs), but his successor, Lloque Yupanqui, obtained the submission of the Cana and Colla people to the south-east, and even built a Sun-temple at Hatun-Colla, the chief city of the latter district. Nor did his successes stop there; another expedition added the tribes of the west shore of lake Titicaca, and some of those on the Desaguadero river, to the growing empire, as well as certain of the peoples dwelling to the westward, as far as the foot of the snowy range dividing the inland country from the plains of the coast. The next Inca, Mayta Ccapac, showed equal energy; proceeding with an army to the Desaguadero river, he crossed the stream by means of a bridge of boats, and, after a great battle with the Colla to the east, subdued the country as far as lake Aullagas to the south, and the region of La Paz to the east. Nor was he content merely to follow in the footsteps of his predecessor; the mighty gorge which confines the waters of the Apurimac to the southwest of Cuzco was spanned with a bridge, a great marsh beyond the Chumpivilca people was crossed by means of a causeway, and the Inca army pursued its way victorious to lake Parinacochas and thence on to Arequipa (see Fig 7, *b*). So far Garcilasso; but other authors give no indication of operations outside the Cuzco valley (with the exception of a foray into Andahuaylas, mentioned by Montesinos) until the reign of Ccapac Yupanqui, the successor of Mayta Ccapac, though Cieza states that the latter prince died when he was making preparations for an expedition to the south-west. But with regard to Ccapac Yupanqui, the fourth ruler, all the historians agree in making the region to the southwest of Cuzco, Condesuyu, the main scene of his military operations, though Garcilasso credits him with further conquests in the south-east also, as far as Potosi. His account would seem to show that hitherto there had been no real conquest of the Collao, but that the Inca had been content to make incursions, which amounted to little more than military displays, into the country, and to accept a nominal submission. But this time an opportunity occurred for a more vigorous policy and the history of the campaign affords an excellent illustration of the methods by which the Inca were able to add large regions to the territory they had already acquired, and explains the rapidity with which their empire grew. As might be expected the people of Cuzco were not the only tribe to form the nucleus of a confederation, nor were the Inca the only chiefs who cherished dreams of empire. In the Collao to the south-west a chief of the name or title of Zapana had in early times united a number of tribes under his sway, and his successors, ruling at Hatun-colla, had maintained the power which he had gained. At last a rival chief arose, of the name of Cari, who established himself at Chucuito on the western bank of lake Titicaca and made many successful raids upon the surrounding country, including the islands of the lake. The Zapana of the time tried in vain to reduce the upstart, but without success, and finally both parties appealed to the Inca for assistance. Garcilasso and Cieza give rather different accounts of subsequent events, but the account of Cieza seems the more probable. According to this, the Inca with considerable skill played off one claimant against the other, and finally, when both sides were weakened, stepped in and annexed the whole territory. By this means a large region already accustomed to imperial rule was added to the Inca dominions. Whether these events occurred in the reign of Ccapac Yupanqui, as Garcilasso avers, or two reigns later under Uiracocha, according to Cieza, is not of great importance; the chief point to be noted is that the conquest of the Collao preceded the Chanca invasion which so nearly destroyed the Inca empire.[1]

The fifth Inca, Rocca, is said to have improved the water-supply of Çuzco, and to have founded schools for the education of children of high birth. He also undertook an expedition to the Collao, reaching, according to

[1] The official history of Sarmiento, it is true, places the Colla conquest after the repulse of the Chanca, but for reasons which will appear later this does not seem so probable.

Garcilasso, as far as Sucre; and the same author credits him with penetrating to the Amazonian forests on the north-east, and with extracting an unwilling and, as events proved, utterly insincere submission from certain of the Chanca on the west. A most romantic story is told by Sarmiento of his son and successor Yahuar-huaccac; the name of this prince means "Weeping blood," and is explained by the following incident. When quite a child he was kidnapped by a disaffected chief of the Ayamarca to the south-west of Cuzco, who had desired to marry his mother. His cruel captor ordered him to be killed, but the child, appalled at the prospect of immediate death, wept tears of blood and prophesied ruin and disaster for his would-be murderers. The chief was alarmed, and spared his life, but sent him to a desolate spot to tend llamas in the care of a body of shepherds, from whom he eventually made his escape. This story is told by Montesinos of the fourth chief of his early list, and denied altogether by Garcilasso, who credits Yahuarhuaccac with the conquest of the coast region from Arequipa to Atacama.

The seventh Inca was Uiracocha, whom Cieza regards as the conqueror of the Collao, and at this point the subject of the Chanca invasion arises. Concurrently with the empires of the Inca and of Zapana in the south, a very important confederation had been formed to the north-west and west of Cuzco. The Chanca people, under two chiefs named Uscovilca and Ancovilca, had extended their sway over a number of tribes, and their descendants had become masters of an empire which probably rivalled in extent that of the Inca. For some time there had been a gradually increasing friction between the two powers; the Inca had extorted an unwilling submission from some of the Chanca towns, and the Chanca had made attempts to subdue the small Quichua people, who looked to the Inca for protection. Suddenly matters came to a head, and the Chanca confederacy, led by two brothers, Asto-huaraca and Tomay-huaraca, hurled its united forces against Cuzco. Garcilasso and Montesinos state that the invasion took place at the end of the reign of Yahuarhuaccac, Sarmiento in the reign of his successor Uiracocha, and Cieza in the reign of Uiracocha's incompetent son Urco. Except Cieza none of the chroniclers admit that Urco ever wore the royal fringe, though Sarmiento says that Uiracocha intended him as his successor. But all give the same account of the war. The extent of the Inca empire at this period according to Garcilasso and Cieza respectively is shown in Fig. 7, c. The Chanca host advanced rapidly, and practically without opposition, to the very gates of Cuzco; the reigning Inca fled; and had it not been for the steadfast courage of his ultimate successor (according to the one account Uiracocha, according to the other Pachacuti, the eighth ruler), the Inca domination would have been extinguished. This prince, aided by a few of his relations and some of the more stout-hearted generals, rallied the panic-stricken people and prepared a desperate resistance. He was supported by a contingent of Quichua, but many of the other vassals, who had been hurriedly summoned, waited upon the surrounding hills to see which way the fortune of battle would incline before venturing to take part in the struggle. The fight commenced, and the Inca troops acquitted themselves so well that they were able to keep the foe in check until a large party, detached for the purpose from the main body, fell upon the enemy's flank and threw them into some confusion. The hesitating vassals, seeing this, seized the opportunity to cast their lot in with the defenders, and the result was the complete rout of the Chanca host. This brilliant victory was ever after ascribed to the direct intervention of the god Uiracocha, who was said to have transformed stones into warriors to assist the Inca army, and great honours were paid to this deity after the battle. This point is noteworthy, for Uiracocha was in particular the god of the Collao, and the honours paid to him were probably in recognition of the fact that the Colla vassals by siding with the Inca turned the scale; had they joined the invaders it seems impossible that Cuzco could have been preserved. This fact seems to prove that the Inca had acquired an ascendancy in the Collao before the Chanca invasion. Though the Chanca and the Inca were bound at some period, for political reasons, to come to grips, this struggle had also an underlying religious significance. The Chanca and their allies were supporters of the low form of huaca-worship which the children of the Sun were continually striving to suppress. Excess of zeal in this direction had brought about the fall of the early empire, and the later rulers showed greater diplomacy. Provided that the Sun were recognized as the chief object of worship, they refrained from active interference with such local cults as did not involve human sacrifice and vicious practices, and it seems as if on this occasion by a timely concession the support of the Collao was assured now and for the future. The reigning Inca who deserted the city was held by that act to have abdicated the throne, and the prince who saved the fortunes of the empire assumed the insignia of power. There is little profit in discussing the identity of this Inca. Those who support the claims of Uiracocha state that he adopted the name of the god, who appeared to him in a vision, predicting the onfall of the Chanca and promising his aid. On the other hand there is the point that Pachacuti bore the title only accorded to a great reformer. The fact remains that the conquest of the Chanca confederacy added to the Inca empire an even greater stretch of territory on the west and north-west than had accrued to it in the south when the region ruled by the Zapana was subdued. The sketch-map Fig. 7, c shows the extent of the Inca influence at the time of the Chanca invasion as given respectively by Garcilasso and Cieza; while Fig. 7, d gives the limits

to which it attained under Pachacuti. In looking at
these it must be remembered that the hold of the Inca
on the country west of Cuzco was little more than nominal
until after the conquest of the Chanca, which followed
immediately upon the failure of their invasion. One
of the effects of this conquest was to open to the Inca
the road to the coast, with the result that after a sharp
struggle the maritime valleys from Arica to Truxillo
were added to the empire. Some little confusion has
resulted from the fact that both Pachacuti and his warlike son bore the same name, Yupanqui, and it cannot
be said for certain at what point the conquests of the
one ended and those of the other began ; but the matter
is of little consequence ; the chief point of interest is
that in the course of three reigns, respectively of Pachacuti, Tupac Yupanqui and Huayna Ccapac, the Inca
dominion grew from a comparatively small confederation to the great imperial state which was found by the
Spaniards (Fig. 7, e). Of these three Inca, Tupac Yupanqui was not the true heir to Pachacuti, but was
selected in place of his elder brother, Tupac Amaru, in
consequence of his ability as a general. Tupac Amaru
acquiesced in the arrangement, and afterwards served
his brother faithfully as a trusted commander.

However, before the campaign against the coast valleys
commenced, important events had occurred in the south.
The chiefs of Tucuman sent ambassadors offering their
homage, and friendly relations were established with the
people of Chile. According to Cieza no actual expedition was made to Tucuman until the reign of Huayna
Ccapac, but there is little doubt that this province became part of the Inca empire. Remains of Inca type
are very common there, and the ease with which the
region fell into the hands of the Spaniards, as compared
with the neighbouring districts of the north-west Argentine, can only be explained by the supposition that it
was fully under the control of the Inca. As regards

Chile, Montesinos states that Yahuarhuaccac had married a daughter and a niece to two Chilean chiefs, and that their children came to pay a visit to their uncle Uiracocha after he had become Inca. After being entertained with lavish hospitality, they returned to find their country in a state of rebellion. They appealed to the Inca with the result that they were re-established in power, but as vassals of Cuzco.

The operations in the north and west were more important; from the Chanca country, now thoroughly reduced to submission, a slow advance was made through Xauxa, Bonbon and Huanuco as far as Caxamarca. But this time the expeditions were no mere military demonstrations; every foot of the ground traversed was assured before further advance was made; a chain of fortresses was built, and a great road constructed which ensured the possibility of rapid communication. The northward advance of the Inca troops was marked by an interesting occurrence. The conquered Chanca had been compelled to furnish levies for the expedition, and a part of their forces were under the command of a chief named Hanco-huallu, who had taken part in the invasion of Cuzco but had been pardoned. This chief could not bear the subordinate position to which he was now reduced, and, with a large number of followers, fled rapidly in a northerly direction, crossing the Andes and disappearing in the forests near the Marañon.

The chief of the Caxamarca region offered the most obstinate resistance to the Inca forces, and here the latter came into collision with the highly-cultured people of the the valleys round Truxillo, who came to the assistance of the ruler of Caxamarca. Once in possession of the strip of highlands bordering the coastal plains, the Inca next proceeded to conquer the coast itself. This was a lengthy and difficult task. The maritime valleys were inhabited by a numerous and warlike population whose culture, in some respects, surpassed that of the Inca, and the hot climate of the coast proved insupportable to the invading highlanders for any length of time. The question of religion was also involved. The Sun, whose worship the Inca insisted should be accepted, was no benefactor to the coast-people, whose life was one long struggle against drought. But the Inca was firm; arrangements were made by which the invading troops were relieved every few months, the valleys were closely invested, and finally the sources of the only water-supply were seized. Rain on the coast was a phenomenon of great rarity, and practically the only water came from the mountains. By means of a wonderful system of reservoirs and aqueducts it was distributed over the coasta districts, and large tracts of what had been uninhabitable desert were thus brought under cultivation. But the very engineering skill, which enabled the coastal tribes to bring their water-supply from a distance inland, contributed to their overthrow. The aqueducts were too long to admit of adequate defence, and, as soon as the upper channels fell into the hands of a foe, the choice lay between submission on the one hand and starvation on the other.

The habitable valleys of the coast were grouped under several rulers; much the same culture prevailed throughout the whole district, and the inhabitants were known to the Inca under the common name of Yunca. In the south, Yca, Nasca and Pisco seem to have formed one group; Chincha was ruled by a prince of the same name, and the valleys between this point and Pachacamac were controlled by a chief named Chuquimancu. From Pachacamac to Huaman a more powerful chief, Cuismancu, held sway, and from here to Truxillo stretched the domain of the most powerful of all, Chimu. But if the last-mentioned chiefdom was the largest, the kingdom of Cuismancu was the most important from a religious point of view. At Pachacamac was a great temple to the deity of that name, who was revered throughout the maritime district, and received the homage of countless pilgrims from other valleys. At Lima was a hardly less celebrated shrine, where the god Rimac ("The Speaker") delivered oracles to those who came to inquire the will of heaven. Of such importance were these two divinities that the Inca permitted the continuance of their worship, and even made offerings himself at their respective temples. At the same time he caused a magnificent Suntemple to be built at Pachacamac in a more exalted position than the older shrine. A concession of this nature no doubt made the conquest of this region of the coast easier ; but in the kingdom of the Chimu a fierce resistance was made from valley to valley, and the chief only gave way when he was invested in the Santa valley in the north of his realm. Cieza places the conquest of the coast after that of Quito, and represents it as taking place from north to south, but as the Chimu had assisted the chief of Caxamarca against the Inca, it seems more likely that the latter preferred to subdue the maritime districts before proceeding further north. Flushed with success, the Inca about this time undertook an expedition of far greater difficulty. A large body of troops was sent across the eastern cordillera to the Amazonian forests, which stretched unbroken from the foot of the chain to the Atlantic. Efforts were ·made to penetrate the country from several points, and the Inca troops forced their way through the dense undergrowth and over trackless swamps, continually harassed by the arrows of the savages, with whom they could never come to grips. A body of them penetrated so far that they shrank from the perils involved in a return, and settled with one of the less hostile tribes, where they were found by Spanish explorers of a later age. Little was done in the way of conquest, but a few of the tribes on the fringe of the forest were subdued, a tribute of macaws, monkeys, honey and wax was levied, and a number of coca-plantations were prepared. In the north the way was now open to the empire which had been established by the rulers of Quito, and the conquest of Ecuador, commenced by Tupac Yupanqui, was finally effected by Huayna Ccapac. This has already been sketched in the last chapter, and it has been mentioned that the river Ancasmayu was fixed as the northern boundary of Inca rule. In the south the great Atacama desert was traversed by a road constructed across it; and the Chilean tribes beyond were conquered as far as the river Maule. An attempt to penetrate still further southward brought disaster upon the invaders at the hands of the nomad Araucanians, and the Maule was finally accepted as the southern limit of Peruvian power. In one other quarter the Inca arms suffered defeat. East of the Bolivian province of Charcas was a region of dense forest and morass inhabited by a fierce and uncultured people called Chiriguano. For two years an army strove to subdue the region, but, as among the Anti further north, the physical features of the district provided insuperable difficulties, and it was obliged to retreat baffled. Before the end of the reign of Huayna Ccapac the Inca empire had reached its greatest extent, and almost immediately the news arrived of the advent upon the coast of white and bearded strangers.

Subsequent history is well known, but for the sake of completeness it may be summed as briefly as possible. Huayna Ccapac died before Pizarro made his attempt upon the country. He left two sons, Huascar, the legitimate heir, and Atahualpa. To Atahualpa he left the kingdom of Quito, or so it was claimed, and thus sowed the seed of dissension between the two brothers. Never before had the empire been thus divided, and the act was a direct violation of the customary law governing the succession. The supporters of Atahualpa alleged that he was the son of Huayna Ccapac by the last prin-

H

cess of Quito, and thus tried to substantiate his claim to the chieftainship of Ecuador. But Sir Clements Markham has shown that this can hardly have been the case. After a short period of extreme tension Atahualpa marched upon Cuzco, supported by the northern army of occupation and some of the best fighting tribes of Ecuador. Huascar was defeated, and fell into his hands, and Atahualpa assumed the supreme power. Whether he ordered a general slaughter of the nobles who supported his brother is uncertain ; at any rate, he refrained from taking the life of Huascar himself, until he feared that the Spaniards were about to support his cause. With the capture of Atahualpa by the Spaniards, and the subsequent murder of Huascar, the history of the Inca empire ends for the purposes of this work.

CHAPTER V—PERU : GOVERNMENT

THE constitution of a people, like its language, being the product of its past, is always a little behind the needs of the present ; anything like radical change in the method of government is always repugnant to the people at large, and one of the distinguishing features of good statesmanship is to adapt the old machinery to the performance of new tasks, so that the changes necessitated by altered circumstances shall be as little apparent as possible. Judged by this standard the Peruvians were remarkably fortunate in their statesmen ; the primitive constitution of the village community had been expanded to fit the needs of a great empire, yet the inhabitants at large, except those of the capital, can have been conscious of little change in their circumstances, save in the direction of increased prosperity and security. From within, the great bureaucracy which directed the communistic system must have been hardly apparent, while the benefits of the communistic system itself were visible to every eye. The Inca system has sometimes been represented as decadent at the time of the Spanish conquest, as a mechanical and soulless tyranny ready to collapse at the first impulse from without. This is not so. In popular language it was in every sense a "going concern," and the very ease with which the Spaniards achieved their conquest when once they had laid hands upon the motive power within the bureaucracy, bears witness, not to the effeteness of the latter, but, on the contrary, to the remarkable control which it exercised throughout the whole empire.

In the earliest times the Peruvians seem to have

lived in small independent communities, or groups of such communities, ruled by the heads of families, but in war accepting the leadership of some distinguished warrior who bore the title of Sinchi. Under such circumstances it was inevitable that men should arise who, having gained the position of war-chief, would encourage the tribe to adopt an aggressive policy in order to retain their power. Gradually a few of the neighbouring tribes would be conquered and absorbed, and the Sinchi, from the continual exercise of his authority when upon the warpath, would begin to acquire influence in times of peace also, and would finally attain the position of chief. By further conquest and alliance the embryo state would expand, the individual tribes would not necessarily change their communistic manner of life, nor their former leaders, only the latter would be subordinated to the chief of the paramount tribe. In a country where nearly all families claimed descent in some miraculous manner from a lake, a stone, a tree, or an animal, the claim of the ruler to divine lineage would be hailed with no surprise, for his ancestor would be magnified with him, and would soon attain the status of a tribal god. In some such way the miniature empires of the Colla and Chanca must have developed, as well as that of the Inca.

The basis of the Peruvian social system was the family, and the people were divided into a number of *ayllu*, or lineages ; at Cuzco these ayllu were divided into two groups, living in different parts of the city, and called respectively Hanan-Cuzco and Hurin-Cuzco ("Upper Cuzco" and "Lower Cuzco"). The origin of this twofold division is obscure, and is explained differently by different authors. Manco Ccapac, Lloque Yupanqui, and Inca Rocca have respectively been credited with the arrangement, while Montesinos makes it date from as far back as the fifth reign of his early list. It is probable that it was of early date, since it was not peculiar to the Inca. The two chiefs who led the Chanca invasion are said to have ruled respectively over the Hanan-Chanca and the Hurin-Chanca; so it is not unlikely that the institution may be connected with the early empire of pre-Inca times. As to its meaning, nothing can be said. The two divisions may have represented two original tribes of a confederacy, or they may conceivably have been connected with some exogamous form of marriage. If the latter they must be very ancient, for the Peruvians tended, as far as our knowledge goes, far more in the direction of endogamy than exogamy.[1] While the Inca state was yet small, the primitive communistic system continued in operation without much supervision; but as the empire grew, and tribe after tribe was added to it, an official class gradually sprang into existence, whose duty it was to see, not only that every man performed his share of work, but also that the products of united labour were fairly distributed. The idea of constant supervision, so repugnant to the Anglo-Saxon temperament, was neither new nor distasteful to the Peruvians. Individual freedom meant nothing to them, and obedience to a superior was a habit. Superstitious to a degree, they were always ready to credit a conqueror with supernatural powers, and readily acquiesced in a new ruler when the change brought no alteration in their individual prosperity. The contrast in this respect between the Peruvians and Araucanians is most striking; the latter form the subject of a later chapter, but we may anticipate by saying that among them individual freedom was a creed, as among our own forefathers, which rose superior to any supernatural terrors. And when a people as a whole is prepared to perish rather than submit, it is unconquerable. Hence it is not surprising that the Inca empire ceased at the river Maule.

[1] Endogamy = the practice of seeking a wife within the group; exogamy = the practice of seeking a wife outside the group.

Of the growth of the huge bureaucracy which the Spaniards found in Peru, little can be said, but it is probable that it only began to be evolved from the primitive communism when, under Pachacuti, the policy of effective conquest and colonial expansion was seriously inaugurated. Later its ramifications extended to every hamlet of the empire. The latter, for the purposes of administration, was divided into provinces, each ruled by an hereditary Curaça who had power to impose local by-laws in accordance with the customary code of the Inca. Under the Curaça was a hierarchy of officials, ranging from sub-chiefs to subordinate inspectors whose responsibility was limited to the supervision of no more than ten heads of families. A strict census was kept of the population and resources of each province, and the returns were sent regularly to Cuzco. In accordance with the census, tribute was imposed, and, as money was a thing unknown in Peru, all tribute was in kind. Of this tribute the most minute records were kept, and the system by which the imperial accounts were registered deserves a short description. No form of writing can be proved to have existed under the Inca. It is true that Pachacuti is said to have had certain events recorded by paintings on boards, but we have no warrant to suppose that these paintings approximated in any way to a hieroglyphic script. Montesinos, again, says that under the older empire writing was practised on stones and banana-leaves, but the statement is in the highest degree doubtful, and we possess no single trace of corroborative evidence. But if they had no form of writing, the Peruvians had invented a very serviceable substitute, the *quipus*. These quipus (Pl. IX, 2) were cords on which were made knots of almost infinite multiplicity. For the purposes of reckoning, each form of knot represented a different number, and each string a different subject; to some of the strings,

PLATE IX

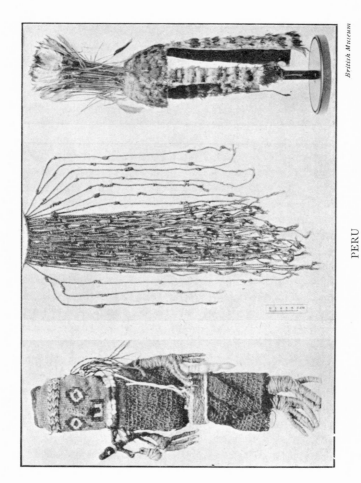

British Museum

PERU

1. DOLL.   2. QUIPUS   3. FEATHER-WORK HEAD-DRESS

COAST NEAR TRUXILLO

subordinate strings were attached (as can be seen in the illustration), serving as footnotes, and the strings forming one set of accounts were arranged as a fringe along a master-string. An indication of the nature of the objects enumerated was furnished by the colour of each string, and the combinations of colours and types of knots gave an almost endless variety to the uses to which this method of recording could be put. It is even said that events were recorded by means of the quipus, and the statement is not incredible, since the system was in the hands of professional accountants, Quipucamayoc, who gave their whole lives to its study and elaboration.

The census made, and the local resources estimated, it remained to impose the tribute, which consisted in the performance of the various tasks necessary for the maintenance and defence of the individual and the state. From two classes of work no man was exempt except by special privilege, agricultural labour and military service, but apart from this, those individuals who were masters of a particular craft were not set to work at anything else. Weaving and spinning were matters of common knowledge, but mining, metallurgy, stone-working and the like, were the tasks of selected artisans. Whether a time-system was in vogue, or whether a man's tribute consisted in the performance of a definite piece of work, is uncertain, since Garcilasso, who gives the best account of this communal labour-system, seems to contradict himself, but probably the system varied according to the nature of the task. No one was allowed to be idle except the sick ; and even the aged, the deaf and blind, and young children, were accorded tasks suited to their limited capacities. It was because the whole of the labour was in the hands of the state that the Inca were able to achieve such marvels in the way of building and road-making ; but the *corvée*-system was not abused, the extent of a man's services, as said above, was limited

(probably in this case by time) and his labour was interrupted by regular rest-days on which he was en-
couraged to hold festival with his fellows. As for the
artisans, their task consisted solely in the manufacture
of definite articles, their material being supplied them ;
and, in the same way, each man received wool for spinning and weaving sufficient for the needs of himself and
his family. The various manufactures and the field-
produce were collected by the officials, and sent to the
chief city of the province at a fixed time ; there they
were registered by the Quipucamayoc in the presence of
the Curaça, and were henceforward at the disposal of the
state. The officials themselves did not labour, their services in the matter of supervision being regarded in the
light of tribute ; and the Inca class, those who were of
the blood royal by birth or *ex officio*, were exempt from
tribute altogether. Besides this no actual tribute was
exacted from youths below the age of twenty-five, but
they might assist their father in the performance of his
allotted task, or he might employ them in the performance of household duties or the tilling of the land allowed
him by the state. In any case, the subordinate inspectors
saw to it that they were not idle. But if no one, save
the members of the ruling caste, was altogether exempt
from some kind of labour, at least there was no poverty.
The produce of the state lands was stored ready for the
victualling of an expedition, or for the relief of a famine
in any quarter of the empire, and the condition of the
peasant in Peru approximated nearer to the ideals of the
doctrinaire socialist than in any country in the world.
But it was at a price which perhaps the natives of no
other country would consent to pay. From the cradle
to the grave the life of the individual was marked out
for him ; as he was born so would he die, and he lived
his allotted span under the ceaseless supervision of
officials. His dress was fixed according to his district ;
he might not leave his village except at the bidding of

the state, and then only for state purposes, he might not even seek a wife outside his own community. An individual of ability might perhaps rise to be one of the subordinate inspectors, but the higher ranks were inexorably closed to him. Even his own family was not entirely under his control, for his daughters, if of exceptional beauty, might be taken by the state to serve in one of the " convents " described later.

Each new province, as it was added to the empire, was organized after the same fashion. Though the Inca empire grew so rapidly, it was not built in haste. The *corvée*-system enabled the ruler to call up enormous masses of men, and to relieve them at reasonable intervals, and it seems to be a fact that actual force was not employed until all the resources of diplomacy were exhausted. The regions already annexed were assured by the building of fortresses and government residences, and there followed in the track of the army a whole host of officials, road-makers and artisans, by whom the country was organized on the accepted lines. Further security was ensured by an ingenious expedient. Large sections of the indigenous population were deported to some distant province of similar climate, and their places filled by others of whose fidelity there was no question. The mutual suspicion which was bound to endure, at any rate for a period, between the new-comers and the old inhabitants rendered anything like organized revolt impossible. Deported colonists were known as *mitimaes*. The same system was employed to relieve a congested population, and to bring under cultivation fertile lands which lay fallow for lack of husbandmen, and resulted in the introduction into many regions of forms of produce before unknown there. Mitimaes sent to a district hitherto uncultivated were accorded certain minor privileges, and their tribute was remitted for a given period until the land was well under cultivation. The communal system enabled supplies of grain to be sent from the fertile valleys to the sterile pasture-lands of the high country for the support of the numerous shepherds who watched the state flocks. At first, at any rate, the former ruler of a newly conquered district was not deposed, if he promised allegiance to the Inca, but was established as Curaça. At the same time an Inca governor was appointed to the province, to command the garrison and to receive the tribute, but not otherwise to interfere with the government of the people except in emergency. But in later times, according to Sarmiento, Tupac Yupanqui deposed the existing chiefs throughout the country, and appointed officers of his own. The heirs of the Curaça were sent to Cuzco to be educated, and were thus hostages for the fidelity of their parents, at the same time imbibing all the Inca traditions.

Rapid communication between the most remote districts and the capital was secured by roads, which in their way are marvellous examples of primitive engineering. Two main routes led from the northern extremity of the empire to the southern, the one following the coast-line, the other the lofty region between the cordilleras. These were connected by cross-roads, such as those between Cuzco and Nasca (Wiener), Xauxa and Lima (Cieza), Pampa and Huaura, Chavin and Paramonga, Caxamarca and Zaran (Wiener). Of the two, that in the highlands was by far the more difficult of construction and Cieza writes of it as follows :[1] "One of the things which I admired most in contemplating and writing down the affairs of this kingdom, was to think how and in what manner they can have made such grand and admirable roads as we now see, and what a number of men would suffice for their construction, and with what tools and instruments they can have levelled the mountains and broken through the rocks to make them so broad and good as they are. . . . Some of them extended for over one

[1] From the translation by Sir Clements Markham.

thousand one hundred leagues, along such dizzy and frightful abysses that, looking down, the sight failed one. In some places, to secure the regular width, it was necessary to hew a path out of the living rock ; all of which was done with fire and their picks. In other places the ascents were so steep and high that steps had to be cut from below to enable the ascent to be made, with wider spaces at intervals for resting-places. In other parts there were great heaps of snow, which were more to be feared, and not at one spot only, but often recurring. Where the snows obstructed the way, and where there were forests of trees and loose clods of earth, the road was levelled and paved with stones when necessary." It was even the custom some-times, when an Inca travelled, to disregard the road made by a predecessor, and to construct a new route. Thus Cieza speaks of three or four roads in the neighbour-hood of Vilcas, and states that he once lost his way on one of the older tracks, believing it to be that still in use. On the coast the difficulties were less, and the road was broad, paved with stone slabs, protected by walls and shaded by trees. But, where it led through the desert, the presence of moving sand-dunes rendered a paved way a waste of time. In such places the route was marked by long poles set in the earth at short dis-tances, many of which ultimately served the improvi-dent Spanish conquerors for firewood ! The roads were made and kept in repair by local labour, each province being responsible for the section passing through its territory, and, in the desert parts, the in-habitants of the nearest villages were called out to per-form the work and were supplied with provisions until the completion of their task.

The main routes met in the centre of Cuzco, forming four cross-roads. According to Wiener, the mountain road to the north ran through Xauxa, over Cerro de Pasco, past Huanuco Viejo and Chavin, to Caxamarca ;

that to the west, to Nasca, where it turned north, and followed the coast to Tumbez, proceeding thence inland *viâ* Loja and Cuenca to Quito, and so to the Ancasmayu. That to the east, led to the Andes beyond Paucartambo; and that to the south, *viâ* Arequipa, to Arica, whence it must have crossed the Tarapaca and Atacama deserts to Coquimbo. Another southern route kept to the highlands, proceeding through the Collao and along the western shore of lake Titicaca to Tiahuanaco. From here there was possibly an extension to southern Bolivia, and even into the north-west Argentine; at any rate traces of Inca roads have been found recently in that locality.

Along the main roads were established a series of small huts, and in each hut were posted two men, who watched the road in each direction. If it were necessary to send a message to the capital, the provincial official would communicate it to one of the men at the nearest post-house, who immediately started to run as fast as he could to the next, which was about half a league distant. As soon as he drew within ear-shot he commenced to shout his message, and as soon as it was understood, one of the watchers would dart off on the road to the next post, and so the message was carried to its destination. The posts were set at short intervals in order to allow the runners, or *Chasqui*, to cover the distance at the top of their speed; the Chasqui themselves were selected for their swiftness of foot, and each remained on service for a stated period during the year, thus paying his "tribute" to the state. By this means, in spite of the precipitous nature of the road, a message could be transmitted from Quito to Cuzco, a distance of over a thousand miles as the crow flies, in eight days. Quipus were also handed from Chasqui to Chasqui when it was necessary to send a communication of greater length. The system is attributed to Pachacuti. Along the route were also constructed *tambo*, "inns" or storehouses, which formed provision depôts for the use of expeditionary forces or those who travelled on state affairs (in fact there were no other travellers).

The provinces were visited periodically by high officials who went a round of inspection, and at the same time listened to complaints; these were registered and referred to Cuzco whence judges were sent to administer justice. But it was only the most serious offences which came before them ; in each village was a magistrate who tried cases of less importance, and inflicted summary penalties in accordance with a definite code. The various subordinate inspectors were obliged to report the smallest misdemeanours to their superior officers, under pain of suffering double the penalty attached to the offence ; the local judges kept strict account of the cases which had come before them, and the quipus on which these cases were recorded were liable to scrutiny by the travelling inspectors. Serious crime, or indeed crime of any sort, seems to have been exceedingly rare ; partly no doubt owing to the elaborate system of supervision, and partly owing to the fact that the ordinances of the Inca were regarded as divine commands, but partly also by reason of the natural docility of the Peruvian. Then too, as regards the most serious offences of all, a man's relations, and even his entire village, were held responsible for his acts and shared his punishment. This system of collective responsibility is common in primitive communities, and invariably proves to be an extremely efficient check upon crime. Children were not exempt from the law, and special punishments were allotted to them, but their fathers were punished at the same time, because a child's naughtiness was held to be the result of bad up-bringing. The chief punishments were flogging and death, fines of course did not exist among a people where there was practically no private property. Besides the regular inspections there were also occasions, occurring at irregular intervals, when the

Inca himself made a visitation of his empire, a proceeding which, in the days of its greatest extent, occupied several years.

The ruler himself lived in divine state, and bore the title of Sapa Inca, or Only Inca; the title Inca was also assigned to all males of royal blood generally, married Inca being called Atauchi, and the sons of the ruler, Auqui. Women of royal blood were called Palla, the unmarried daughters of the ruler, Ñusta, and his chief wife, Ccoya. It was a rule for the Sapa Inca to marry his sister, who thus became Ccoya, but the antiquity of the practice is at least doubtful. The idea which seemed to underlie it was that the purity of the succession should be preserved as far as possible, for it was only the sons of the Inca and Ccoya who were the rightful heirs to the kingdom. Of them the eldest had first claim, but, as in the case of Tupac Amaru, eldest son of Pachacuti, he could be superseded in favour of one of his brothers if the exigencies of the moment demanded. The Inca generally formed a ruling caste, sharing in the divine origin of the head of their clan; they were possessed of numerous privileges, such as exemption from tribute, and were distinguished by various *insignia* of which the most important were the two large studs worn in the lobes of their ears. To such an extent were these ornaments the peculiar privilege of their class, that the Spaniards gave them the name of *Orejones*. The badge of sovereignty was a fringed cord called *llautu*, of vicuña-wool, wound three or four times round the head. In the case of the ruler the fringe was red, in the case of the heir, yellow; and the higher officers, such as viceroys, seem to have borne similar fringes of other colours. Another ornament, peculiar to the Sapa Inca, was a golden diadem in which were fixed two wing-feathers of the bird called Coraquenque; his garments, a long tunic and a square cloak, were made of the finest vicuña-wool, and he sat on a

throne of gold supported by a large plate of the same
metal. Before him was carried a banner, blazoned with
the rainbow, the badge of the royal house. The Inca's
court was brilliant in the extreme; all the utensils of
the royal household were of gold or silver, and magnificent gardens were attached to the palace in which every
kind of plant was imitated in the precious metals. Not
even his own relations could enter the presence of the
ruler without removing their shoes and carrying burdens
on their backs, expressing thus the sense of their own
unworthiness. When he travelled abroad to visit the
provinces he was carried in a wooden litter resplendent
with gold and jewels, and furnished with curtains which
could be drawn when the divine inmate desired privacy.
The bearers were all chosen men, inhabitants of certain
provinces, who gave their services by way of tribute,
and had undergone long training in the art; while in
front went runners whose duty it was to remove the
slightest obstacle from the path lest the bearers might
stumble, an offence punishable, it is said, with death.
The whole resources of the empire were at the service
of the Inca. Large bodies of selected labourers drawn
from the provinces built his spacious palace in Cuzco and
his hardly less magnificent residences in the suburbs,
whither he retired to refresh himself when tired with the
cares of the state. All the gold and silver produced
throughout the country was royal property, and even the
other Inca and the Curaça only employed ornaments
and utensils made from the precious metals by his permission. For him the inhabitants of the many "convents"
spent their days in weaving clothing from the wool of
the vicuña and llama; of these the finest were reserved
for his personal use, while the rest were distributed
among the other Inca.

When a ruler abdicated or died, one of the highest
officials was appointed to act as regent, since it was necessary for the heir to prepare himself for his new office

by a long and severe fast. The heir then received the fringe, *llautu*, in the great Sun-temple at Cuzco, and was henceforward absolute ruler of the empire. It was necessary that the coronation ceremony should take place at Cuzco, and one of the chief reasons why Atahualpa was regarded as a usurper was the fact that he assumed the fringe at Tumebamba.

Such then was the Peruvian constitution ; at the head the divine ruler ; next, the Inca nobility, who held the principal offices of state ; next the Curaça who were not Inca, but who were often permitted to adopt certain of the Inca *insignia*, notably the ear-studs ; next, the humbler members of the great official hierarchy, and finally the populace.

In connection with the noble class an institution of the greatest interest was the ceremony called Huara-chicu, at which the youths of high birth were admitted to a kind of chivalrous order. This ceremony was closely connected with the very ancient and holy *huaca* called Huanacauri, the origin of which has been related above. It is said that just before Ayar Uchu became a stone, he laid upon his brother Manco a command that after the foundation of the prospective city he should be regarded as the patron of all the youths of the clan on the occasion when they were admitted to manhood. It seems probable that the ceremony was extremely ancient, and dated from pre-Inca days. It is almost undoubtedly the survival of some primitive initiation ceremony, such as exists among so many barbarous peoples, at which the youths were dedicated to the god, and proved their manhood by submitting to numerous ordeals more or less severe. After a six-day fast, in which the near relations participated, the candidates took part in a foot-race from the sacred Huana-cauri hill to the fortress at Cuzco. The winner received great honour, and was selected as captain over his companions. So writes Garcilasso, but another author, also of Inca blood, states that the race took place from the city to the Huanacauri hill where were placed certain animals typical of swiftness and sluggishness.

A more severe test than the foot-race was provided by a sham fight in which one half of the candidates attempted to storm a fort held by the other half; blunted weapons were used, but severe wounds were by no means infrequent. The struggle lasted for one whole day, and on the next the attacking party assumed the *rôle* of defenders, and *vice versâ*.

Next followed a series of individual competitions in various athletic exercises, and in the use of different weapons, javelin, bow, and sling, in which candidates of similar age were pitted one against the other. Their vigilance was proved by long spells of sentry duty, their fortitude by scourging with wands of osier, while their self-control was made the object of the following peculiar test. A skilled warrior brandished a club or spear close to the faces and limbs of the novices while they, as Garcilasso says, "were expected to stand as immovable as rocks beaten by sea and wind"; the slightest sign of flinching, the mere blinking of an eye, brought disgrace upon the unlucky candidate.

The thorough nature of soldierly training among the Incas is well illustrated by the fact that the young aspirant to military honours was expected to be proficient not only in the use of arms, but also in their manufacture, and, further, in the preparation of sandals, a matter of great importance in a country so extended as ancient Peru, where a campaign entailed a series of long and wearisome marches. Provision was also made for the moral training of the candidates in a series of lectures delivered by men of distinction in which ideals, strangely similar to those of Spanish chivalry, were set before them—ideals which in practice often suffered a distortion as great as those of their conquerors.

At the conclusion of the month of probation the

I

candidates were brought before the ruler to receive at his hands the *insignia* of their new rank, "without which," Garcilasso writes, "as the books on knighthood would have it, they were virgins unable to bear arms." The occasion was one of great solemnity. The ruler, surrounded by the highest princes of the blood, received the homage of each of the candidates in turn, and with his own hands conferred upon him the most important mark of the dignified position to which he had attained, by piercing his ears with a golden bodkin. The holes were not allowed to close, but were gradually enlarged until they could support ornaments of considerable size. Such ornaments, as remarked above, were the mark of the ruling caste.

After this honour the candidate passed before the Inca who ranked next in authority to the ruler, and received from him a pair of cloth shoes of the pattern worn by the ruling class—a proceeding which Garcilasso compares to the investiture of a Spanish knight with spurs. After this he was conducted to another apartment where other Incas of high rank clad him in the loincloth, *huara*. This proceeding ranked next in importance to the piercing of the ears, which was a royal privilege only to be conferred by the Son of the Sun himself; but, in so far as it marked the boy's attainment of his majority, it gave the name to the whole ceremony. The presentation of the shoes, it is said, was not an essential part of the investiture, but was regarded rather in the light of a reward for the hardships undergone during the month of probation.

As remarked above, no Inca who had failed to pass through the whole course of initiation could hope for an honourable position either in civil or military life. Even the heir-apparent himself was not exempt from any of the ordeals to which the other candidates were submitted. In fact, it is recorded that he was treated with greater rigour than his comrades, for it was held, in proportion as his destiny was higher than theirs, his probation should be more searching; the wider his experience in the toils and hardships of war, the more ready would be his recognition of good service on the part of his future subjects. For a similar reason his clothing during this period consisted of the "vilest and most wretched clothes that can be imagined," so that his future prosperity might not render him blind to the evils of poverty, but that, inspired by the sympathy of experience, he might indeed merit the royal title of Hacchacuyac, the meaning of which is "Lover and Benefactor of the Poor." During his novitiate his exalted rank secured him but one distinction; the prize for victory in the foot-race from the sacred hill of Huanacauri to the citadel was awarded him as of right.

His investiture also was similar to that of the rest, with the exception that two other *insignia* were conferred upon him as the future ruler. One of these was an axe with a blade of copper, which was put into his hands while the word "Aucca-cunapac" was pronounced; a word pregnant with meaning in so far as it signified "for the punishment of tyrants, traitors, the cruel, the perfidious, and the false." "All this and much more is meant by the word 'aucca,'" writes Garcilasso. The second was the fringe of yellow wool which was bound upon his temples.

In the matter of the upbringing of their children the Peruvians were by no means over-indulgent. Infants were kept fastened in their cradles, and were never taken in the mother's arms when fed, because it was thought that otherwise they would want continually to be nursed. As soon as the infant was weaned, an important ceremony, including the ritual shearing of the hair, took place. At this, the first lock was cut with a stone knife by one of the elder relations, who stood to the child in the relation of godfather, and the rest of the relations followed in order of precedence.

Or, according to another account, the ceremony was inaugurated by the eldest uncle. After this the child received a name, and the proceedings terminated with a feast at which presents were given to him. In the case of the heir to the empire these gifts were exceedingly magnificent, and included offerings brought or sent by the various provincial Curaça ; while the high-priest of the Sun cut the first lock from his head. For the children of the Inca nobility, special schools were erected in Cuzco, where instruction in religion, history, the arts of war and government, was given them by special professors. They were also taught to read the quipus to some extent, and were trained in astrology and music. The foundation of these schools was associated with the name of the Inca Rocca, and Pachacuti is said to have reorganized and extended them ; but it is probable that some such form of instruction for the youths of the ruling class existed before, on lines similar to that practised by certain more primitive peoples, as, to give one instance, the Whare-kura of the Maori. In fact Montesinos states that the 42nd ruler of his early list founded a "university" at Cuzco, and that the 78th re-established it at Tampu-tocco. The children of the provincial Curaça were allowed to share in this instruction, but the rest of the population were excluded from any part in "higher education." It was held sufficient to teach them the employments of their fathers, and the rulers feared that by over-education they might "become proud and endanger the commonwealth." This was part of the price they had to pay for the benefits which they received under the communal system.

CHAPTER VI—PERU : DAILY LIFE AND OCCUPATIONS

THE Peruvians were primarily agriculturists, and though the valleys were extremely fertile, yet throughout the greater part of the country cultivation was carried on under difficulties. Large tracts of the interior were situated at such an altitude that maize could not ripen there, and, under ordinary circumstances, were unable to support a large population. On the rainless coast agriculture was, normally, only possible in the neighbourhood of the rivers, none too numerous, which had their sources in the mountains; and their fertilizing influence extended but a short distance from their actual banks. Where the climate was favourable, the very uneven nature of the country, and the steepness of the mountain-slopes, rendered special measures necessary for the retention of the soil, and here too arrangements had to be made for irrigation.

For agricultural purposes a threefold division of the land was made. Certain tracts throughout the empire were reserved for the Sun, and the revenues from these were devoted to the maintenance of the temples and ministers of the state religion. Part of the remainder was divided among the population at large according to their needs; and the rest was royal property. Each head of a family received a plot for himself, with additional plots for each child. When a son married, he took over the control of that portion which his father had received at his birth, but when a daughter married, her portion lapsed to the state. If the population of a neighbourhood increased, part of the crown-lands passed into their hands.

The cultivation of the land, like everything else, was controlled by special officials, and the inhabitants of the village laboured in common. The local "church-lands" received the first attention, and next the lands apportioned for the use of the villagers. Even here a certain precedence was observed, in that the fields of the widows, aged and sick, came first. This rule was carefully observed, and Garcilasso mentions that, in the time of Huayna Ccapac, a local official of Chachapoyas was hanged because he arranged that the lands of a certain Curaça, to whom he was related, should be tilled before those of a widow. The crown-lands came last. From these crown-lands the ruler portioned out estates to the members of the nobility and the provincial Curaça, and the produce of what remained was reserved for his own maintenance, the needs of the army, and the relief of famine. Each day the local overseer announced which fields were to receive attention; the men assembled with their digging-sticks, long stakes with sharpened points and a foot-rest, and, acting in concert to the cadence of a song, proceeded to turn up long furrows. The women followed behind to break up the clods and pick out the weeds. Later when the crop was sowed—and where seed was lacking it was supplied from the state granaries—the services of the less able-bodied were employed to scare the birds from the growing crops. On the coast the digging-sticks were often shod with copper blades, many of which have been discovered, and textiles have been found with inwoven scenes depicting cultivation. On these are seen men equipped with such spades working among the crops, while others, armed with blow-guns and slings, protect the produce from the birds fluttering among the leaves. Every available inch of fertile ground was used for cultivation where the climate allowed, and we are even told that one of the Inca ordered the destruction of a number of villages in the neighbourhood of Cuzco in order that the land might be devoted to agricultural purposes. One of the chief features of the Peruvian landscape is constituted by the terraced mountain-slopes. Here long series of parallel walls were built of rough stones, one above the other, each inclining slightly inwards in order to support the weight of the earth with which the space between it and the hill-side was filled. By this means a series of horizontal surfaces, similar to a flight of stairs, was obtained, decreasing in depth as the mountain was ascended. These terraces, called locally *andenes*, belonged mainly to the state, since they had been constructed by state-labour. One terrace could be reached from the next by rude stair-ways of flat stones projecting from the face of the containing-wall, and the whole were watered by an extensive irrigation-system.

The aqueducts of Peru constitute a feature which has deservedly moved the wondering admiration of the early chroniclers. By their means alone was the coast enabled to support the large population which existed there before the Spanish conquest; and it is owing to the fact that the Spaniards failed to maintain the system that large tracts of country, formerly reclaimed from the desert, are now abodes of utter desolation (see Pl. XIV). Many of these aqueducts and reservoirs on the coast dated from pre-Inca times, but the Inca did much to extend the range of their utility ; some have survived to the present day, though the source whence they draw their water has in many cases never been discovered. In a note in his edition of Cieza de Leon, Sir Clements Markham describes the irrigation system of the Nasca valley. " In 1853 I examined the irrigation channels of this valley very carefully. All that nature has supplied in the way of water is a small watercourse which is frequently dry for six years together ; and at best only a little streamlet trickles down during the month of February. The engineering skill displayed by the Incas in remedying this defect is astonishing.

Deep trenches were cut along the whole length of the valley, and so far into the mountains that the present inhabitants have no knowledge of the place where they commence. High up in the valley the main trenches or *puquios* are some four feet in height, with floor, roof and sides lined with stones. Lower down they are separated into smaller *puquios* which ramify in every direction over the valley, and supply all the estates with delicious water throughout the year, feeding the little streams which irrigate the fields. The larger *puquios* are several feet below the surface, and at intervals of about two hundred yards there are manholes, *ojos*, by which workmen can get down into the channels and clear away any obstruction." Inland there were aqueducts of even greater extent; Garcilasso mentions one constructed by the Inca Uiracocha, which was twelve feet deep and wide, and traversed a distance of no less than one hundred and fifty leagues. In this part of the country, too, the difficulties which the engineers had to surmount were more considerable. The principle of the arch was unknown to the Inca, and they were consequently unable to carry their watercourses across a ravine of any dimensions. Thus if the bed of a stream were encountered, they were forced to make a long detour so as to carry the aqueduct round its source. The aqueducts were furnished with sluices which enabled the flow into the subsidiary channels to be regulated. Experience had taught the Peruvians how much water was necessary for the irrigation of a given quantity of land, and each land-holder was allowed the flow for a period corresponding to the size of his holding. If he neglected to make proper use of the supply, he was liable to punishment by flogging.

Besides the principle of irrigation, the Peruvians were also familiar with that of manuring the crop. This too seems to have been practised by the coast people before the Inca conquest. The desert sand near the sea was removed until the moist subsoil was laid bare ; in this small holes were made, and in each were placed a few grains of maize together with the head of a small sardine-like fish which occurs in great numbers on the coast. But besides fish-manure, the great stores of guano found on the islands off the coast were freely utilized. Under the Inca rule the various islands were apportioned among the different coastal villages, and trespass was severely punished. Inland other forms of manure were used.

A large variety of crops was cultivated throughout the empire, but, where the climate allowed, maize, of several kinds, formed the staple produce. In the loftier altitudes of the interior, however, maize could not be grown, but the hardy quinoa, a kind of buckwheat, took its place. Here too the potato flourished as well as in the lower country, and the oca, another tuber, was also of economical importance where it could be grown. Maize was usually eaten whole, roast or boiled, owing to the labour involved in grinding ; from the grain was prepared the national drink of the country, *chicha ;* the leaves were eaten as a vegetable, and another form of intoxicating beverage was extracted from them after they had been chewed by the women ; from the stalk a syrup was expressed ; and from the immature grains an oil was manufactured. Quinoa was usually eaten in the form of porridge, but chicha was also made from it when maize could not be procured. From the potato a preparation was made called *chuno,* which even now forms the staple food in the high country of the Collao. The process was as follows: after being exposed for some time to the frost, the potatoes were pounded and dried in the sun. So treated, they provided a fare which, if extremely insipid, was at any rate nourishing, and could be stored for a considerable length of time. Manioc, ground-nuts, beans, gourds, tomatoes and the guava, were also reared in the localities which suited them. A plant of considerable economical importance was the maguey, or American aloe ; the pith was much used by wood-carvers ; the sap of the leaves was employed as a medicine ; and the fibre was made into ropes, string, and thread for weaving. Syrup and a kind of vinegar were also extracted from it, and the roots when pounded furnished a soap and a hair-dye. But the most highly-prized product of Peruvian agriculture was the coca, the narcotic and sustaining properties of which are well known to medical science at the present day. The leaves were chewed, together with lime or bone-ash,[1] and were held in such estimation that they were re-served for the Inca. Large plantations were prepared, especially in the eastern province, and were tended with the greatest care ; the leaves were plucked one by one, dried in the sun and preserved in baskets. Coca figured as an offering in most religious ceremonies.

But the Peruvians were also a pastoral people, and their flocks were of the greatest importance to them. The *fauna* of Peru includes a species which may be re-garded as typical of the country. This is a species of ruminant, allied to the camel and known by the general name of llama ; and its appearance is too well known from the specimens present in all zoological gardens to need a particular description. There are in fact two species, both wild, the huanaco and the vicuña, but two domestic varieties of the huanaco existed in great numbers, the llama proper and the alpaca. Of the two latter the llama was the larger, and was employed chiefly as a beast of burden, though its wool was used for cloth-ing, and its flesh for eating and as an offering to the gods. The alpaca furnished a larger fleece, but the finest garments, reserved for the Inca, were made from that of the vicuña. From the wool of the huanaco, cloth of a coarse quality was woven, and the flesh was also an important article of diet, though it was not esteemed so

---

[1] It has been said that lime was not used in times previous to the conquest.

good as that of the llama. At the time of the Spanish
conquest the herds of llama and alpaca had attained
enormous proportions in the highland country, herds of
five hundred being considered of no account; on the
coast the animals could not live, owing to the heat, but
remains have been found there of individuals which
must have been imported for sacrificial purposes under
the Inca rule. As the only beast of burden in the country, the llama was invaluable, especially as it is very
tractable, easy to feed, and exceedingly sure-footed, a
quality much to be desired among the dizzy heights of
the inland roads. For carrying purposes it required no
harness, the load was simply arranged in a cloth so that
it hung in two equal portions on each side of the animal's
body. On long journeys as many as twenty-five beasts
were allowed to one load, since the animal is not capable
of great endurance, and it was therefore necessary to
make frequent changes. The llama and alpaca were
classed according to colour, and, if an animal were produced which differed from the rest of the herd in this
respect, it was transferred to another flock. The wild
species were hunted, together with other game.

Drives were organized on a large scale in which the
ruler often took part, and in which fifty or sixty thousand beaters were employed and as many as thirty
thousand head of game were taken. The chief quarry
was the huanaco and vicuña, of which the females and
the best males were merely sheared and let go, but the
beasts of prey, such as pumas, bears, foxes, and wild-
cats, were killed. When the beaters, after traversing a
wide expanse of country, had penned the game within
a narrow circle, the animals were secured by means of
the *bolas* or killed with sticks and clubs. The wool of
the huanaco, being coarse, was divided among the
common people, that of the vicuña was reserved for the
Inca, who shared it with the members of his family, and
no one was allowed to wear garments made of it with-

out permission. The flesh of the animals killed was eaten by those who participated in the hunt, but quantities of it were also dried and preserved in the storehouses for the use of troops on the march. Meat so preserved was called *charqui*, a word which is of particular interest, since from it is derived our term "jerked" beef. These

Fig. 8.—Hunting scene, from a vase, Truxillo.

hunts took place only at stated intervals in order to allow time for the fleeces of the huanaco and vicuña to grow. The llama and alpaca were also sheared periodically.

In the matter of the herds, as in other respects, the Spaniards showed their usual improvidence, and the numbers were sadly reduced within a very short period after the conquest.

An interesting hunting scene is shown in Fig. 8, a

vase-painting dating from the pre-Inca period of the coast. Here a hunter is seen armed with a spear-thrower and hurling darts at deer within the circle of hunting-nets.

Dogs were used for hunting, and it is noteworthy that remains of three varieties of dog, all differing from that of Europe, have been found on the coast. The largest of these was an animal of medium size with slender head and legs, and was probably used for watching the house (and, in the interior, the herds) and for hunting. The second was a short-legged dog, somewhat resembling a dachshund, which, to judge from a vase-painting, was also used in the chase. The third was a kind of pug, probably kept as a lap-dog.

Besides hunting, fowling by means of nets was largely practised, especially on the coast, where the abundance of bird-life is reflected by the designs on the pottery and textiles (Pl. XX, 2 and 3). The blunt arrow-heads found on the coast were probably used for birds (Pl. XXVI, 4). But in the maritime districts fishing ranked next in importance after agriculture. For this purpose balsas, as described on p. 60, were used, but they were quite small and carried only one or two passengers ; sails were not in use. This form of craft is still seen on lake Titicaca (Pl. XIII, 1). According to Garcilasso the harpoon was the principal apparatus employed, one of which made of copper with two barbs is shown in Pl. XXVI, 6, together with another with stone head and copper barb (Pl. XXVI, 8) ; but small nets and hooks were also used. The hooks were of bone or copper, and were furnished with a stone sinker (Pl. XXVI, 5), but no information is forthcoming as to the baits employed. The fishing appliances on Pl. XXVI come from Arica, and are akin to the culture of the Chilean coast; but objects of a similar type were used further north also. A spirited fishing scene is shown in the vase-painting reproduced in Fig. 9. Here a coast-Indian kneels on a balsa constructed of reeds ; he is

FIG. 9.—Fishing scene, from a vase, Truxillo.

hauling at a line at the other end of which is a hook firmly fixed in the jaws of a monstrous fish. Bird-headed creatures, probably sea-spirits, assist in the pro-

FIG. 10.—Warriors fighting, from a vase, Truxillo.

pulsion of his craft, which by the addition of grotesque heads has been given the semblance of a sea-monster.

The dress of the Peruvians was based upon two garments, the robe and the tunic. The latter was in its simplest form an oblong strip of cloth, folded across the shorter diameter, and sewn down the sides ; a hole was made in the centre for the head, and the side seams were left open at the top corners for the arms (e.g. Fig. 10, left-hand figures). Short sleeves were sometimes added (e.g. Fig. 8). The tunic was often confined with a belt, which in the art of the coast is often represented as a double-headed snake (Fig. 10), and the men usually wore a very abbreviated form of breeches (as in the same illustration). The tunic of the women reached nearly to the feet, and a robe was worn over this also. Speaking generally the material used on the coast was cotton, in the interior, wool, but the conquest of the country by the Inca had brought about a considerable interchange of products at the time of the discovery. Naturally there was considerable difference in the quality of clothing, according to the rank of the wearer; only the coarser forms of cloth were allowed to the peasantry, while the finest of all was reserved for the Inca. Ornament varied in the same degree ; some of the best textiles, especially those of the coast, are gorgeous in the extreme, displaying great variety of colour and inwoven designs (Fig. 23), with fringed and embroidered decoration, and further ornamented with feathers and small plates of silver and gold. In the interior, however, the colours were far more sober, browns, yellows and dark reds predominating. Feathers were applied to cloth to form mosaic designs, and head-dresses of this work, crowned with plumes, form some of the handsomest objects yielded by the graves in the coast valleys (Pl. IX, 3). It has already been remarked that the inhabitants of different regions could be distinguished by their form of head-dress. On the coast before the Inca conquest a greater latitude was allowed, to judge from the pottery (Pls. XXI and XXII). Conical or flat-topped caps seem to prevail, frequently with flaps covering the ears and back of the head and sometimes passing under the chin so that the features alone could be seen.

PLATE X

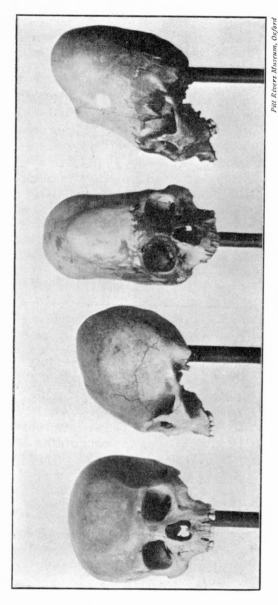

Pitt Rivers Museum, Oxford

PERU

ARTIFICIALLY DEFORMED SCULLS: 1, 2, FROM THE COAST; 3, 4, FROM THE HIGHLANDS

Some such form of head-dress must have been preserved
under the Inca, since Cieza states that the Yunca went
" muffled like gipsies." Inland, in the Collao, close-
fitting conical caps with ear-flaps were also worn, a pattern which has survived to the present day (Pl. XIII, 2),
but there were small local differences. The people of
Andahuaylas wore their hair in a number of plaits made
up with woollen cords, while those of Urcos were distinguished by a black fillet. The Huanca wore a sort
of wreath of wool, about three inches broad; the inhabitants of Caxamarca, a fillet composed of a number of
cords, while those of Chachapoyas confined their hair
by means of a sling, a weapon with which they were
particularly expert. The *llautu*, or fringed braids, which
were worn by the ruler and his heir have already been
mentioned, and it must here be stated that the governing class were also permitted to wear a braid coiled round
the head. The significance of this ornament lay in the
colour, red for the reigning Inca, yellow for the heir,
and black for the highest class of nobles. The hair itself was cut according to rank, and, contrary to the
Colombian custom, its length varied inversely with the
status of the individual. Thus a closely-cropped head
was the privilege of the ruler, and more flowing locks
the badge of servitude. Women wore the hair long.
The ear-stud was another sign of high rank, and no one
was allowed to wear one of these ornaments equal in size
to those of the ruler. But though the right to wear the
ear-stud was generally confined to the Inca class, it was
sometimes conferred upon the inhabitants of a district as
a special mark of favour. Thus the people of the Yucay
valley were granted the privilege, while the Quichua,
in return for their services against the invading Chanca,
were not only allowed to wear ear-studs, but also to bear
a llautu of a certain pattern and to wear their hair shorter than other tribes. The pottery of the coast shows
that studs were worn in the ears (Pl. XXI) and lower lip

K

(similar to Fig. 33, *b*), and that the nose was pierced for the reception of gold ornaments similar to those of the Colombian tribes, in the days before the Inca conquest.

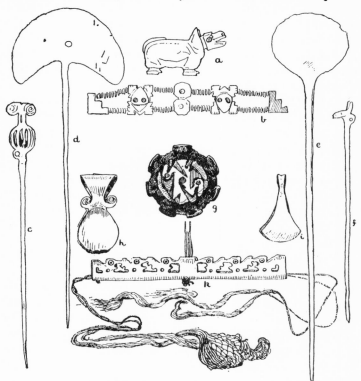

FIG. 11.—*a* Stone figure of llama, inlaid.   [*British Museum.*
           b Necklace of shell, wood and turquoise.
        c-f Copper pins.
           g Mosaic ear-stud.
h and *i* Silver tweezers.
           k Bone balance-beam with "pans" of netting.

In the maritime districts ear-studs were usually of wood, carved in open-work, or inlaid with shell and turquoise (Fig. 11, *g*). Beards and moustaches were not worn, but the hair was plucked out by means of small silver and copper tweezers, of which numbers have been found, especially in the coastal region (Fig. 11, *h* and *i*). The coast people of early days seem to have been peculiar in wearing stockings, unless indeed the markings on the legs of the figures represented in the vase-paintings are meant for painted ornament (Figs. 10 and 15), but some form of foot-covering was universal throughout Peru. Sandals, called *usutas*, were made of llama hide or vegetable fibre, very similar to those worn by the monastic orders in Europe, were fastened to the feet by means of cords. The early coast people, however, seem to have evolved a kind of slipper, which was worn probably by the more important men.

Many forms of ornament besides those mentioned above were in vogue, and again the graves of the coast have provided more evidence than those of the interior. Necklaces (Fig. 11, *b*) of small beads of coloured shell and turquoise are common, often interspersed with larger beads of carved wood and shell in the form of animals and human faces, of which the details are inlaid with shell of another colour or with turquoise. Finger-rings, anklets and bracelets of silver and gold are also found, while the pins used by women for fastening their cloaks are common throughout the country (Fig. 11, *c-f*). These are of two principal types, one with a flat semi-circular head, the other with a head modelled to represent that of a llama, the latter being more common in the highlands. These are made of silver or, more frequently, of copper, and were called *topo*. Head-deformation was practised locally, principally on the coast and in the Collao. The maritime people applied boards to the heads of their infants so that a flattening was produced along the forehead and at the back of the head, while a corresponding expansion took place at the sides (Pl. X, 1 and 2). In the Collao the fashion was different; here the aim was to prolong the crown in the form of a cone (Pl. X, 3 and 4). The extent of distortion produced in either case was considerable, and skulls have been found which exhibit an almost incredible degree of deformity. Tattooing also was practised on the coast, patterns similar to those on the textiles being produced in a bluish pigment.

The subject of habitations next arises, a subject which it is extremely difficult to treat shortly, and at the same time to give an idea of the astonishing facility with which

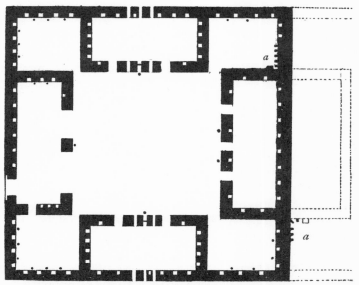

FIG. 12.—Plan of Inca dwelling, near Ollantaitambo.

the Peruvians of the inland region, possessing no metal but copper for the manufacture of tools,[1] and relying solely on human labour for the traction of great weights, handled enormous masses of stone. Speaking generally the buildings on the coast are composed of clay, those of the highlands, of stone, and this antithesis holds true to the extent that after the Inca had conquered the coast,

---

[1] The copper, as will be seen later, nearly always contains an element of tin, and is therefore a bronze ; but this element was purely accidental, and not intentionally added as an alloy.

PLATE XI

CHULLPAS : NEAR LAKE TITICACA

PERU

INCA HOUSE : NEAR OLLANTAITAMBO

they erected there buildings of the type characteristic of their own region, but of the local materials (Pl. XIV and XVI, 1). Nevertheless along the whole coast there is no important site where stone was not employed to some extent in building, though its use was usually confined to the foundations of walls. Inland the more humble dwellings were constructed of stones of convenient size piled together with or without mortar, and furnished with a gabled roof of thatch. Some of the buildings of this character still remain in the neighbourhood of Ollantaitambo (Pl. XI and Fig. 12). Here the buildings forming a dwelling are arranged round a court and enclosed with a wall; the principal building is furnished with an upper storey, approached from the outside by means of a stairway of stone slabs projecting from the enclosing wall (Pl. XI, 1, and Fig. 12, a, a). Some of the rooms are provided with small windows, giving on the court, and the walls are furnished with a series of niches, probably used as cupboards, alternating with projecting stones pierced vertically. The position of these pierced stones is marked on the plan, Fig. 12, by dots; in them were probably fitted pegs to which the looms were attached. The dwellings of the more important men, and especially the palaces of the Inca, were far more elaborate. On the island of Titicaca, in the lake of that name, is a building of which the main features can still be traced. It is rectangular in plan, and divided into a number of similar apartments. These apartments are arranged in isolated series, and the rooms of each series are interconnected, and approached by an outside door. The ceilings are vaulted, not by means of a true arch, which was unknown to the Peruvians, but by making the upper courses of masonry overlap inwards until the space could be bridged by a single slab. On the surface so obtained a second series of rooms was built, with an open promenade in front from which a magnificent view of the lake and the surrounding mountains could be obtained. This upper storey was approached, not from the ground-floor, but from the hill against which the palace was built. The doors are of the characteristic Inca pattern, with jambs inclining inwards (as the niche in Pl. XIII, 2), bridged with a single stone slab as lintel, and the rooms are furnished with numerous niches, and also windows, of similar shape. In this case clay has been used as mortar, and the whole covered with a yellow stucco, while the recessed portions of the doorways have been coloured red. Not all the palaces were stuccoed, and in such cases no mortar was used, but the regularity of the stone-laying was remarkable. It is noteworthy that the principle of bonding the corners of buildings, of which the Mexicans were ignorant, was well known to the Peruvians. Most of the palaces in Cuzco were of this latter type, a type which is well exemplified in the masonry of the Intihuatana figured on Pl. XVII, 2. Level ground is not a common feature of the Peruvian Sierra, and buildings of this nature were generally erected on a series of terraces, similar to those used for cultivation, but far more carefully constructed. Where the terraces were long, the monotony was usually broken by a series of niches, such as appear in the upper terrace of Pl. XII, 2, and each terrace was approached from that below by means of slabs projecting from the wall, or by a graded way. Even the most pretentious buildings were roofed with thatch, but to judge from the roof, existing until recent times, of a ruin known as the Sondor-huasi, the thatching was of a very elaborate and ornamental nature. In this building, according to Sir Clements Markham, it was no less than five feet thick, and we may well believe Cieza when he states that such roofs were impervious to fire. Inside, the wall-spaces were adequately broken by niches, and the walls were further ornamented with gold plates and jewels. The niche (Pl. XIII, 2) as a means of decoration seems to have existed from the earliest times ; it forms the main

PLATE XII

PERU
UPPER TERRACE, FORTRESS OF OLLANTAITAMBO

PERU
LOWER TERRACES: OLLANTAITAMBO
(From Wright's "Old and New Peru," by permission of Messrs. Barry & Sons)

feature of the great blocks found near the site of Tiahuanaco (Pl. XVIII, 1), to be mentioned later, and survived in the clay-built buildings of Inca times on the coast, as may be seen in Pl. XIV. Many of the Inca buildings were of great size, and though figures are not attractive, it may be as well to give the dimensions of the temple erected by the conqueror of the Chanca, Uiracocha or Pachacuti, in honour of the god Uiracocha by whose aid the enemy was defeated. This temple was peculiar in some respects, in so far as the greater part of the central wall, 40 feet high, was built of clay bricks. The shape was oblong, and the roof was gabled ; the building was furnished with an upper storey, floored with stone slabs, extending from the outer walls to that in the centre, and supported by rows of pillars. The central wall was pierced by numerous doorways, 14 feet high, with, probably, wooden lintels, and the length of the building was no less than 330 feet (according to Squier), the breadth being 87 feet.

There are many fortresses in the provinces, and no general description is adequate to picture them, since the plan of each was adapted to the particular locality. One of the best-preserved is at Huanuco Viejo. This is a rectangular building standing on a terrace and approached by a broad flight of steps. The walls are furnished with a cornice, and measure, on the exterior, about 16 feet high, on the interior, about 5, since the ground-level within has been artificially raised. Close at hand are the remains of a town, laid out in the usual orderly manner, with a palace and baths. At a short distance, on a terraced hill, are a number of small buildings, not only square and oblong, but also round, roughly built of unsquared stones. Circular buildings are not common in Peru outside the Collao, where, especially at the north end of lake Titicaca, are found numbres of peculiar erections known as *chullpa*, usually supposed to be the mausolea of the ancient Colla chiefs. Remains of two of these chullpa are seen in Pl. XI, 2, and they were constructed as follows. A domed structure of loose stones was first built, and round this was erected a facing of beautifully fitting blocks, so as to form a tower greater in diameter at the top than at the bottom, and furnished with a projecting cornice a short distance below the summit. To reduce the weight of these blocks, their lateral faces were hollowed; and the tower was provided with two entrances, both very small. One of these was in the centre of the summit, and was covered with a slab. The other was at the foot. The suggestion has been made that they were granaries, but Squier certainly found human remains in most of those which he explored. Square chullpa are also found. The Inca were accustomed occasionally to build in circular form ; one end of the great Sun-temple at Cuzco formed a perfect apse, and in the fortress of Chancayillo in the Casma valley, described by Squier, there were two circular double towers affording a view of the whole of the valley. These towers were surrounded by three walls, the outer with five, the next with four, and the inner with one, entrances, most of them protected with a curtain-wall, and in no case opposite one another. But by far the most picturesque fortress is that of Ollantaitambo (Pl. XII), to the north of Cuzco, which guarded the Vilcomayo valley, one of the few passes to the plains of the Amazon. The description of the locality given by Squier is so good that it merits quotation. " Their principal works were built .... at a point where a low ridge extends nearly across the valley. This ridge had been terraced up with high vertical walls, rising from the very bed of the stream on every side, to the height of nearly one hundred feet. Held by any considerable body of men, it commanded completely the passage of the valley. The river pours with arrow-like rapidity between these terraces and the rocky escarpment opposite, along the face of which runs the narrow and dizzy pathway over which all travellers to Ollantaitambo are obliged to pass. From this point forward for a league, the valley is narrowed to a mere cleft between mountains rising in rugged masses, but with almost vertical fronts, to enormous elevations. The brain reels in straining to discern their splintered summits. Dark and chill, this is one of the grand *portadas*, or mountain gateways, of the Andes, leading to the plains of the Amazon, of which the early chroniclers write with undissembled awe. The river looks black and sinister in the subdued light, and its murmur subsides into a hollow roar. The shrubs of broom become scant and small, and their flowers are few and mean. In front rises forever the white, ghastly, Chicon." Two main forts overhanging the river guard the approach to the citadel, which is built on a rocky spur. The citadel is approached from the plain beneath over a series of magnificent terraces (Pl. XII, 2), and is protected from above by a complicated series of walls abutting on precipices. At the summit of the terrace is a confused series of ruins and huge stone blocks, some of which can be seen in the illustration, and a platform faced with enormous slabs (Pl. XII, 1), the largest of which measures roughly 13 by 7 by 5 feet. Many of the ruins date, no doubt, from pre-Inca days ; not only do we find the large sculptured blocks characteristic of the " megalithic " period, to which allusion will be made later, but another form of stone-laying appears. Great polygonal blocks are surrounded by others of less magnitude, but each accurately cut to fit its neighbours. Many walls of this type are found at Cuzco, and some idea of the labour involved in their erection may be gained from the illustration on Pl. VII, 2. A smaller polygonal style is seen in Pl. XIII, 2. It must be remembered that no mortar was used in the construction of this type of masonry, and that the joints are so close as not to admit of the introduction of a knife-blade between the stones. But the most stupendous example of this type of building is presented by the Sacsahuaman fortress which guards the northern approach to Cuzco. This consists of three parallel walls, each over three hundred yards long, built with re-entering angles, so that an attacking force must always expose its flank to the defenders. The nature of the masonry can be seen in the illustration Pl. XV, and it need only be said that some of the stones at the salient angles attain dimensions such as 17 by 12 by 7 feet. To this fortification many additions were made by the later Inca, probably in the form of buildings at the summit of the hill, but it seems almost certain that the great walls must be of far earlier date. Apart from the fact that these blocks required individual fitting, their transport must have afforded considerable difficulty. It is said that Quito was built with stones brought from Cuzco, but though this is almost incredible, yet even the two short leagues, which separated Ollantaitambo from the quarries whence the red porphyritic blocks were transported, could not have been traversed without tremendous labour, considering the nature of the ground. Near many of the more important works, large stone blocks lying deserted bear witness to the difficulty of carriage, and were known by the picturesque name of " tired stones." As to the method by which these blocks were extracted from the quarry, nothing is known, but it is believed that holes were bored and wedges of wood inserted ; water was then poured on, and the expansion of the wedges caused the rock to split. In buildings of what may be called the older type, such as portions of Ollantaitambo, and at Tiahuanaco, yet to be described, T-shaped clamps of copper were countersunk in the blocks to hold them firmly together.

On the coast very different conditions prevailed. Here stone was not readily procurable, and was only occasionally used for the bases of walls and, mixed with earth, for

PLATE XIII

2. INCA WALL WITH NICHE : CUZCO

PERU

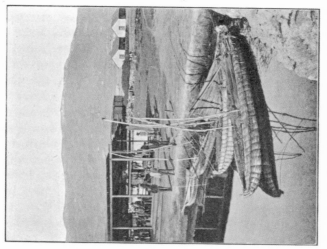

1. MODERN BALSAS : LAKE TITICACA, BOLIVIA

the platforms on which the more important buildings were erected. The earliest remains are composed of rough balls of clay or mud pressed together when still in a moist state, but the majority are of large bricks known as *adobes*. A still later form consisted of a kind of concrete of mixed clay and pebbles, called *pilca*. The early coast-dwellers were masters of their material, and their buildings were often of far more ornamental a nature than those of the Inca. The hard and durable algarroba wood was chiefly

FIG. 13.—Types of dwellings on the coast, from vases ; Truxillo.

used in building, and also canes to form the skeleton of the adobe walls. Simple huts were built entirely of canes and roofed with mats ; indeed in this region, where rain was a rarity, roofing was not important. A good idea of a dwelling of this type may be gathered from Fig. 13, *a–c*. *a*, from a vase, shows the hut in section ; the beams on which the roof rests are supported by forked poles, and the exterior of the roofing is ornamented with projections resembling club-heads. *b* and *c*, also from a vase, give the exterior of the building, with its ornamental roof-crest, and an indication of the ridge-pole which supports it.

But the ruins show far greater complication. Two sites are of particular importance ; Truxillo, the seat of the great chief Chimu, conquered by the Inca, and Pachacamac, the realm of Cuismancu and the site of the famous temple. The first has not been thoroughly surveyed, but the details given by Squier afford some indication of its nature.

The general plan of the coast settlements is very unlike that of Inca towns. Though they were laid out with equal, or even greater, care, and the different wards were separated by streets at right angles, yet each ward, even each section of a ward, is enclosed in its own containingwall, and is accessible from only one entrance. Chamber opens from chamber and court from court in bewildering succession, and many enclosures can have been approached only along the walls of the rest. The presence of pathways along the tops of walls seems to have been quite a feature of coast architecture, and has been especially remarked at Pachacamac. From the top of the wall an incline led down to the interior of the court or dwelling which had no other entrance. At Truxillo the various wards were built with great symmetry, and most of them contained what appears to be a *plaza* with, perhaps, shops grouped round it, and a reservoir. In one of the wards is an extensive terrace in which are rows of small subterranean chambers, each entered from above and entirely unconnected. This has been supposed to be a prison, but was more likely a series of workshops where the artisans of Truxillo performed their appointed tasks. Chambers have also been discovered the walls of which show traces of fire, and the presence of metallic slag seems to prove that they were furnaces for the smelting or working of metal. The ruins of Pachacamac have been more thoroughly explored, thanks to the labours of Uhle, the first scholar to attempt excavation on proper scientific lines in Peru. His researches both here and elsewhere have been of the very greatest importance to South

PLATE XIV

By permission of Prof. Max Uhle

PERU

INCA PALACE : VALLEY OF PISCO

American archæology, as will be seen later ; for the present we are merely concerned with the nature and architecture of the ruins. The ward system appears also in Pachacamac, but a difference exists between this site and Truxillo. Here we have a number of great terraced palaces, probably the residences of nobles, each surrounded by a complexity of less important structures, which must have been the dwellings of their numerous retainers. But each of these wards is surrounded by its wall, and can only be entered through the palace-gate, which is, moreover, well guarded by lesser buildings, and opens upon a tortuous passage easily capable of defence. It seems possible that the ayllu-system extended to the early coast-dwellers, and that each ward was the residence of a particular ayllu.

It has been said that the Yunca were more apt to decorate their buildings than the Inca. The finest examples of ornamentation are found at Chanchan, near Truxillo, where the adobe walls are frequently covered with elaborate *relievo* designs in stucco. A good example of this kind of work is shown in Pl. XVI, 2. But some walls were finished with a flat stucco surface on which frescoes were painted. Unhappily none of these exist in perfect form, but traces have been found at Truxillo, Paramonga, Pachacamac, and elsewhere. The most imposing remains on the coast, however, are the huge stepped pyramids, forming burial-places, and the terraced substructures of the temples with their shrines at the summit. At Pachacamac there are two temples, which Uhle has been able definitely to assign to their respective deities. In the plain is the older, dedicated to the eponymous deity of the place, standing on an artificial terraced plateau of some 4700 square yards and surrounded by a large enclosure. Outside the entrance to the latter is a double colonnade, and a number of small buildings, probably intended for the housing of the pilgrims who visited the temple. The Sun-temple, constructed under the Inca *régime*, occupies the summit of a neighbouring hill; the hill itself is terraced and provided with graded ways and staircases, and the south-west or principal façade is ornamented with large niches of regular Inca type. Two groups of buildings may still be discerned on the summit. Terraced pyramids of huge bulk, now unfortunately much impaired by the excavations of treasure-seekers, occur at intervals along the coast, and it is as difficult to realize the vast amount of labour which must have been expended in the manufacture of the adobes of which they and the other remains are composed, and in the placing of those adobes in position, as to estimate the toil which went to the building of the stone fortresses and palaces of the highlands. It is certain that the population of the coast must have been very large, but the unfortunate policy of the Spanish conquerors, and especially their failure to maintain the aqueducts, brought about a rapid degeneration. At the present time the only witnesses to the former prosperity of the region are the numerous remains of once thronged palaces and towns, situated, like the Inca Palace in Pl. XIV, in an environment of utter desolation.

A few words on bridges may conclude the chapter. In dealing with small streams, such as those which flowed through the city of Cuzco, the banks were lined with masonry, and the bed spanned by large slabs resting on corbels projecting from the walls. Larger rivers, such as the Apurimac, were provided with suspension-bridges. Five large cables of osier were stretched from bank to bank, and made fast to the living rock, or to huge masses of masonry specially constructed for the purpose. Three of the cables, each as large as a man's body, served as the floor, and were protected from wear by a layer of hurdles; the two others played the part of hand-rails, and were connected with the former by interlaced boughs. Such bridges were extremely strong, though they required constant repair, and served for the passage of men and beasts. Floating bridges on bundles of reeds were also used in places where the current was not strong, but needed replacing more often. Occasionally travellers were conveyed across a stream in a large basket running on a cable, and, where this means of transit was adopted, special watchers were appointed whose duty it was to assist in pulling the passengers across.

CHAPTER VII—PERU : BURIAL AND RELIGION

HAVING considered the habitations of the living, it will be as well to turn our attention to those provided for the dead. The question of the disposal of the dead was of great importance throughout Peru, since, as will be seen, some form of ancestor-worship was practised throughout, both on the coast and in the Sierra. Belief in the continued existence of the soul after decease was found practically everywhere, though the accounts of its fate varied locally. Garcilasso states that there was a kind of heaven and hell, for the souls of the good and wicked respectively, and also that some form of resurrection was expected, for which reason all hair-combings and nail-parings were carefully stored in holes in the walls. Arriaga writes that, according to the people of the Sierra, departed souls went to a place called Ypamarca, crossing over a great river by a bridge of hairs (recalling the spider's web boat of Chibcha tradition), while the coast folk of Huacho believed that they were carried to the guano islands by sea-wolves. Elsewhere the dead were believed to be escorted to the other world by black dogs, and numbers of these animals were bred and cared for, to be sacrificed on the occasion of a funeral. The custom, almost universally prevalent, at any rate in early times, of interring the favourite wives and even retainers with important individuals, also bears witness to a belief in the continued existence of the soul. At the same time, by a natural confusion of thought, the actual body was regarded as in some way sentient, since frequent offerings of food and especially drink were made at the tombs, and the mummies were brought out at stated

intervals and ceremonial feasts were held in their honour. The term 'mummies' is used for want of a better,
but there is no evidence that any preservative preparation was injected into the body. Sometimes the internal
organs were removed, and, in the case of the Inca, preserved in golden vessels in a temple twelve miles from
the capital; but the preservation of the body was due
mainly to the extra-
ordinarily dry atmo-
sphere of the coast
and the higher sierra.
Inland the body, ar-
ranged in a squatting
position, was usually
wrapped in a gar-
ment of fine cotton,
enveloped in many
wrappings of cloth,
and finally in a tight-
ly fitting reed mat
secured by a net. The
face was sometimes
left exposed, as at
Xauxa, where the
dead were sewn up
in fresh llama-skins
and preserved in the

FIG. 14.—Mummy, from the coast ; Ancon
(after Reiss and Stübel).

houses. The stone burial-towers of the Collao have
already been mentioned. On the coast two or more
bodies are often found in a single mummy-pack, and
the wrapping is rather more elaborate. At Ancon,
where so many graves were explored by Reiss and
Stübel, the dead were arranged in a contracted position
and the fingers and toes carefully wrapped in cloth. A
number of bandages were wound round the body, which
was then packed in cotton, leaves or seaweed, and made
up into a rectangular parcel with more wrappings. To

L

many of the mummy-packs, irrespective of the number of bodies which they contained, a false head was added, furnished with eyes of shell or silver, a nose of wood and a wig (Fig. 14). The actual form of grave differed according to locality. In the highlands natural caverns, often enlarged by artificial means, were employed as mausolea, and the bodies were arranged in a seated position round the walls or in niches. Many of these mortuary caves are situated in the face of some inaccessible cliff, and the dead must have been lowered there by means of ropes. The entrance was always carefully concealed with masonry. In many parts of Peru, especially in the neighbourhood of Cuzco, occur outcropping rocks which have been carved with stairways, seats, and all manner of intricate channels leading from small reservoirs. Usually some sort of grotto or deep niche has been cut in the lower portion of these rocks, and human remains have been found in them. Uhle has suggested that these were the burial-places of important individuals, and that the small basins or reservoirs were intended for the reception of libations, which were supposed to reach the dead by means of the channels leading from them. It is also possible, however, that the rock was supposed to be the dwelling-place of some huaca, for whom the libations were intended, and that the presence of the bodies was due to a desire to be buried at the shrine of the huaca of the ayllu, just as the royal mummies were preserved in the temple of their clan-god, the Sun. Evidence of this desire occurs at Pachacamac, where burial within the temple precincts was regarded as a great privilege only to be granted to individuals of exalted position. The same authority also suggests that the numerous seat-like carvings, almost invariably called " Seats of the Inca," one of which is shown in Pl. XVII, 1, were also connected with a festival to the Sun, at which the mummies were brought out from their sepulchres and shared passively in the ceremonies.

PLATE XV

Photo. Underwood

PERU

Masonry of the Sacsahuaman Fortress : Cuzco

On the coast the burials show great variety, but two main forms may be distinguished, the excavated grave and the pyramid. Grotto-burial seems not to occur, except at Paramonga; but even here it is not certain that the graves are not those of the later Inca population, since they have not been properly explored, and the locality was an important military post, fortified by Pachacuti with a magnificent citadel. The graves of Ancon, which may be taken as roughly typical of the whole coast, exhibit this variety to a considerable degree. Shallow pits, deep shafts with or without niches, single subterranean chambers, or a series of such chambers arranged at different levels in a diagonal direction, all occur; and the more important are lined with masonry, pilca or adobes. Some form of protection from the superincumbent earth is nearly always present, sometimes a regular roof, sometimes merely a reed mat or a fragment from a huge jar. The habit of providing the dead with some such shelter, again seems to imply that they were regarded as in some way sentient, especially as we are told by Arriaga that the natives were continually disinterring the bodies of those who had been accorded Christian burial, and disposing of them secretly after the pagan fashion, because, it was thought, they were oppressed by the earth. Arriaga, it is true, writes of the interior, where the practice of cave-burial prevailed, and the idea of inhumation no doubt was the more repugnant to the native mind. Burials occur both singly and in groups, and some of the graves are literally packed with mummies, in which case the more important are always at the top. With the dead, especially on the coast, was buried their personal property, and to this fact we owe most of our knowledge of the ethnography of the maritime districts. Garments, textiles, weaving apparatus, arms, implements, ornaments, domestic pets (such as dogs, parrots and monkeys) and even children's dolls (Pl. IX, 1) are found all along the coast, together with great stores of pottery, of which the finest comes from Truxillo and Nasca. The coast, in fact, is one vast grave-yard, and, in the words of Cieza, " It is certainly a mar-vellous thing to see the great quantity of dead bodies that there are in these sandy and barren mountains, with their clothes now worn out and mouldering away with time." In the interior of the country the associated objects are fewer. But though we have been able to a great extent to reconstruct the culture of the Peruvians through their custom of depositing the cherished possessions of the dead with their bodies, yet this very habit has con-tributed to the loss of a great deal of important evi-dence. Unfortunately many of the utensils are of gold and silver, and the burial-places have attracted the atten-tion of treasure-seekers innumerable from the earliest days of the Spanish conquest. For example one of Gon-zalo Pizarro's captains is said to have taken more than fifty thousand dollars' worth of treasure from a tomb at Yca. The damage wrought by "excavators" of this sort is incalculable, but the material is vast, and still offers magnificent opportunities to a properly trained archæo-logist, who would carry on the work so ably initiated by Professor Uhle. Burial within the precincts of the dwelling was sometimes practised, and numerous graves have been found among the ruins at Pachacamac. The custom of urn-burial is very rare in Peru, and seems to have been practised only in the case of twins who died young. The urns were kept in the house. As stated above the mummies of the rulers and their con-sorts were preserved in the Sun-temple at Cuzco, seated in order round the wall, near the image of the Sun, on golden chairs. At the conquest they were secretly re-moved, but five of them, including the bodies of Uira-cocha, Tupac Yupanqui and Huayna Ccapac, were dis-covered by the Licentiate Ondegardo and were seen by Garcilasso, who describes them as follows: "The bodies were so perfect that they wanted neither hair, eye-brows nor eye-lashes. They were in their clothes such as they had worn when alive, with the llautus on their heads, but without any other sign of royalty. They were seated, in the way the Indian men and women usually sit, with their arms crossed over their breasts, the right one over the left, and the eyes cast down as if they were looking on the ground."

Important ceremonies took place in all the provinces at the death of the reigning Inca, a feature of which was the recitation by selected poets of all the feats performed by the deceased, and which were renewed at stated intervals for a whole year. A peculiar custom connected with the demise of a ruler was the following. His palace with all its contents, including the gold and silver furniture, was left exactly as it was at his death, and did not pass into the possession of his successor; even the staff of servants, it is said, was still maintained. This custom accounts in a large measure for the great quantity of gold which the Spaniards found in Peru at their arrival, since each Inca was obliged to supply himself with an entirely new outfit of the utensils necessary to his rank. Solemn mourning ceremonies were also practised in the case of individuals of exalted status, and of the coastal chieftains. We are told that it was the custom to open the graves of the latter at intervals, and to renew the clothes and food placed within them; and in some places burials have been found which seem to support this statement.

The subject of the religion or religions of Peru is one of great complexity, and really deserves a whole volume to itself. The material is extensive; most of the early chroniclers, some of whom were of Inca descent, give valuable information concerning the beliefs and ceremonies of the people, and the writings of the early missionaries are of the highest importance in this respect. In its main outlines the religion as found by the Spaniards was fairly homogeneous in character throughout Peru, since the local cults of which it was composed were the product of a common psychology. But very great differences existed in the quality of the beliefs, and, from the cultural standpoint, those of the peasant population differed from those held by the educated Inca as widely as the primitive village cults of India from the highest tenets of Hinduism. The objects of worship may be divided roughly into four classes : creator-gods; the heavenly bodies, Earth and Sea; *huaca ;* and personal fetishes; but it must be remembered that the distinction is artificial, in so far as we have no knowledge that it existed in the native mind. With the cult of the huaca, ancestor-worship was inseparably bound up.

Of the creator-gods, the name of Uiracocha has already been mentioned as that of the deity worshipped by the rulers of the pre-Inca empire who came from the Collao. Uiracocha is closely connected with Tiahuanaco, the megalithic site at the south end of lake Titicaca. Here he is said to have carved men in stone or modelled them in clay, and to have transported them miraculously to certain caves, rocks, trees and streams in the various provinces, whence they issued as the ancestors of the different tribes. To him is attributed the creation of the sun and moon, and he held power over lightning and thunder. After the creation he travelled northwards through the country in the guise of an elderly man with a long beard, and performed various miracles with the aid of a magic staff, finally disappearing over the sea in the neighbourhood of Porto Viejo. The latter part of the myth probably represents the conquest of the country by his worshippers. His full name is given as Con Ticsi Uiracocha, and appears to be derived from some language other than the Quichua dialect, which was the official tongue of the Inca empire at the time of the Spanish conquest. In other parts of the Collao this creator who held power over the heavenly bodies was known as Ton-

PLATE XVI

PERU

PORTION OF THE "CONVENT," INCA PERIOD: PACHACAMAC

PERU

STUCCO WALL DECORATION: CHANCHAN, TRUXILLO

*(Both subjects from Wright's "Old and New Peru," by permission of
Messrs. Barry & Sons)*

apa and Tarapaca, and his cult seems to have extended as far south as the north-west provinces of the Argentine Republic. The Quichua name for the creator was Pacha-camac (the " Soul of the Universe "), and this Pacha-camac was identified with Uiracocha. As we have seen, an important centre of his worship was the coast town of that name ; but the fact that the name is Quichua seems to prove that the deity to whom the early temple was erected was not the Quichua Pachacamac, but mere-ly identified with him by the conquerors of the coast. Whether this identification took place in Inca or pre-Inca times it is impossible to say, but the latter hypo-thesis appears almost the more probable, since the name Pachacamac had become very deeply rooted on the coast in the neighbourhood of the famous shrine. Santillan states that here the primitive name for Pachacamac was Irma. Uhle quotes an interesting myth from the coast which shows Pachacamac in conflict with the Sun. Pacha-camac created a man and woman, but omitted to provide them with food ; the man died, and the woman appealed to the Sun for assistance. The Sun gave the woman a son, and taught the pair to live upon the wild fruits of the earth. Pachacamac, enraged at his interference, killed the son, but buried the various portions of his body in the earth, and created from them the various cultivated plants. From the teeth sprang corn, from the bones yuca, and from the flesh other vegetables and fruits. The Sun however gave the woman another son, who was named Wichama, but in his absence Pachacamac slew the woman, who by this time was very old. Wichama in wrath pursued Pachacamac, but the latter disappeared in the sea, and Wichama vented his rage upon the rest of mankind by scorching up their land and turning many of them into stone. This myth, which has been interpreted as representing the course of the seasons, seems to have been influenced by the beliefs of the inland region, since Pachacamac, as well as Wichama, is represented as the son of the Sun. In the parched maritime districts the Sun was not regarded as a benefactor, and Sun-worship was not practised until imposed by the Inca ; it is unlikely, therefore, that the local creating and preserving deity should have been connected with the destroyer.

In the upland province of Huarochiri, which is nevertheless near the coast, another creating deity was found, here called Iraya, and identified with Uiracocha. It would appear that the inhabitants of this place had moved inland from the seaboard, and the stories which have been preserved by Avila concerning Iraya resemble in some particulars the myths of the god of Pachacamac. It is rather in tone than in actual details that this similarity exists ; the great gods of the coast are not nearly such dignified beings as those of the interior. They adopt a variety of animal-forms as disguise, and play all manner of tricks on men and the other gods. In fact some of the tales of Huarochiri might almost have been transported direct from the coast of North-west America. Though the conduct of Iraya at times befits a huaca of low order rather than a creator, yet he is given all the attributes of Uiracocha as well as the name. Uhle identifies him with Irma-Pachacamac, but though he may have represented Irma, it does not seem possible that the inhabitants regarded him as equvalent to Pachacamac ; for the latter is mentioned in the same myth in terms which seem to make him quite a different person. These few details give some idea of the intricate nature of the problem, and of the manner in which the theology of Peru had been complicated by conquest and reconquest, and also, in all probaiblity, by intrusive elements from further up the American coast. One fact seems to result, namely, that many, if not most, of the Peruvian tribes worshipped each a supreme creator-god, and that the attributes of these creator-gods were sufficiently similar to admit of their identification when the cults came into contact.

The next class of objects of worship, the heavenly bodies, the earth and the sea, are to some extent connected with the third class, the huaca, and it will be as well here to explain shortly this puzzling term. Huaca, though a substantive, is best translated by " holy," although its meaning is even more extensive. It was applied to material objects which were honoured with a cult, rocks, lakes, animals, and mummies of ancestors, to temples, graves, and to the offerings which were made at shrines; and even to objects and individuals departing in some way from the normal, as, for example, a double-yolked egg or a person with a hare-lip. At the present day it is the term usually applied to an ancient grave. For the purposes of this chapter it will be used as a generic term for the first of these classes. As a matter of fact the Sun, though the name huaca was never applied to it, must originally have belonged to this class, since it was the clan-god of the ruling family of Cuzco ; but the Sun-cult had increased in importance with the spread of Inca power, until it became the state religion. The Sun-temple, or Curicancha (" House of Gold ") at Cuzco is said to have been founded by Manco, but it was rebuilt and expanded by later rulers. Part of the building exists to-day incorporated in the monastery of Santo Domingo. The golden glories of the Curicancha have often been described ; the walls, built of accurately fitting rectangular blocks of stone, were covered with sheets of the precious metal and studded with jewels; one end formed an apse which contained the image of the sun, a huge circular plate of gold which has never been discovered.[1] Near the main building were four other shrines, one ornamented with silver and dedicated to the Moon, another, similarly decorated, to the Planets, a third to the Thunder and Light-

---

[1] The golden plate which fell to the share of Leguisamo and which he gambled away in a single night seems to have been a smaller emblem of this divinity.

ning, and the fourth, which was lined with gold, to the Rainbow. But Sun-worship was not confined to the Inca; indeed most of the people of the Sierra seem to have adored Inti or Punchao (the Sun) as a benefactor, and, as we have seen, the cult extended through Ecuador up into Colombia. Another divinity which received worship was the Earth, which under the name Pachamama, " All-mother," was regarded as the personification of fertility. On the coast, at Truxillo, the Moon, under the name Si, was worshipped as the ruler of tempests by the subjects of Chimu ; but generally throughout this region the Sea occupied the place held by the Sun in the highlands. At Truxillo the ocean was called Ni, while to the Inca, who also paid it reverence when they penetrated to the coast, it was known as Mamaccocha, " Mother Sea," and it was especially invoked as a preserver from sickness. The huaca were innumerable, and, as said above, appear to have been closely connected with ancestor-worship. Each ayllu claimed descent from a common ancestor, and this ancestor might be a rock, lake, river, tree or animal, or some supernatural personage later transformed into a stone, beast or bird. Whatever the ancestor, it was adored by the ayllu in common. Thus certain of the Colla, who believed they had issued from lake Titicaca, paid offerings to the lake ; a section of the Chanca adored a puma from whom they believed themselves to have sprung, and so forth. Arriaga states that a certain village worshipped an ancestral huaca in the form of a stone eagle, which was found together with four mummies, said to be those of its human sons, the parents of the tribe. Where the huaca was an animal, the descendants, especially on the coast, seem to have worn costumes representing the supernatural ancestor at stated festivals, and many of the vase-paintings appear to represent the dances which took place on such occasions (Fig. 15). Here we have men clad in masks and dresses to represent deer, foxes, scorpions, bats, owls, condors, falcons, pelicans, lobsters, crabs and fish. Some of these designs may represent the huaca itself, combining its human and animal aspects, but Garcilasso states that, at the great feast of the Sun at Cuzco, the various deputations from the provinces appeared clad in the costumes of the animals from which they claimed descent. It is possible that the paintings representing combats between warriors adorned in dresses of this sort may represent contests between the men of different ayllu (e.g. Fig. 10, *a*, where one of the fighters is dressed as a bat). Animals held as huaca, and possibly, though we do not know for certain,

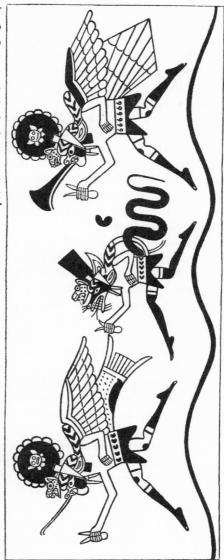

FIG. 15.—Men in ceremonial masks and dresses.   From a vase; Truxillo.

regarded as ancestors, were, white llamas in the Collao, jaguars and serpents among the Anti, dogs among the Huanca, snakes and condors in Chachapoyas, and certain fish and crustaceans on the coast. In the interior the cult of rocks appears to have been extremely extensive, as indeed throughout the whole Andean region. Mention has already been made of the rocks sculptured with steps, niches, basins and channels, at which offerings were made and where the important dead were deposited. In the case of inanimate huaca such as these, some natural confusion seems to have existed in the native mind as to whether the object itself was divine, or merely the habitation of some indwelling spirit. Arriaga, for instance, mentions a rock which had been the huaca of a particular village, but was disturbed, and he goes on to describe how the huaca left the rock in the form of a parrot and disappeared into another rock which in consequence became huaca. One of the most celebrated of the sacred rocks in Peru was that on the island of Titicaca, which, at any rate in later times, was associated with the Sun, and was faced by a large temple dedicated to that deity. The qualification is added, because here too the Inca may have appropriated an important local huaca for their own deity. From the history we gather that certain of the Inca attempted to put down the huaca-worship, but on the whole, especially in later times, they were broad-minded, and were satisfied that the Sun should be accorded the premier position. When a province was conquered, the local huaca, if movable, were deported to Cuzco, there to act as hostages for the good behaviour of their worshippers. Much of the huaca worship was also incorporated in the Sun-cult, and it has been mentioned that the ancestral mummies were paraded, and dances performed in honour of the huaca, at festivals which were held in honour of the Sun.

The care which was everywhere lavished on the dead,

PLATE XVII

PERU

1. "SEATS" CUT IN THE LIVING ROCK: NEAR TITICACA, BOLIVIA
2. THE INTIHUATANA: NEAR PISAC

and the preservation of the bodies in mummy form, called *malqui* on the coast, and *munaos* in the highlands, has been illustrated in the earlier part of the chapter. It need only be repeated here that respect for the wants of the departed entered very largely into the daily life of the people. Constant offerings were made to the ancestors, especially at the season for sowing ; and in Andahuaylas when the fire threw out sparks it was believed that the family forbears were hungry and thirsty, and chicha and maize were thrown upon the fire. If an owl or a lizard on the roof uttered cries soon after a death, the inhabitants supposed that the deceased required attention, and measures were taken to supply the necessary offerings.

The lowest order of sacred objects (which also fell under the term huaca, used in its widest sense) included the personal and household fetishes known as *conopa* on the coast and as *chanca* in the sierra. These were usually small stones of peculiar shape or colour, crystals, and, after the Spanish conquest, unfamiliar objects such as a piece of sealing-wax or the foot of a glass goblet. Even the ruling Inca possessed personal fetishes of this nature, called *huauqui* or " brother." That of Manco was a miraculous bird, named Inti (Sun), that of Sinchi Rocca, a stone fish, while Lloque Yupanqui possessed an "idol," named Apu Mayta. The huauqui of the Inca Uiracocha is said to have been a gold statue representing the lightning, and the god Uiracocha is said to have appeared to him and given him a two-headed snake as his personal guardian. This fact is interesting, since the belt of various forms of ceremonial dress is represented in the art of the coast (Fig. 10) as a double-headed serpent, and no doubt is intended to represent power over the lightning and thunder.[1] Such personal fetishes were

[1] It is interesting to note, further, that the belt of the principal figure on the relief at Tiahuanaco (Fig. 17) also terminates in monstrous heads, which may be meant for those of snakes and not of pumas as is

buried with the owner, but the family conopa were inherited by the eldest son, together with the dresses used
in the festivals held in honour of the huaca, and constituted
one of the extremely few forms of individual property
existent in Peru. With the conopa and chanca may be
grouped other forms of fetishes, stones in the form of
maize-heads (Fig. 27, *d*) and potatoes, which were supposed to confer fertility on the crops, and figures of llamas
(Fig. 27, *b*), which were believed to perform a like service
for the herds. Some of the latter were furnished with
a hollow in the back in which offerings were placed
before the figure was buried in the pastures. The use
of these llama figures as fertility-charms has survived
to the present time among the people of the Collao.
Another variety of fertility-charm was the *zaramama*
("maize-mother"), a doll made of maize-stalks, a double
head of maize, or one which was of unusual shape or
colour ; these, which have many parallels among agricultural communities all over the world, were carried
by the participants in the harvest festivals and afterwards burnt in honour of the lightning. Certain stones
in the fields and aqueducts received offerings at the time
of sowing, while the bodies of twins who died young
were preserved in vases in the hut, one individual of
a twin being supposed to be the child of the lightning.
Infants born feet first were similarly honoured, and all
cradles were regarded as sacred, and were sprinkled with
chicha and adjured to protect the youthful inmate. In
the life of the peasantry no doubt the lesser objects of
worship played the leading part, since they were supposed to exercise an influence on every action ; the more
important were only adored on stated festivals or at
times of especial difficulty, when sickness occurred, or
when a journey had to be undertaken.

usually believed. As will be seen later there is reason to believe that
this figure represents the creator sky-god who had power over the
lightning.

The service of these almost innumerable deities, from the Sun to the conopa, required the existence of a regular hierarchy of priests, who interpreted their wishes, proclaimed their oracles, and received offerings in their names. The head of the hierarchy was the priest of the Sun at Cuzco, who was always a near relation of the ruler, and bore the title of Villac Umu. His ceremonial robes consisted in a long ungirt tunic and a cape ; a plate of gold representing the sun adorned his head, another of silver his breast, and his garments were richly ornamented with precious metals and jewels. He was allowed to marry, but his life was hedged about with many restrictions, in compensation for which he was paid a reverence second only to the divine ruler himself. The Sun-worship in each province was superintended by an Inca, under whom ranked a number of vicars appointed from among the relations of the local Curaça, assisted by priests of inferior degree. The higher ranks were supported entirely out of the revenues derived from the lands set apart for the Sun, while the lower orders, who performed their functions in rotation, received state support only as long as they were on duty ; at other times they lived the lives of ordinary individuals. The provincial and local huaca were also served by priests, and even the malqui and conopa had ministers of their own according to their degree. Under the Inca the creator-gods alone, as a general rule, were without temple or priesthood. The point of view seems to have been that they needed no offerings, since all was theirs. The temple of Uiracocha was an exception, and was built to commemorate the victory over the Chanca, while that at Pachacamac had originally been erected to the creator-god of the coast who was only in later times identified with Pachacamac. The worship of the creator was spiritual rather than material, in fact, as Garcilasso says, they " worshipped him in their minds." Among the Peruvians, as among every people where a great difference in education exists between the upper and lower classes, the beliefs concerning the supernatural powers varied according to the status of the individual. Huayna Ccapac, we are told, harboured doubts concerning the divinity of the Sun itself, since he remarked that it was obliged to perform an appointed journey, presumably at the bidding of some higher power ; and some of the prayers to Uiracocha, which luckily have been preserved, bear witness to the spirituality of the religious beliefs held, at any rate by the ruling class. One of these given by Molina and translated by Sir Clements Markham, runs as follows : "O Creator ! O conquering Uiracocha ! Ever-present Uiracocha ! Thou who art equal unto the ends of the earth ! Thou who givest life and strength to mankind, saying let this be a man, and let this be a woman ; and as thou sayest so thou givest life, and vouchsafest that men shall live in health and peace and free from danger ! Thou who dwellest in the heights of heaven, in the thunder and in the storm-clouds, hear us, and grant us eternal life ! Have us in thy keeping, and receive this our offering, as it shall please thee, O Creator ! "

The oracular functions of the gods were most important in Peru, and some of the shrines, notably that of Rimac ("The Speaker"), at what is now Lima, was especially famous ; but most of the huaca were supposed to utter responses through the medium of their priests. Besides the oracular shrines, counsel was sought of numerous diviners, who employed various means of discovering the will of the supernatural powers. Some distributed grains of maize in random heaps, foretelling good or ill luck according to the odd or even number of the grains ; others pronounced judgment from the dreams appearing to them while sleeping on a garment of the inquirer. Others again prognosticated good or evil fortune from the twitching of various muscles (as among the Chibcha), from the inspection of the entrails of a *cuy* ("guinea-pig"), or from fire. (The last form of divination is said to have been that practised by the original inhabitants of the Cuzco valley.) Sometimes a certain kind of spider with long legs was stirred with a stick until some of its legs fell off, and the number and position of the severed limbs provided the answer. But one of the most important methods was to inflate the lungs of a young llama and to read the reply in the pattern made by the blood-vessels. Unauthorized practitioners of the black art were also supposed to exist, especially on the coast, who cast sleep upon their victims and sucked their blood or devoured their souls.

An important part was played in religion by the establishments called Aclla-huasi, which corresponded very closely to the convents so familiar to the Spanish conquerors. These were attached to most of the Sun-temples, and contained a number of young virgins, under the care of certain duennas called *Mamacona*, who spun and wove the garments worn by the highest class and the Inca, as well as those dedicated to the Sun. The inmates were chosen chiefly for their beauty from all over the kingdom by special officers, but even members of the royal family received their education in one of these establishments. They slept in small cells, which were visited three times in the day, and were kept in seclusion from the outside world. At a certain age the fairest were selected for the harem of the ruler, others were given in marriage by him to Inca of high position and Curaça, others again entered the service of religion, vowing perpetual virginity, and serving as Mamacona or as handmaids in the Sun-temples. The last were regarded with the most reverential respect. The practice of reserving virgins for the service of a deity seems not to have been confined to the Inca, since Arraiga states that in Conchucos a maiden was dedicated as wife to a stone huaca called Chanca. Remains of Aclla-huasi still exist ; one at Cuzco, which at the conquest became a

M

Christian nunnery, one at Pachacamac, and one on the island of Titicaca in the lake of that name. The plan of the Pachacamac convent (Pl. XVI, 1), described by Uhle, corresponds very closely with that at Titicaca, figured by Squier. The buildings are arranged round three sides of an oblong court, of which one of the long sides is left open. Along the side facing the open space are a number of small cells which must have formed the sleeping-chambers of the inmates, while the other apartments were reserved for ceremonial use and the housing of the Mamacona and the " lady superior." One of the duties of the chosen maidens was the preparation of chicha used in offerings to the Sun, but they also seem to have contributed their own persons in the form of human sacrifices.

The question of human sacrifice has been hotly debated from early times. It is quite certain that the practice was common among many tribes before the establishment of the Inca *régime*, and it is equally certain that the Inca suppressed it, if not entirely, at any rate to a very large extent. Garcilasso protests vigorously that the Inca never made human offerings, but the majority of the chroniclers, including such trustworthy authorities as Cieza, are against him. Recently archæology has given its verdict in favour of the existence of the practice. Uhle found in the precincts of the Sun-temple at Pachacamac a cemetery of women all of whom had been strangled. It was evident that these were not women who had broken their vow of chastity, or had been guilty of any other serious crime, since the bodies were sumptuously clad and surrounded with their possessions and well-decorated vases. It seems certain, therefore, that these had been sacrificed to the Sun. Molina and Gavilan describe the sacrifice. The victims were selected proportionately from the different tribes, and, after the needs of the capital were supplied, the remainder were despatched to the various provinces and distributed among the important shrines. They travelled in regular convoys, those children who were too young to walk being carried in the arms of their mothers. With them they bore many other offerings, and received the adoration of all whom they met on the journey. Most were strangled, but some had the neck broken with an implement of stone, while the throats of others were cut, and their faces anointed with their own blood, which was also sprinkled on the shrine. In other cases the hearts were offered to the divinity. They were buried in special cemeteries together with the vessels which they had been accustomed to use in life. No doubt the practice of human sacrifice was limited to occasions of the highest importance and was therefore rare ; certainly the Inca took measures to ensure that such offerings should be made only with state sanction and under state control. Other offerings, almost infinite in variety, were made to deities of every degree, from the Sun to the humblest conopa. Of these perhaps chicha and coca were the most common, and the latter was deposited at the stone cairns, *apacheta*, which marked the summits of mountain passes, a custom which still survives. Maize, fruit, brightly-coloured feathers, shells, and cuys were offered to the minor objects of worship, while llamas were reserved for the more important festivals held in honour of the huaca and the Sun. In these cases the beast was ornamented with garlands and tethered to a stone ; the heart was torn out and offered to the deity, while the blood was sprinkled on the offering and on the huaca. The maize and coca which were used for such purposes were usually grown in special plantations reserved for the use of the shrine, while the most important huaca possessed large herds of llamas, those belonging to the Sun being vast in extent and scattered widely throughout the empire. Offerings of gold, silver and jewels were practically restricted to the Sun.

Pilgrimages were often made to the more important shrines, notably that of Pachacamac. Here special residences were erected for the use of pilgrims, since they had to undergo a lengthy purification before they were permitted to enter the temple precincts. According to Hernando Pizarro, a fast of twenty days had to be observed before the worshipper was admitted to the first court, and this fast must be prolonged for a year before he might ascend the highest terrace upon which the temple stood. Fasts of this nature, consisting in a strict limitation of diet, including abstinence from all condiments such as salt and red pepper, were invariably necessary before ceremonial purity could be attained. Besides this, a form of confession was often prescribed, which was made before a special priest, who employed a form of divination to ascertain if the confession was genuine and complete. The priest drove a thorn into a fragment of shell, and observed if the latter broke into two or three pieces. In the former case the penitent had to recommence his confession. Pilgrimages were also made to the sacred rock on the island of Titicaca, and here too the visitor was obliged to make confession and take means to purify himself of sin before he was allowed to deposit his offering at the Kentipuncu ("Humming-bird Gate") and pass through to the holy ground. Other forms of purification consisted in ceremonial washing and a changing of garments.

A description of the various festivals which were held at stated seasons of the year is beyond the scope of this book. The material which exists on this subject is large, and will form an important section of that general work on the religion of Peru which some day must be written. A few words may, however, be said concerning the two most interesting, Intip Raymi, the great feast of the Sun, and Situa, at which all evil was banished from the city of Cuzco. Raymi, which lasted

nine days, took place in June, and was celebrated by all
of the ruling caste who could be present, together with
deputations from the provinces headed by the Curaça.
The worshippers prepared themselves by a fast, and
assembled before sunrise in the great square. All wore
their finest jewels and ceremonial garments, and the
scene must have been one of great magnificence. When
the sun rose all prostrated themselves in adoration,
until the ruler stood, and, taking two vases of gold, full
of chicha, emptied one into a golden vessel connected
by a conduit with the temple. This was a libation to the
Sun. He next drank from the other, and the rest of
the liquor was poured into small cups which were distributed among the members of the royal family. The
Curaça also received cups of chicha manufactured by
the maidens dedicated to the Sun. The Inca and his
relations next entered the temple and offered up the
precious vessels from which they had drunk, together
with other objects of silver and gold, while the less
exalted assembly waited in the square. A black llama
was then sacrificed, and the lungs inspected ; if the
omen were unfavourable, another victim was tried, and
again another. But if after the third attempt the signs
were still unpropitious, the ceremony proceeded no
further, and all manner of disasters were apprehended
during the coming year. If the omens were favourable,
a large number of other llamas were sacrificed, and their
hearts and blood offered to the Sun, the flesh being reserved for the subsequent feast. For this, a special bread
was prepared from maize, which on ordinary occasions
was eaten simply roasted. It was considered necessary to
prepare new fire by a ceremonial method for the sacrifices and banquet. On the eve of the ceremony the
sun's rays were concentrated on a wisp of cotton by
means of a concave mirror worn on the bracelet of the
Villac Umu. Torches kindled at the flame so obtained
were conveyed to the temple and the Aclla-huasi, where

the sacred fire was constantly maintained until the next year. If the day were cloudy the ordinary fire-sticks were used, but the omen was considered bad. The chief feature of the ceremonial banquet was the enormous quantity of chicha which was consumed. The drinking-vessels were all of the same size, and a regular etiquette was observed. One of the assembly would approach another with two cups, and invite him to drink; each emptied one of the vessels, and the challenger returned to his seat. The invitation always came in the first instance from the superior in rank, and the other was supposed to return the compliment at a later stage. The ruler also sent cups of chicha to selected individuals with a similar invitation, and the person so honoured replied in the same fashion ; the Inca expressing his esteem by the quantity which he drank from the goblet handed him by his subject.

The Situa festival was held in August, and the principal huaca (such as were movable) were transported from all over the empire to take part in the proceedings. At this season the rains began, which were usually accompanied by much sickness, and the ceremony was of a prophylactic nature. All strangers, deformed persons and notoriously unlucky individuals, were required to leave Cuzco. Four bodies of armed men, all of high rank, formed up in the square, and, at a given signal, rushed each along one of the main roads leading to the provinces, brandishing their weapons and shouting " Go forth all evils." When they had run a certain distance, others took up the cry, which was thus passed on by relays of armed runners until a stipulated river was reached where they bathed and washed their arms. Meanwhile the inhabitants of the city came to their doors and shook their mantles, crying out " Let the evils be gone." That evening there was a dance and a feast, of which the remnants were thrown into the rivers. Next day the figures of the Sun and huaca, and the mummies of the important dead, were brought into the square and ceremonially washed, and the Inca poured a libation to the Sun as at the Raymi festival. The day was passed in feasting and games, thanks were given to the creator for permitting his worshippers to survive another year, and prayers were offered for preservation during that to come. On the succeeding days large sacrifices of llamas were made, and the feasting continued, the persons temporarily expelled from the city being permitted to return and share in the proceedings. A final sacrifice of llamas and cloth terminated the festival, and the provincial embassies were permitted to return laden with gifts, the Curaça being on this occasion allowed the privilege of litters. This feast was said to have been established by Pachacuti.

One point ought to be mentioned in conclusion of this chapter. A tradition of a great deluge seems to have existed throughout the highlands of Peru, as in Colombia. Most of the legends place it immediately before the coming of Uiracocha, and two of them relate that warning of the impending flood was given to the eventual survivors by their llamas. It is strange how this deluge-myth not only pervades practically the whole of the Andean region of South America, but extends also to many regions in the northern portion of the continent.

CHAPTER VIII—PERU : THE SEQUENCE
OF CULTURES

HAVING sketched the ancient history of Peru as far
as we know it, and given a few details regarding
the beliefs and general culture of the people, it is now
time to deal with the question how far the archæology
of the country can explain, or be explained by, the foregoing chapters. Whatever view may be taken of the
value of the writings of Montesinos it is evident that
the short list of Inca, concerning which most of the
chroniclers are in agreement, does not take us back to
the earliest form of culture of which remains are found
in the country. Apart from the fact that we find in Inca
records stories of the discovery of mighty ruins, the
evolution of the several varieties of the llama species,
two of which have never been found in a wild state, requires a longer period than that covered by the list ;
while the evolution of the cultivated varieties of maize
and potato can only be explained by long centuries of
agricultural activity. We have seen that a certain locality called Tiahuanaco, situated at the extreme south of
lake Titicaca, is closely associated with the creation-
myths current among the Inca and Colla. Here it was
that Uiracocha, coming from the south, made mankind
and the heavenly bodies, and here are found the ruins
which most excited the astonishment of the later Inca
conquerors. These ruins, of which a careful survey was
made by Stübel and Uhle, and which have been further
unveiled by Courty of the Créqui-Montfort expedition,
stand in a desolate plain thirteen thousand feet above
the level of the sea. The most noticeable feature is a

large mound, resembling a ruined step-pyramid, concerning the origin of which there has been much dispute. Some have held that it is natural, but the recent discovery of a series of walls, apparently terrace-walls, and of a large stone-lined drain leading from the summit to the foot, proves that this mound, even if it be not entirely artificial, has at least been considerably modified and enlarged by the hand of man. But the mound, though the most conspicuous of the remains, is the least

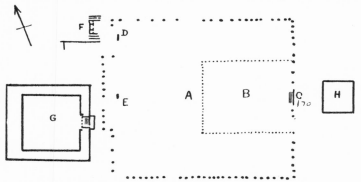

FIG. 16.—Sketch-plan of the megalithic enclosure at Tiahuanaco.

A. Great enclosure.
B. Artificial depression.
C. Stairway (Pl. XVIII). 170
D. Monolithic gateway (Pl. XIX). 171H. Small enclosure.

E. Large monolithic slab.
F. Small chambers.
G. Enclosure with double wall.
H. Small enclosure.

remarkable. In the plain at its foot is a large rectangular enclosure, roughly about 90 by 80 yards, marked out by rows of enormous monoliths of dressed sandstone (Fig. 16. Two of the monoliths appear in Pl. XVIII, 2). One of the largest of the monoliths measures over 12 feet high (above ground), 6 feet wide, and 4 feet thick, and the weight has been estimated at over 26 tons. The sides of the enclosure face the points of the compass, and the western end is recessed as shown in the plan. The great monoliths in their present condition, standing some sixteen feet apart, bear some resemblance to the stone circles of this continent, but the most recent excavations have proved that they were connected by a wall, built of stone blocks without mortar, and that the enclosure was entered by a staircase of large monolithic steps in the centre of the eastern side (Pl. XVIII, 2, and Fig. 16, *c*). Within the enclosure is a rectangular depression (Fig. 16, *b*), to which the stairway gives immediate access, and opposite the stairway, to the east of the great enclosure, is a smaller square enclosure (Fig. 16, *h*), built in the same manner, but with grotesque heads sculptured in relief on the supporting columns of the wall. Immediately west of the great enclosure, is a third, intermediate in size between the other two, and furnished with a double wall (Fig. 16, *g*) ; and at the north-west corner is a small building with three cell-like apartments (Fig. 16, *f*). The two lesser enclosures are furnished with stone-lined drains, which have not yet been fully excavated. Within the north-west corner of the great enclosure is the famous monolithic gateway, shown in Pl. XIX and Fig. 16, *d*), which is the most remarkable ruin in America. The term ruin is used advisedly, because at some period it has been broken in two pieces, but, since the photograph reproduced in the plate was taken, the two fragments have been placed in their proper relation. Cut from a single block of andesite, it measures 10 feet by 12 feet 6 inches, and the weight is estimated at over 9, or, according to another authority, over 12, tons. Along the "lintel" runs a frieze, cut in relief, representing a large figure, shown full-face, flanked on either side by three rows of smaller figures in profile, and beneath this is a second narrower frieze of sun-faces and meanders terminating in condor-heads.

The central figure is shown in Fig. 17. It represents a being in human form with abbreviated legs, the head surrounded with rays terminating in puma-heads and circles. Similar puma-head decoration is seen on the fringes of his tunic skirt and sleeves, his belt, and at the

PLATE XVIII

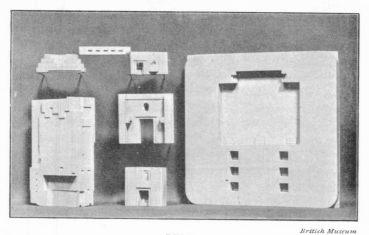

PERU

MODELS OF CARVED STONES : TIAHUANACO, BOLIVIA

(Scale : 1/200TH)

British Museum

PERU

THE MONOLITHIC STAIRWAY : TIAHUANACO, BOLIVIA

end of the engraved band which runs from each eye down his cheek. On his chest he bears an ornament representing an animal with a fish-like body, curved into a semilunar shape, and with a head similar to those

FIG. 17.—Central figure of Pl. XIX (scale $\frac{2}{13}$; after Stübel and Uhle).

which fringe the skirt of the tunic, supported on an indeterminate object flanked by bands terminating in condor-heads. This object is repeated on the ornamental bands which run from his shoulders to his belt. In each of his hands he holds a kind of staff, the butt-end of which is carved to represent the head of a condor, but here the resemblance between the two ceases. The upper portion of that in the right hand is single, and a small condor rests on the inner surface of the extremity; that in the left hand is double, each branch terminating in a condor-head. The figure stands on a kind of throne, again ornamented with heads of the condor.

The lesser figures (Fig. 18) are arranged in three rows on either side of the principal figure, and the figures composing each row resemble one another and those of the row opposite. Each figure represents a man in ceremonial bird-like dress, with wings and a tail, while those of the central row wear bird-masks also. All are crowned with fringed diadems; in the case of the figures in the top rows, the diadem represents a condor with uplifted head and tail; in the centre rows, possibly a fish; in the bottom rows, a puma; while the fringes of the diadems, and the wings and tails of the dresses, terminate in fish- and condor-heads. The figures in the top and centre rows bear

FIG. 18.—Side figures of Pl. XIX (scale ⅕; after Stübel and Uhle).

staves similar to that in the left hand of the central figure,

PLATE XIX

PERU

MONOLITHIC GATEWAY : TIAHUANACO, BOLIVIA

(From Wright's " Bolivia," by permission of Messrs. Barry & Sons)

except that they are ornamented with fish-heads; those in the bottom rows carry staves similar to that in his right hand. Any vacant spaces on the bodies of the figures are filled with bird- and fish-heads, a wing is represented behind the eye, and an engraved band runs down each cheek, terminating in the head of a fish or the tail of a bird.

The reverse side of the gateway is furnished with a number of deep niches, the two largest of which appear to have been fitted with doors. Its present position cannot be explained, and it has probably been moved from its original site at some period unknown. Other monolithic gateways, entire and in fragments, with ornamentation of a similar type have also been found in the neighbourhood. Other remains discovered in the great enclosure are a large slab opposite the centre of the recess in the western side (Fig. 16, e), and a monolithic statue; but though a trench has been driven across it from east to west, no trace of other buildings has been found. Several colossal statues have been discovered in the neighbourhood, many of them holding goblets similar in shape to those on Pl. XX, 9, and Fig. 26, and ornamented in relief with designs conceived in a style exactly similar to those on the gateway. Not far from these ruins, to the south-west, is a site strewn with stone blocks in the utmost confusion in front of a low horse-shoe-shaped mound. Many of them are of colossal proportions, and all of them worked with a skill hardly paralleled, and never surpassed, in the archæology of any country. Of these a few models [1] are shown in Pl. XVIII, 1, which affords but a poor idea of the great variety of their forms. With them is shown an even larger slab, measuring about 13 ft. 6 in. square, which lies to the east of the great enclosure, and suggests the floor of a small shrine. The angles of these blocks are extraordinarily true, and the presence, in many cases,

---

[1] Constructed from the particulars given by Stübel and Uhle.

of counter-sunk fittings for copper clamps (many of which have been found in this neighbourhood) shows that they must have been intended for, or perhaps actually composed, a building or buildings ornamented with niches. These blocks show that the art of architecture must have attained some degree of perfection, since they can only have been fashioned in accordance with a preconceived plan. Any attempt at reconstruction is, unfortunately, rendered impossible owing to the fact that the builders of the neighbouring town of La Paz used this wonderful site as a quarry from which to obtain ready-dressed blocks for the construction of their houses and the paving of their market-place.

On the most recently excavated carvings, traces of paint have been found; for instance Courty discovered a puma-head with blue eyes and a red mouth, and it seems probable that all the reliefs and statues were originally ornamented in similar fashion. To return to the monolithic gateway, various explanations of the frieze have been suggested. As far as the central figure is concerned, the mind turns naturally to the great creator-god associated with the locality, Uiracocha. The rays round his head may well represent the llautu or royal fringe, which, according to one of the chroniclers, typified the rays of the sun ; while the semi-lunar breast-ornament suggests the plate worn by the Villac Umu, which symbolized the moon. The objects which he holds are more difficult to explain ; it has been suggested that they are respectively a club and a bolas, but a more likely theory identifies them with a spear-thrower and a quiver of darts.[1] Such *insignia* well befit the god who dwells " in the heights of heaven, in the thunder and in the

---

[1] Even this explanation is not entirely satisfactory. The object in the left hand seems to resemble the ornament on the tunic, which in its turn resembles the design below the puma-headed fish. This last, especially, can hardly be regarded as either a bolas or a quiver containing two darts. I must confess, however, that I am at a loss for a better explanation.

storm-clouds." Moreover, as we have seen on p. 157, the double-headed belt may typify the lightning. The continual repetition of the condor and puma, animals sacred throughout practically the whole of the Andean region, constitutes a fitting ornament to the dress of the supreme deity. The subsidiary figures would then represent the members of three ayllu, each clad in the dress of the huaca of their respective clans; and it is worth mentioning in this connection that the immigrants led by Manco from the south to the Cuzco valley are said by Sarmiento to have been divided into three ayllu.

The art of Tiahuanaco is distinguished by certain well-marked features, notably a remarkable boldness and certainty of outline, recalling in some respects that of the north-west coast of North America, and also by a number of peculiar conventions. Of the latter the principal are the three-fingered hand (Fig. 17), the circular nostrils of the puma-heads when shown in profile, and the angular S-shaped ear attributed both to birds and beasts. The two latter features are well shown on the fragment of a beautifully carved stone cup illustrated in Fig. 26. Pumas and condors painted in a style exactly similar to the carvings, are found on the pottery vessels, of which the most typical are the beakers shown on Pl. XX, 7–9.

At the ruined fortress of Chavin de Huantar, far to the north of Tiahuanaco, the discovery was made of a remarkable stone, some twenty-five feet long, which had fallen from the façade of the building. This monolith is of diorite, rectangular in shape, and, though the fortress itself is of Inca construction, is evidently of far greater age. The design engraved on one surface is shown in Fig. 19, and is traced from a photograph which the writer owes to the courtesy of Professor Uhle. The design is confused, but a little study reveals a figure bearing a distinct resemblance to the central figure of the Tiahuanaco frieze, though the style is very different.

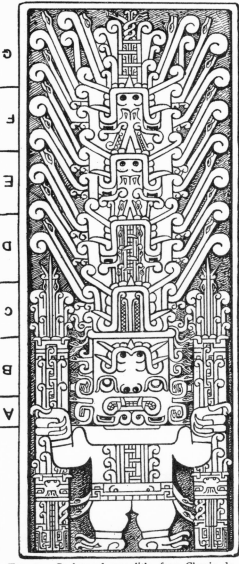

FIG. 19. Sculptured monolith, from Chavin de Huantar. (Lima Museum.)

In each hand he holds a staff, and these staves, unlike the objects held by the Tiahuanaco figure, are exactly similar, though they are too overloaded with ornament for their exact nature to be determined. Round his waist is a belt in the form of a grotesque face, terminating at each extremity in a double fillet furnished with eyes. But the most curious feature of the figure is the head, which is quite inexplicable until the figure is turned upside down. When this is done, a series of monstrous faces (B–F) can be distinguished issuing one from the mouth of the other, furnished with formidable tusks and surrounded with rays resembling conventional ostrich-feathers and fillets with eyes. From the mouth of the last face protrudes a tongue, G, also overloaded with conventional ornament. The principal face, B, has underneath the eyes the U-shaped mark so often seen in the conventional faces of the Maya, and, to anticipate, this U-shaped mark is replaced in the pottery characteristic of Nasca, by a simple horizontal band (see the faces on the vase Pl. I, Fig. 2). Over the principal face is a diadem, A, with a puma-head in front, like those worn by the figures in the lowest row of the Tiahuanaco frieze. The full-face position of this puma-head is expressed somewhat conventionally by placing two profiles face to face and joining the mouths; when each half of the puma-face is regarded as a profile, the shape of the nostril suggests strongly the conventions of Tiahuanaco art. Below the principal face follow the subsidiary faces in order, C, D, E and F, each issuing from the mouth of the other, the series terminating in a tongue, G. A grotesque face of similar character can also be seen on each staff immediately below the elbow of the figure. Both in general appearance and in certain details, though not in all, this remarkable figure bears some resemblance to the Maya carvings of Yucatan, while the reversed position of the head and the "ostrich-feather" rays can be paralleled in some of the reliefs of Ecuador (Fig. 3). The position of the personage portrayed, and his attributes, seem to connect him with the god of the heavens; the rays may well be those of the sun, the staves thunderbolts, while the reversed position of his multiple heads may indicate in conventional fashion that his gaze is turned skyward. But for any closer parallel we must leave the sierra and descend to the coast. Here we come into direct contact with the results achieved by Uhle, whose long researches, carried out on scientific principles, have at last given us the material on which to base a system of comparative chronology.

In his excavations at Pachacamac, he discovered that

N

the celebrated temple, erected to the god of that name, had at an early time been enlarged. At the foot of the original wall, and in ground covered by the later additions, he discovered a cemetery, containing pottery ornamented in the unmistakable style of Tiahuanaco (such as the designs shown in Fig. 20). In a stratum of earth above the original ground-level, but still beneath

FIG. 20.—Designs in the Tiahuanaco style on vases found near Truxillo.

the later buildings, he found burials containing pottery ornamented in a style apparently derived from the last. Again, at the foot of the more recent construction, another series of graves was examined, which contained black ware of a type common on the coast (Pl. XXI, 2–5), associated with vases of Inca type. In another cemetery similar black ware was found without Inca remains. It has thus been proved, at any rate for this region, that four periods can be distinguished : that of Tiahuanaco, that

PLATE XX

PERU

POTTERY TYPES:

1, 2, 3. TRUXILLO   5. ARICA

4. INCA   6. RECUAY, NEAR TRUXILLO

7, 8, 9. TITICACA

(Scale : 1-3, 1/6TH ; 4-9, 1/5TH)

distinguished by a style derived from the former (generally known as the red-white-black period, from the colours in which the vases are painted), that of the black pottery, and that of the Inca. The Tiahuanaco style, as it appears on the coast, is distinguished from that in the highlands by the more conventional style of the painting, and by the far greater variety of colours employed; but the figure shown in Fig 20, *b*, unmistakably represents the personage on the great monolithic gateway, and the objects which he holds are more easily recognizable as spear-throwers of the type shown still more realistically in Fig. 8. Vases painted in this style are found throughout the whole coast, from Truxillo to Nasca. But though the Tiahuanaco style appears as the oldest of the series at Pachacamac, it does not hold this position in every site. In Truxillo, from the archæological evidence collected by Uhle, it was preceded by vases painted in masterly fashion in red on a white slip, and others modelled with a skill which even a modern artist might envy (Pls. XX–XXII). Here too follow in order the red-white-black type, the black, and the Inca.

The fine painted ware is associated with walls constructed, not of adobes, but of clay balls, piled together and left to dry in position. At Moche, near Truxillo, are two large pyramids, built in this style, but now so weathered as to present the appearance of natural hills; and at the foot of one is a cemetery, with walls of similar construction, containing the fine painted ware. In the mass of the pyramid itself have been found graves containing vases in the Tiahuanaco style, and the inference is that the pyramid was used as a burial-place after it had become obsolete as a place of worship. This assumption is supported by the fact that burials of the Tiahuanaco type have been discovered in ground full of fragments of the fine ware. The conclusion is almost inevitable that, at Truxillo, the Tiahuanaco style is later than the finer vases.

The style of the oldest ware from the Truxillo district is, as said above, well shown in Pls. XX, XXI, and XXII ; but though it differs in many respects from that characteristic of Tiahuanaco, a closer study reveals certain peculiar similarities. Take for instance Fig. 15. Here we have represented, apparently, a ceremonial dance ; the figures wear dresses and masks to represent animals, the first a falcon, the second a fox, the third a pelican, and the head of each is crowned with a head-dress in the form of a puma or tiger-cat. Each again carries an object, the exact nature of which cannot be determined, but which is divided above the hand into two projections. The attitude of the personages depicted, the animal dresses, especially those with bird wings and tails, the puma head-dresses, and the bifid object in the hand, all recall the series of minor figures on the great gateway at Tiahuanaco. That the scene represents some ceremony important in the life of the people is obvious from the fact that, in a series of two hundred and fifty of these vases recently acquired by the British Museum from the Chicama valley, it occurs no less than fifteen times. The animal head-dress and the belt terminating in animal heads, such as worn by the central figure in the Tiahuanaco frieze, are found as constant features on vases where human figures are depicted (Fig. 10), while condor-heads are also common as terminals (e.g. to the bands depending from the knives held by the figures in the same illustration). If we turn now to the Nasca and Yca valleys in the south, we find yet another style of pottery, of which two examples of the finest type appear on Pl. I. Here the decoration, though far less free than that of the Truxillo vases, surpasses the latter in the variety of the colours employed. Vases moulded to represent human figures are as rare at Nasca as they are common at Truxillo, and in this respect Pl. I, Fig 1, is not typical, though the painted ornament is ; but the crest projecting from the side of the head-dress is quite in the Truxillo style (e.g. Pl. XXII, 8), and the designs on many of the vases, both from Yca and Nasca, show a close correspondence with Truxillo art. Again we find figures clad in animal dresses, though the style, being more conventional, is in this respect more closely allied to that of Tiahuanaco; another feature recalling the Tiahuanaco art is the fringe of faces to the tunic of the figure on the vase, Pl. I, Fig. 2 (compare Fig. 17). But the closest parallel by far to the Nasca style is constituted by the Chavin monolith, to which the figure on the vase shown on Pl. I, Fig. 2, bears a distinct resemblance. In both cases we have the same exuberance of detail, as if the artist did not know when to stop, the same multiplication of heads, encircled by the same "ostrich-feather" rays. Sometimes, too, the head of a figure is shown in reversed position, as on the Chavin monolith, while the idea of faces or figures issuing from the mouths of others is often expressed in the designs of the Nasca vases. The figure in Pl. I, Fig. 2, holds two serpents, and, as we have seen, the serpent probably typified the lightning in Peru. It is conceivable, therefore, that here too we have a representation of the all-powerful sky-god who seems to have figured at the head of the Peruvian pantheon. Two of the features shared by the respective styles of the Nasca pots and the Chavin stone, viz. the reversed heads and the rays, appear also in the stone carvings of Manabi; but the art of the latter locality and that of Nasca have another point in common. In both the spider appears as an ornamental motive, conventionalized in much the same manner.

Excavations carried on by Uhle in the Lima valley, show that the Nasca art, or a style derived immediately from it, prevailed here also at an early period, and was associated with a class of building resembling the early mounds at Moche.

Pottery in the Tiahuanaco style is also found under conditions which suggest a later date. It is of particular interest to note that in this neighbourhood the earliest graves contained bodies buried extended at full length, that is to say in a position extremely rare in Peru. In the graves in which pottery of the Tiahuanaco style was found, however, the dead were arranged in the usual contracted posture, though at Tiahuanaco itself bodies buried in a horizontal position were found by Courty.

The Nasca style is, moreover, found at Pachacamac, though not in relation with the stratified graves at the foot of the ancient temple, but from the evidence yielded by the neighbouring valleys, it may be assumed that the Nasca style is here too the earliest. At Chancay and Ancon, pottery of a style related to that of Nasca also occurs, but in these localities remains of an even earlier date are found. These are the relics of a primitive fishing population, who did not possess metal, but used implements of bone, and, though very unskilled in weaving, manufactured basket-work of good quality. Their pottery is not painted, but engraved. These remains are found in shell-heaps, similar to those which, as will be seen in a later chapter, fringe the Chilean coast, some being at a considerable distance from the sea. This primitive population came in contact with the makers of the fine painted ware, and in many of the graves pottery of the Nasca type is common, showing that they plundered the graves of the settlers from Nasca, and used their pots, besides, towards the end of their period, copying the Nasca designs. At Chancay the Tiahuanaco style follows next, and it is possible to trace the development of the red-white-black from it ; and again the evolution of the black and white type, so characteristic of this neighbourhood, by the omission of the red pigment. Upon this last style supervenes that of the Inca.

The conclusion, therefore, seems to be inevitable that the Tiahuanaco style is later *on the coast* than certain local styles, exemplified in that of Truxillo and that of Nasca, but that a connection, at any rate psychological, underlies all three. Turning now to the south-east of the

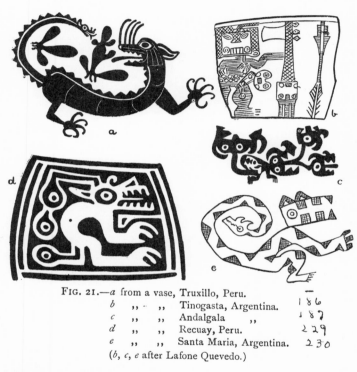

FIG. 21.—*a* from a vase, Truxillo, Peru.
  b   ,, - ,,   Tinogasta, Argentina.
  c   ,,   ,,   Andalgala   ,,
  d   ,,   ,,   Recuay, Peru.
  e   ,,   ,,   Santa Maria, Argentina.
  (*b, c, e* after Lafone Quevedo.)

Tiahuanaco district, we find what appear to be certain traces of the Tiahuanaco style in north-west Argentina. For instance the engraved potsherd found at Tinogasta shown in Fig. 21, *b*, bears a close resemblance to the central figure of the Tiahuanaco gate; and the monster, Fig. 21, *e*, from an engraved vase from the Calchaqui valley, resembles as closely the animal from a painted red-white-black vase found at Recuay (Fig. 21, *d*); and the designs of the red-white-black ware, which is found along the coast from Truxillo to Pachacamac, are themselves derived from the art of Tiahuanaco. The question becomes more complicated when practically the same monster is found on many of the older Truxillo pots (Fig. 21, *a*), treated with the freedom characteristic of the art of that region.

The black pottery (Pl. XXI, 2–5), common on the coast from Truxillo to Pachacamac, next demands attention. It is found in greatest quantities in the neighbourhood of Truxillo, and, though it is indisputably more recent than the Tiahuanaco style of pottery, it is superior in technique even to the fine pots characteristic of the early Truxillo period. But though the makers of this black ware were better artisans, they were far inferior as artists. Since the colour of the vases did not admit of painted decoration, the potter was compelled to employ moulded and engraved ornament alone, and the modelling, though based upon the early Truxillo style (e.g. Pl. XXI, 5), is far inferior to it. From the excavatory evidence it is clear that this black pottery was the predominant type in the region of the coast above mentioned during the period immediately preceding, and subsequent to, the Inca conquest.

The problem presented by the researches of Uhle is by no means easy of solution, but it is possible to base upon them a tentative reconstruction of the early history of Peru. Excluding the primitive fishing population mentioned above, the earliest inhabitants seem to have been fairly homogeneous; though three culture-centres may be distinguished, at Truxillo, Nasca and Tiahuanaco, which seem to have sprung from a common root, though they developed, at first in isolation, on different lines. In the north, the art of modelling was found at its best, extending into the region of Manabi, and painting occurred in its freest and most vigorous style. In the south, the art developed in the direction of colour, but lost in effect through over-luxuriant conventional-ization. In the highlands, it maintained a severer style than at Nasca, and found its fullest expression in stone, achieving results unparalleled in America. "In the highlands" is written advisedly, since many authorities hold that the cyclopean structures beyond the immediate region of Tiahuanaco, such as the ramparts of the Sacsa-huaman fortress at Cuzco (Pl. XV), portions of the fortifications at Ollantaitambo (Pl. XII, 1), and the larger polygonal style (Pl. VII, 4), are relics of this early cul-ture. These three centres were flourishing when a new phase becomes evident ; the art of Tiahuanaco appears throughout the coast, not indeed in stone, for stone was lacking in this region, but in pottery, and, locally, in textiles. The general supersession of the coastal styles by this inland art can hardly be explained except on the hypothesis that the highlanders overran the mari-time region, and the inhabitants of the latter adopted the style of their conquerors. It is obvious that most of the vases, painted in the Tiahuanaco style, which have been found on the coast, are the work of local artists ; instead of the simple black and white pigments found in the neighbourhood of Tiahuanaco itself, a variety of colours often appear (as can be seen in Fig. 20, where they are indicated by shading), and polychrome designs are typical of the Nasca art and its derivatives. Moreover in many cases the artist, working in an un-familiar style, loses the vigour of the original design, and even in some cases misunderstands it.[1] Nor was the Tiahuanaco influence exerted only in the direction of the coast, since traces of it can be seen also in north-

[1] Uhle divides the Tiahuanaco style as found on the coast into two periods ; Tiahuanaco style proper, and a later derived type which he terms "Epigonal." It seems almost impossible to make a definite dis-tinction, there must from the first have been considerable variation according to the skill and intelligence of the artist, but still a gradual transition seems to have taken place from the "classical" Tiahuanaco designs to the later style of the coast.

west Argentina. The Tiahuanaco domination seems to have lasted long enough to extinguish the local arts, except at Truxillo, which was perhaps the last region to be reduced; and, when its influence waned, a new style, still bearing a relation to the imposed art, appeared, the red-white-black, and its later derivatives.

But the uniting of the maritime region under a single, if only temporary, control, had produced considerable intercommunication between the various coastal districts, so that the distribution of the red-white-black type was fairly uniform; and when a degenerate variety of the older art made its appearance in the black ware of Truxillo, it spread readily down the coast to meet at Pachacamac the advancing wave of Inca culture. The Chavin stone is as yet unexplained, and certainly provides a difficulty. Like as it is to the Tiahuanaco sculptures, it bears a closer resemblance to the painted style of Nasca. It is probably the result of the reaction of the Nasca art on that of Tiahuanaco, and it may well be that, just as the Tiahuanaco style is later on the coast than that of Nasca, so the Nasca style is later in the highlands than that of Tiahuanaco. It is interesting to note that this Nasca-Chavin style seems also to have reached the north-west Argentine, as can be seen from the detail from a vase engraving shown in Fig. 21, c.

If this interpretation of the archæological evidence is correct, there seems yet more reason to believe that the account of Montesinos is based on genuine tradition, garbled and perverted it is true, but containing nevertheless a substratum of fact. The rulers of his early list, viewed in this light, become the sovereigns of the Tiahuanaco empire. Whether the seat of government remained fixed at Tiahuanaco, or whether it was transferred to the more fertile Cuzco valley, it is impossible to say, at any rate Cuzco and Ollantaitambo must have been two of the most important frontier fortresses of the early empire. It is quite true that a difficulty is consti-

PLATE XXI

PERU

1. Carved stone vessel : Cuzco
2-5. Black pottery : Truxillo
6-8. Red pottery : Truxillo

(Scale : 1, 1/12th ; 2-5, 1/9th ; 6-8, 1/6th)

tuted by the fact that pottery of the Tiahuanaco type has not been found in the highlands north of Titicaca, but the archæology of the highlands is very imperfectly known. No graves of undoubtedly early date have been discovered (except at Tiahuanaco itself and in Titicaca island) and the climatic conditions in this region are not favourable to the preservation of remains for a great lapse of time, as in the coastlands, except at great altitudes such as the Titicaca region itself. It may be that the conquest of the cordillera north of Ollantaitambo has been transferred by Montesinos from the latter Inca empire to the period covered by his early list of kings, and that the Tiahuanaco dominion may have been confined to the Collao and the coast ; but this leaves the Chavin monolith unexplained. However, in the present imperfect state of our knowledge an entirely satisfactory explanation cannot be expected ; it is only possible to put forward a tentative theory which must be modified in accordance with future researches. It is worth while calling attention to a tradition which, according to Garcilasso, existed among the inhabitants of the Chincha valley. They stated that in former times they were a powerful people, making frequent *razzias* in the Collao. Though Garcilasso discredits the tradition, it may have been based on fact, and may have called forth reprisals on the part of the Tiahuanaco rulers, leading to the conquest of the coast. It is probable, too, that some such intercommunion took place, owing to which designs such as that shown in Fig. 21 filtered through from the coast to the Argentine.

An interesting point in connection with the representations of the creator-god of Tiahuanaco and his worshippers has not hitherto been noticed. On looking at Fig. 17 it will be seen that the engraved bands running down each cheek from the eye contain two engraved circles, and the same feature is observable in the case of the lesser figures (Fig. 18). In the vases painted in similar style from the coast (Fig. 20) these bands containing circles are particularly noticeable. The circles strongly suggest tears, and the probability that they were actually intended as such is greatly strengthened by the fact that masks, on which tears were painted, were worn by the Chibcha at the ceremonies held on the occasion of the harvest (see p. 32). As the Tiahuanaco god was evidently a sky-god, it is probable that these tears represent the fertilizing rain, and the fact, that no such symbolism occurs in the art of the coast before the introduction of the Tiahuanaco style, can be explained by the circumstance that rain was extremely rare in that region. The early chronicler explains the tears on the Chibcha mask as an appeal to the pity of the supreme powers, but it is quite possible that he did not fully understand the meaning implied, and that here too they were symbolical of rain, especially as the ceremony was connected with the harvest. A pottery head with what appear to be indications of tears has been found in Ecuador and is figured in Gonzales Suarez' *Atlas Arqueologico*, Pl. VII, *a*. On the fine funerary vases characteristic of the Diaguite region in north-west Argentina, tears are also represented (Fig. 28, *a*,[1] and it may be that the children whose bodies these vases contain were sacrificed to the sky-god worshipped there. The same feature is seen on the fine bronze shown in Fig. 30, *a*. Still more interesting does the question become when it is noticed that grooves running from the eyes over the cheeks are a common characteristic of the idols of the ancient inhabitants of Jamaica,[2] especially as these grooves were evidently emphasized by inlay, probably of shell. Some of the anthropomorphic vases from the island of Marajo

[1] It is a noticeable fact that the double-headed snake, which, there is reason to believe, typified the lightning, frequently appears on these vases ; see the illustration quoted.

[2] See Journal of the R. Anthrop. Inst., Vol. XXXVII, Pls. XLVIII and XLIX.

in the Amazon estuary also seem to show traces of painted tears, after the fashion of the Argentine urns, but this is not so certain. In any case the convention seems extremely widespread, and appears to imply that the fundamental ideas underlying the religions of a great part of South America and the early population of the Antilles were closely akin.

This is a convenient place at which to deal shortly with the question of external influence on South American culture. Many archæologists in the past have found it difficult to believe that the culture of the Andes at its highest could be of indigenous origin, and have sought its source in Egypt, China and other parts of Asia, Polynesia and the fabulous Atlantis. At the present time it is recognized that, given an environment where the conditions of life are not too arduous, there is no reason why a culture of a high type should not develop independently of other culture-centres; and that external influence ought not to be inferred without explicit evidence. As we have seen, the evolution of the different varieties of llama, and of the potato-culture, imply centuries of settled life; while the fact that the American languages stand, structurally, apart from those of the rest of the world proves that any immigration which may have taken place from elsewhere can have been but inconsiderable. Traditions of immigration exist, as has been stated, at Manabi and Lambayeque, and Garcilasso writes that the people of Chincha preserved the tradition that their ancestors had come from a far country. Montesinos, again, chronicles the arrival of immigrants upon the coast. The Lambayeque legend is the most important, since it preserves the names of the chief and his successors, and the titles (or names) of his chief officers. The legend is related by Balboa, and it is well known that the early Spanish chroniclers were very accurate in the transcription of native words, both as regards Peru and Oceania. Mr. S. H. Ray, one of the leading authorities on Oceanic languages, fails to identify these terms with any Polynesian or Melanesian dialect, and states that, in his opinion, they bear far greater resemblance to some American tongue. The inference is that the Lambayeque immigration proceeded from some other point of the American coast ; and if this is the case with the Lambayeque immigration, why not with the others ? Certainly the two following facts in combination tell in favour of an indigenous origin for the Andean culture ; firstly, the purely " American " character of the languages, and secondly the homogeneity which seems to underlie the Andean culture from Colombia to Bolivia and the highland provinces of the northwest Argentine. Another point is worthy of attention. Any people arriving on the Pacific coast must have been skilled seamen, and it seems incredible that, after settling, they should have proceeded immediately to forget their craft, especially as their chief source of nourishment must have been the sea. Yet throughout the whole of the coast of South America nothing but the most primitive form of raft was found, and it appears that sails were entirely unknown south of Tumbez. It is not possible, or even reasonable, to deny that occasionally a stray canoe manned by Polynesians may have made the American coast; it is known that the eastern Polynesians were expert and daring mariners, and there is reason to believe, on the strength of a tradition, that the Maori penetrated even into Antarctic waters. Besides this certain of the food-plants, notably the sweet potato, common in Polynesia, are believed to be indigenous to America. But if occasionally an isolated crew of wandering Polynesians made the American coast they could have had practically no influence upon the indigenous population, even if they settled there, which is very unlikely. They would most probably have come unprovided with women, and if they took wives, permanent or temporary, from among the aborigines, their children would have grown up speaking the mothers' language (for the influence of the mother in this matter is paramount), and practising the local customs. Another important point relative to the Polynesians is the following. From a consideration of the traditions and genealogies collected in various parts of the Pacific it is possible to trace with reasonable certainty the colonization of the islands from west to east and to estimate the date at which each group received its Polynesian population. Now the Eastern Pacific can hardly have been colonized before the middle of the seventh century ; and therefore if the Polynesians had landed on the American coast in sufficient numbers to affect Peruvian culture, some traditions of their arrival would surely have survived. In any case the early culture can hardly have been subjected to their influence. The event of a Chinese crew finding its way across the breadth of the Pacific, and passing by the islands to settle in South America, is almost unthinkable, and in any case could never have occurred with sufficient frequency to have left any impression whatever. Egypt may be disregarded altogether. The possibility of influence emanating from Central and North America is not so remote; the art of Nasca and the Chavin monolith suggests that of the Maya to a certain extent, and there are points of resemblance between the Tiahuanaco and Truxillo styles on the one hand, and the art of the north-west coast of North America on the other, a resemblance which also appears in some of the coast legends. But these resemblances do not amount to much more than a common " American " character, and in the present state of our knowledge we are not justified in admitting more than the possibility of some early intercommunication. Even if we admit this we are forced to allow that the various schools of Andean art, and the culture and beliefs of the eastern half of South America, have developed locally and on separate lines ; and our admission amounts to no more than this, that the art and culture of this region, starting from a common " American " basis, have completed their evolution in South America, and have therefore every claim to be considered indigenous. To presume more than this, in the present state of our knowledge, would argue ignorance of the value of scientific evidence.

[*₊* Since this chapter was written, Dr. A. Hrdlička has published a preliminary note on his researches at Truxillo and Pachacamac. His extensive collection of human remains (including over 1100 skulls from Truxillo) still awaits detailed investigation, but he distinguishes three types which he assigns to three successive periods. First, a round-headed population who made pottery, simple in form and with sombre painted ornament, and who possessed little metal and that chiefly gold. Second, another round-headed people, with pronounced artificial deformation (of the type shown in Pl. X, Figs. 1 and 2), who made better and more brightly-ornamented pottery, used copper freely and some gold. Third, a long-headed type, which appears in small numbers at the time of the greatest prevalence of the deformed type. Until his researches are published fully, it is impossible to say how they bear upon the theories put forward in the above chapter, but at present they seem to support rather than to controvert them.]

CHAPTER IX—PERU : ARTS AND CRAFTS

OF the various products of Peruvian craftsmanship the pottery is the most important archæologically, as may be inferred from the last chapter; it is, moreover, the most important from an artistic point of view. By far the greater proportion of the pottery remains come from the coast; for in the interior the atmospheric conditions are not so well suited to the preservation of ceramics for a long period. Naturally there was great variation in the quality of the ware, both according to locality and period, and according to the purpose for which the vessel was intended, but, in the case of the better specimens, the clay was well-mixed and the firing good. Most of the pottery, red or black, light or heavy, porous or compact, is of the same kind of clay, containing much volcanic detritus. In the better specimens, the fine surface and the thinness of the walls are the result of careful polishing. They are not heavily fired, for the vegetable substances are not entirely carbonized, and the firing must have been performed in the open, probably in a hole in the ground. Throughout the whole of Peru the use of the wheel was entirely unknown, and the remarkable regularity and gracefulness of some of the forms in which the vases were moulded (such as Pls. XX, 1-3, and XXI, 6-8) bear witness to the masterly skill with which the primitive potter handled his material. Undoubtedly the early inhabitants of Truxillo and the neighbourhood take the premier place as workers of clay. Their vases are moulded chiefly in reddish clay, often covered wholly or partially with a white slip and burnished. On this white slip, patterns are painted in red.

o

The variety of designs is endless ; vases are found in the form of human heads or figures (Pls. XXI, 6–8, and XXII, 8–10) modelled with such skill that an excellent idea can be obtained of the personal appearance of this early people, their dress, ornaments, weapons and musical instruments. Warriors with their weapons (Pl. XXII, 10), musicians with pan-pipes, flutes and drums, individuals in ceremonial masks and dresses, personages of monstrous appearance, furnished with formidable tusks (recalling the San Agustin carvings mentioned on page 39), and probably intended for huaca, women carrying children or burdens, are all portrayed ; even the more sombre side of life is illustrated in the vases representing maimed and diseased persons and cripples. The painted type (Pl. XX, 1–3) show regular scenes, representing fishing (Fig. 9), hunting (Fig. 8), combats (Fig. 10) and ceremonial dances (Fig. 15). The animal world is well represented in both types of pottery; land-animals, such as dogs, deer, jaguar and cavies; birds, principally pelicans, falcons, wild-fowl and owls; dwellers in the sea, such as sea-lions, fish, crabs, lobsters and shell-fish, are all to be found. An especially pleasing vase of this class is shown in Pl. XX, 2 ; here a marsh-bird is represented as seated on the vase, while below is painted its nest and young in a reed-bed, and cranes are engaged in catching fish close by. But it is in the representation of the human face that the Truxillo artist excelled, and the character expressed in such masterpieces as Pl. XXI, 6 and 8, and Pl. XXII, 8 and 9, can hardly be surpassed in the plastic art of any country or period. Many pots show conventional designs, continuous spirals, step-patterns, frets and meanders, all drawn with remarkable freedom and certainty. Many of these are evolved from, or combined with, animal designs, as can be seen in Pl. XX, 1. A common feature of the pottery of this neighbourhood is a spout forming a loop-handle, which fulfilled a utilitarian purpose. In the hot

PLATE XXII

PERU

1, 3, 4. SILVER VASES : FROM THE COAST NEAR TRUXILLO

2. SILVER MACE-HEAD : FROM THE COAST NEAR TRUXILLO

5, 6, 7. VASES : FROM THE HIGHLANDS

8, 9, 10. VASES : FROM THE COAST NEAR TRUXILLO

(Scale : 1-4, 1/5TH ; 5-7, 1/7TH ; 8-10, 1/6TH)

and dry atmosphere of the coast a long and narrow neck
was necessary to prevent evaporation of the contents,
while the loop allowed the vessel to be slung on a
baldric so that the owner could carry a supply of drink
with him.   That these vessels were so used is proved by

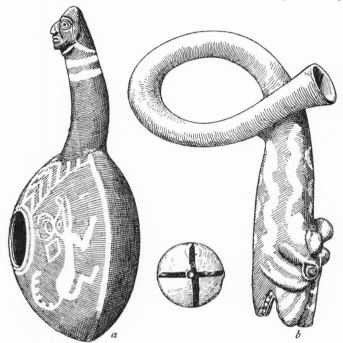

FIG. 22.—*a* pottery vase, *b* pottery trumpet ; from Truxillo (scale $\frac{3}{11}$).
[British Museum.]

the discovery of vases representing men with vases suspended in this manner.   A type of vase almost peculiar
to this locality and period consists of a circular body with
projecting handle, somewhat resembling a saucepan
(Fig. 22,*a*).   The qualification is necessary, since a single
example of this type has been found on the coast of Ecuador, but it must almost certainly have been of Truxillo
manufacture.   Pottery trumpets in the shape of bugles

are also characteristic of this region (Fig. 22, *b*). At Truxillo are found the finest specimens of the black ware
(Pl. XXI, 2–5), which in later times became common far
down the coast. This ware is covered with a plumbago
slip, which takes a fine burnish. It seems that the plumbago ware was known in early times also, since some of
the figure-vases in this style closely resemble those in
the red ware, and are almost as well modelled (compare
Pl. XXI, 5, and XXII, 10). Most of them, however, are
undoubtedly later, and though they are technically
superior to the earlier type, in so far as the ware is of
extreme and uniform thinness, the soul has gone out of
the designs and they have become mechanical. They exhibit, however, an almost equal variety of form, with the
exception of course that they are not found with painted
decoration. The red ware also persisted in later times,
but exhibits an equal degeneration. At all periods vases
with double bodies (Pl. XXI, 3) were found, though
this type was not so common in the early age. The
bodies are connected, and one is furnished with a spout,
the other with a whistle, so that the motion of the liquid
within produced a sound, which was no doubt supposed
to represent the cry of the animal in the form of which
the spoutless portion of the vase was moulded. The
coast vases were often made in sections, the body being
composed of an upper and lower part accurately fitted
together, and subsequently furnished with spout and
handles. At any rate in later times moulds were com-
monly employed, a fact which might be gathered from the
frequent occurrence of identical designs, even if numbers
of the moulds themselves had not been discovered.
The joints were completely concealed by the slip, and
it is only from broken pots that the composite nature
of the vases can be determined. Next to the Truxillo
ware, the most striking specimens of Peruvian ceramic
art are found at Nasca. These are distinguished by
an extraordinary variety of colour, as may be seen

from Pl. I. In this region moulded vases, such as
Pl. I, 1, which represents a man holding a sling, are
comparatively rare, and the painted type predominates,
the variety with twin spouts such as Pl. I, 2, being
especially characteristic. The later pottery of the
province of Yca derived from this early type, is distinguished by a more subdued colouring, and is usually
covered with all-over designs derived from the figures
of birds and fish expressed in the angular method peculiar to basket-work and textiles (such as Pl. XX, 4). Engraved pottery, some of it dating from the earliest times,
is far commoner in southern Peru than on the northern
coast.

In the inland parts the pottery is characterized by great
restraint both in colour and form, especially in the
earliest times. The Tiahuanaco vases are as a rule of
red ware, painted in red and white, but a black engraved
variety has also been found. When the Tiahuanaco
style reached the coast it deteriorated, losing to a great
extent its vigorous simplicity, though gaining in colour.
For instance the design shown in Fig. 20 is painted on
an orange-red ground in white, black, crimson, grey
and buff. The beaker type of vase, as shown on Pl.
XX, 7–9, is especially characteristic of Tiahuanaco, and
the specimens found in the highlands are distinguished
by considerable elegance of form and good proportions;
but jars with single and double handles have also been
found. The beaker type also occurs on the coast,
though all its elegance has vanished, and here the better
examples of the Tiahuanaco art consist in designs painted
on vases moulded in the style of the coast.

It is difficult to write with freedom on the subject of
Cuzco pottery for two reasons. Firstly, the remains
in the highlands are few, and much of the material,
perhaps even the greater part, has been collected on the
coast and in other provinces whither it was carried by
mitimaes; and secondly, the Inca deported many of the

coast-artisans to Cuzco, in order that the capital might reap the benefit of their skill in pottery-making and metallurgy. In this way arose no little confusion in styles, but at any rate certain types can be indicated as characteristic of the dominant people. The principal of these is the type shown on Pl. XXII, 5–7, examples of which are found in every quarter where Inca influence penetrated, from Quito in Ecuador to Copiapo in Chile. In many of the provinces the pattern was copied by the local potters, who further sometimes applied their own style of decoration (as in the north-west Argentine ; see Fig. 29, c) ; but in none of these cases were the products of provincial artists equal to those of the capital. This type of vase seems to have been made in great numbers and all sizes, from a few inches to over 2 feet 6 inches in height. The ware is red, sometimes covered with a white slip, and the patterns are in red. and black. The tones are very subdued, as in all the highland pottery. A small knob may be noticed at the base of the neck; for carrying the larger specimens of this kind of vase, a cord was passed through each handle, and over the knob, which prevented it from slipping off, and the vase was hoisted on the back of the carrier, the cords passing over his shoulders. Another type of pot (also found in Ecuador, the Argentine and on the coast), which is typical of Cuzco, is a round cup, often with a cover, supported on a stem with expanding foot, and furnished with a single loop-handle arranged in a horizontal plane (Fig. 6, c). This type is usually undecorated. Dishes again are regarded as typical of Inca influence, and are sometimes painted on the interior with elaborate designs in the usual subdued colours. But the most pleasing examples of Inca pottery, always excepting the graceful type shown on Pl. XXII, 5–7, are certain fragments found on the island of Titicaca, on which are painted naturalistic representations of butterflies and other insects. The above short

summary, taken in connection with the preceding chapter, will perhaps be sufficient to give a general idea of
the pottery of Peru, though the subject is by no means
exhausted. Many complex questions are
connected with it, and it cannot be treated
fully except in a special work containing
a vast number of illustrations.

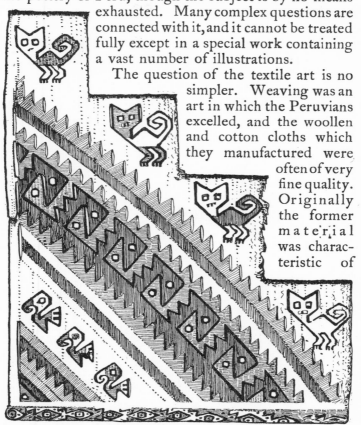

The question of the textile art is no
simpler. Weaving was an
art in which the Peruvians
excelled, and the woollen
and cotton cloths which
they manufactured were
often of very
fine quality.
Originally
the former
m a t e r i a l
was charac-
teristic   of

FIG. 23.—Fragment of textile ; Truxillo (scale ½).   [British Museum.]

the highlands, the latter of the coast, but the establishment of the Inca empire brought about an interchange of
produce, so that the distribution of both became more or
less general.   The coast however furnishes by far the
greater number of textile remains, even of those in the
style of the highlands, owing to the dryness of the cli-

mate. The earliest textiles known are those in the Tiahuanaco style, which is as easily recognizable in tapestry as
in pottery. In the earliest times the loom does not seem

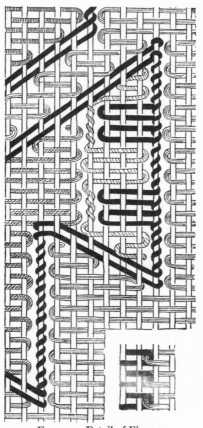

to have been known ;
the warp was arranged
on a frame and the weft
put in by hand by means
of wooden needles, each
wound with thread of a
different colour. The
main outlines of the de-
sign ran parallel with
the warp and weft, and
the design was built up
in patches of colour and
was not surrounded
with an outline in black
as in the pottery. This
method of tapestry -
weaving was followed
later on the coast, es-
pecially in the northern
parts, but with a techni-
cal difference. Where
the dividing line be-
tween two colours runs
parallel with the warp,
it is evident that a slit
must result (e.g. behind
the tails of the birds in
Fig. 23). In the later textiles these slits were al-

FIG. 24.—Detail of Fig. 23.

lowed to occur, and they performed a definite function in
adding emphasis to the design. The technique of this
particular fragment is shown enlarged in Fig. 24 (in
which, however for the sake of clearness, the number
of weft-threads has been reduced by one-half), so that

the structural nature of these slits may be seen; the portion shown being the tail of one of the birds.   But in the tapestry woven in the Tiahuanaco style, no slits occur, the weft-threads of two contiguous patches of colour being interlaced as shown in Fig. 24, inset.   This method of avoiding a slit seems to have been characteristic of the highlands, since it is found in Inca cloth of

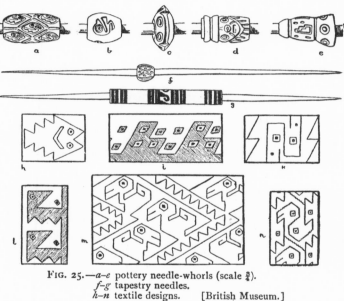

Fig. 25.—*a–e* pottery needle-whorls (scale ¾).
f–g tapestry needles.
h–n textile designs.   [British Museum.]

a later date ; but it appears to have been forgotten on the coast in subsequent times, since in cases where a long slit occurred, it was closed by sewing, or by overlapping of the colours, and not by interlacing the weft.   Long slits, however, were avoided as far as possible by making the main outlines of the pattern run diagonally, and not vertically as in the Tiahuanaco style.   The coastal tapestry is always in bright colours, the earliest in yellow, brown, blue and red; in the later manufactures a more extensive variety of tints is found (as may be seen from

Fig. 23, where the colours are represented by shading), of even greater brilliancy. The needles (Fig. 25, *f* and *g*) with which tapestry was woven were weighted with small pottery whorls, ornamented with engraved and painted patterns; some of these are among the most decorative of the smaller objects found in the coast graves, notably the specimen with a bird design shown in Fig. 25, *a*. Less often they are moulded to represent a human figure or an animal such as a frog, as illustrated in the same figure. But the great bulk of the textile manufactures was produced by true weaving on a loom. The loom employed was a very primitive appliance; the warp consisted of a long continuous thread, passing backwards and forwards between two horizontal rods, which thus corresponded to the warp-beam and cloth-beam of the European hand-loom; each alternate warp-thread passed through one of a series of cotton loops arranged along a third rod; so that, when this rod was raised, every second warp-thread was lifted sufficiently to allow the passage of the shuttle carrying the weft. The warp-threads connected with the loops passed under a thick rod inserted in the warp, and the rest of the warp-threads passed above it; so that as soon as the rod which bore the loops was lowered, the warp-threads connected with it fell below the level of the rest, and, in the technical language of weaving, the " shed " (or aperture between the two series of warp-threads) was divided in the opposite direction, and the shuttle was passed back again. From certain differences in the technique of cloths of the periods characterized respectively by the Tiahuanaco designs and their derivatives on the one hand, and by the diagonally arranged patterns on the other, there seems reason to believe that a change in the form of loom took place; the former being manufactured on a horizontal, the latter on a vertical loom. Various methods of decoration were employed; patterns were woven in the material, or introduced by means of embroidery after manufacture ; designs were painted on the cloth (Pl. XXIII, 4), or the latter was dipped in dye, certain portions being " reserved " from the action of the pigment by being tied tightly so that the dye could not penetrate. Fine specimens of painted and dyed work exist dating from the Tiahuanaco period, and garments have been discovered made up of a patchwork of variously dyed pieces, forming symmetrical patterns in reciprocal colours. Since the warp consisted of one continuous thread wound round the primitive cloth- and warp-beams, the ends appeared as a series of loops. To join two patches together a thread was passed through the end-loops of adjoining pieces, uniting them so closely that they appear to have been woven in a single piece. In the later periods, stripes were often introduced into the fabric by the insertion of warp-threads of different colours, and this method of ornamentation is especially frequent in Inca textiles. Another late development was the employment of a double warp and woof, in two colours, by means of which a double-faced cloth was woven, the pattern appearing in reciprocal colours on each side of the fabric (Pl. XXIII, 3). A peculiar variety of three-ply weaving, which seems practically to be confined to America, was also practised. In many cases patterns were applied to plain cloth by simple embroidery, for which, according to Garcilasso, thorns were used as needles.

As regards designs, considerable variation occurred throughout the long period during which weaving and tapestry were practised. The finer Tiahuanaco patterns are conceived on a bold scale, and the details appear as patches of colour unemphasized by outline except in the case of the painted figures. Later, an outline became a regular feature (Pl. XXIII, 1), and a greater variety of colours was introduced. At the same time the figures became curtailed, a tendency towards symmetrical arrangement showed itself ; with the result that all-over patterns of a geometrical nature were gradually evolved. The modification of naturalistic designs into simple geometrical ornament may be seen from the few examples shown in Fig. 25, and is a frequent feature in the history of decorative art, especially in periods of decadence. The heads of birds are interlocked and repeated (Fig. 25, *k*, *m*, and *n*) until the eye loses the significance of the detail in the geometrical pattern to which its symmetrical repetition gives rise ; and the figures of fish (Fig. 25, *h* and *l*) and heads of beasts (Fig. 25, *i*) suffer similar degradation. The process was no doubt hastened by the application to cloth of patterns taken from basket - work. In basket - work the designs, even though they may be taken from the natural world, are obliged, for technical reasons, to assume a geometrical form. The kinship of later Peruvian textile ornament with basket-work is especially seen in southern Peru,— such designs as Pl. XXIII, 2, being particularly characteristic of Yca. Indeed these basket-work patterns invaded even the pottery, the painted decoration of which became modified according to the conventions of textile art.

Delicate gauzes (Pl. XXIII, 5) were also manufactured during the later period on the coast, consisting of a fine net background on which were embroidered designs characteristic of the period ; and reticules of ornamental network, often in colours, are found in the graves. The textiles of the Inca, like their pottery, were distinguished by the sobriety of their colours, black and brown predominating, though subdued yellows, reds and blues are also found. Stripes and small all-over patterns are the most common, and the garments are remarkable for the excellence of their technique rather than for the brilliance of their hues. Embroidery and the manufacture of double-faced cloth were also practised by the inlanders, and it is possible that the latter may have been introduced on the coast from the highlands. Cloth was

PLATE XXIII

British Museum

PERU

1, 2. TAPESTRY, COAST STYLE
3. CLOTH, INCA STYLE
4. PAINTED CLOTH, COAST STYLE
5. GAUZE, COAST STYLE
(Scale : 1-4, 1/8TH ; 5, 1/4TH)

also ornamented with brilliantly coloured feathers forming patterns, and many beautiful examples of this work,
some with designs in the Tiahuanaco style, have been
preserved. A specimen of this kind of work is seen in
the head-dress figured on Pl. IX, 3.

The preparation from cotton and wool of the thread for
weaving was one of the principal occupations of women.
Garcilasso tells how " even in going from the villages
to the city, or in passing from one house to another on
necessary business, they took with them the means both
of spinning and twisting. On the road they went along
twisting what they had already spun, as being more easy ;
and on their visits they took with them the distaff and
span while they conversed. Those who went along the
roads twisting or spinning belonged to the lower classes.
The Pallas [princesses] of the royal blood, when they
paid visits, caused their servants to carry their distaffs ;
but both visitors and those who were visited were thus
occupied while they talked, so as not to be idle. . . .
If any woman who was not a Palla, even though she
might be the wife of a Curaça or a lord of vassals, went
to pay a visit to a Palla of the blood royal, she did not
bring any work of her own with her. But after the
first few words of the visit, or rather adoration, for such
it was, she begged to be given some work, saying that
she had not come on a visit, but to serve as an inferior
to a superior. The Palla, as a great favour, complied
with this request, and gave some of the work that either
she or one of her daughters was doing; for she did not
degrade her to the level of the servant-girls by giving
her some of their work. This favour was all that the
visitor could wish for, seeing that the Palla thus made
her in some sort on an equality with herself and her
daughter." [1]

In wood-carving, as might be expected, the Peruvians

[1] From the translation by Sir Clements Markham, published by the
Hakluyt Society.

showed much skill, but remains of this perishable nature are few, and consist mainly of small objects, such as caskets, ear-ornaments, and the like. The most interesting examples of this art are certain wood-carvings found buried deep in the guano on some of the islands off the coast. A few of these are shown in Pl. VIII, 4–6, and their style bears a close relation to the older art of the maritime region. Figs. 4 and 6 resemble sceptres, and present a personage seated on a throne (in one case under a canopy), holding, apparently, a vase and a club, and surrounded by a number of animals. The figures bear a remote resemblance to the stone figures discovered at Tiahuanaco, who also hold cups, and the birds and beasts may be condors and pumas, the inevitable attendants of the creator-god. The central figure is carved at the top of a post, and represents a seated man with a cord round his neck. Many similar figures are shown with the hands bound behind them, a feature which has given rise to the supposition that the islands may have been used as penal settlements in early times. That the carvings are of great age is proved by the depth of the guano deposits under which they were found and to which they owe their preservation. Inlaying was widely practised, wood with shell, bone with turquoise, stone with stone of another colour, and shell with shell and turquoise. Some of the inlaid beads of necklaces show a very pleasing contrast of colours. The white shell frogs in Fig. 11, *b*, have eyes of red shell, while the central bead is of mother-of-pearl inlaid with turquoise. The small llama figure (Fig. 11, *a*) is cut from a hard stone, of a faint mauve colour, the eyes are red, and the muzzle and feet were originally encircled by gold bands. Wooden carvings were also inlaid with a kind of coloured mastic, but examples of this art seem to be peculiar to the highlands, and to belong to the late Inca empire. Incrustation of shell-mosaic, set in a matrix of gum, frequently occurs on wooden ear-plugs, such as Fig. 11, *g;* in this specimen the double bird in the centre is of mother-of-pearl, with turquoise eyes, while the surrounding mosaic ground is of scarlet and dark crimson shell. The occurrence of turquoise, proved by the analysis of certain of the inlaid fragments, is interesting, since the nearest deposits of this material which are known to exist are those of Santa Fé in New Mexico. This fact does not necessarily prove connection, since it is possible that turquoise deposits may yet be discovered in South America. Inlaid work has a wide range in America, extending from Arizona through Mexico and the Antilles to the north-west Argentine.

As regards carving in stone, the skill of the Peruvians in handling large masses of sandstone, andesite and diorite has been remarked in a previous chapter. Of smaller objects the figures of llamas (Figs. 11, *a*, and 27, *b*) show considerable skill ; while the stone cup from Tiahuanaco

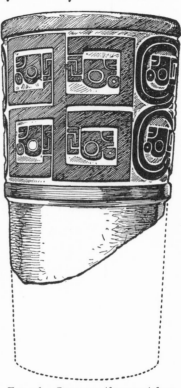

FIG. 26.—Stone cup (fragment) from Tiahuanaco (scale ¾).
[British Museum.]

(Fig. 26) and the mortar carved in the Cuzco style (Pl. XXI, 1), and ornamented with snakes in relief, are veritable masterpieces. The style of building in polygonal blocks, which at least survived into the Inca period, necessitated enormous labour in so far as each stone had to be shaped separately to fit its neighbours. For the purpose of stone-dressing, copper, or at best an accidental bronze, was the only metal available, and it is probable that stone tools were employed, since stone can be worked with stone more easily than with such metal as was at the disposal of the Peruvians. In any case it is difficult to realize the difficulties which must have been mastered in the preparation of such triumphs of the mason's art as are seen at Tiahuanaco.

Of metals, gold and silver were used for ornament and for the manufacture of the utensils used by the Inca and the nobility, and formed an important part of the offerings presented to the Sun. Gold was collected chiefly from the alluvial deposits of certain rivers, but silver could only be obtained by regular mining. The labour was hard, and each miner worked for only a few months in the year, his services being regarded as his tribute to the state. Miners were exempt from the necessity of cultivation, and their fields were tilled for them. We are also told that they were required to be married, in order that they might have someone to prepare their food. Ore was smelted in small pottery furnaces, in the base of which were holes to admit the copper tubes serving as bellows. Through these tubes, the inner end of which was furnished with a small perforation, the metallurgist blew to fan the flames. Some of the silver ore required a greater heat than could be obtained by this primitive method, and other means were called into requisition. Pottery furnaces, called *huaira*, tubular in shape, about a yard wide at the base, but expanding in diameter towards the top, were set up on the loftier slopes of the hills, where they caught the evening breeze, which blows with great force and regularity. Holes were pierced to admit the draught, and in front of each hole was a small shelf, on which a fire was lit in order to warm the air before it entered the furnace. The ore and fuel were placed inside, and the molten metal ran out into a clay receptacle at the base. These huaira were

used at the mines of Potosi well on into Spanish times,
and Acosta writes : "There were in old time upon the
sides and tops of *Potozi*, above five thousand *Guayras*,
which are small furnaces where they melt their metall,
the which were placed like lights (a pleasant sight to
behold by night) casting a light afarre off like a flame
of fire. But at this day there are not above two thousand,
for that (as I have said) they use little melting, but re-
fine it by quicksilver, the which is the greatest profit."
Quicksilver was familiar to the Inca, but its properties
were unknown, and lead was sometimes used as a flux.

Though the methods of smelting were primitive,
there is no doubt of the skill of the smiths ; the ordinary
tools were an anvil of a particularly hard variety of stone,
and copper cubes with rounded corners, of different
sizes, which served as hammers. Gold and silver were
cast, soldered, hammered and inlaid, and the finer examples of the goldsmith's art excited the wondering
admiration of the conquerors. The Inca even possessed
gardens in which the trees and plants were imitated all
"in gold and silver, with their leaves, flowers and fruit ;
some just beginning to sprout, others half-grown, others
having reached maturity. They made fields of maize
with their leaves, heads, canes, roots and flowers, all exactly imitated. The beard of the maize-head was of
gold, and all the rest of silver, the parts being soldered
together. They did the same with other plants, making
the flower, or any part that became yellow, of gold, and
the rest of silver." As remarked above, the vessels and
furniture of a ruler were never used by his successors,
and the quantity of treasure found by the Spanish was
enormous. Some idea of it can be gathered from the fact
that Atahualpa within a few days was able to collect bullion to the value of three-and-a-half millions sterling as
his ransom, and this consisted of worked gold. Unfortunately nearly all the treasure discovered in the highlands found its way to the melting-pot, and the hopes of

P

archæology now centre on the traditions of the treasures which were hidden by the Indians when the conquerors threw off the mask. Most of the surviving remains in the precious metals have come from the deserted cemeteries on the coast; but even these are the less intrinsically valuable, consisting of thin silver cups, often in the form of human heads (Pl. XXII, 1, 3 and 4), which, though of low artistic standard, display great technical skill, in so far as they appear to have been beaten out of a single sheet. The puma-head figured on the same plate is cast solid and appears to have formed the head of a sceptre. In beating gold the Peruvians excelled, and Wiener mentions certain golden butterflies which he saw in the possession of a Spaniard, the wings of which were only one-tenth of a millimeter thick. Even these delicate objects, the intrinsic value of which was very small, were melted down and sold as bullion ! Gold was worked by the old inhabitants of Tiahuanaco, and a beautiful embossed plate is figured by Baessler in *Ancient Peruvian Art*, Pl. 145.

But the implements of everyday use were made of copper, and in this copper is usually found a percentage of tin. The percentage is always low and variable; thus Mortillet[1] gives the percentage of tin in copper implements, including two T-shaped cramps from Tiahuanaco used in stone-building, as varying between $5·83\%$ and $7·70\%$. Near Potosi the variation is greater, from $2·10\%$ to $10·72\%$; while in the north-west Argentine it is greatest of all, from $1·57\%$ to $16·53\%$. It seems almost certain that the presence of tin is accidental, since it is found in greatest quantities in those implements which require it least. Of copper were made the characteristically shaped knives of Inca times, such as Fig 27, *c*, as well as spade-blades, spiked club-heads (in the form of Fig. 5, *b*), of which a variety especially characteristic

[1] Congrès Préhistorique de France, 1905, *Le Bronze dans l'Amérique du Sud.*

of the Inca culture is shown in Fig. 27, *a*, pins for dresses (Fig. 11, *c–f*), tweezers for pulling out hair on the face (Fig. 11, *h* and *i*), chisels, and a whole host of other implements and ornaments, including the crests worn by warriors on the coast, as exemplified in the Truxillo

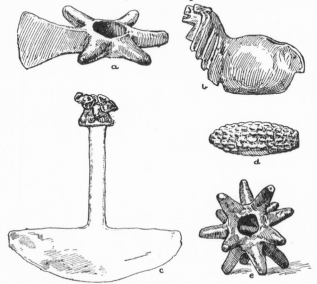

FIG. 27.—*a* copper mace-head.
b stone llama.
c copper knife.
d stone maize-head.
e copper bolas-weight.
All from the highlands (scale ⅓).
[British Museum.]

vase shown in Pls. XXI, 5, and XXII, 10. The clubs used on the coast seem to have been furnished with a star or ring of metal or stone, as shown in Pl. XXI, 5; in paintings they have exactly the form of the roof-ornaments in Fig. 13. Stone mace-heads, with flanges or points, have also been found in the highlands. Shields were of wood, both circular and square (e.g. Pl. XXI, 5, and XXII, 10), and darts and spear-throwers of the type shown in Fig. 8 were used throughout the coast, and in all probability in the highlands also. The bolas, as described on p. 246, was used in southern Peru and Bolivia, and the weights were either of stone or of metal, as shown in Fig. 27, *e*. Slings were common throughout (e.g. Pl. I, 1), and the blow-gun also occurred, though the only evidence for its presence is a painted textile from Pachacamac. This weapon is of course common among the savages of the Amazonian forests. The knives used in fighting by the early inhabitants of Truxillo seem to have resembled in pattern the so-called axe-heads of Cuenca, as may be seen from Figs. 5, *k*, and 10. It is possible that the Cuenca specimens were also used in the hand, and that the hole at the butt may have served for the attachment of a cord to wrap round the wrist.

It seems perhaps a contradiction to speak of the literature of a people who had no writing, but the Inca possessed at least the germs of a literature in the commemorative songs sung at the funeral ceremonies of rulers and great men, in their love-songs, and in their hymns to the Creator and the Sun. More than this they seem to have recited dramatic poems which amounted to plays. Salcamayhua mentions these, and states that they were of four kinds, including farce and tragedy. One has come down to us, and is strangely reminiscent of a modern melodrama. At one time it was thought to be of post-Spanish origin, but Sir Clements Markham has shown from internal evidence that the bulk of the work at any rate dates from an earlier epoch, though it may have been modified in form after the conquest. It is called Ollantay after the hero, a noted warrior, who, alas, is not of Inca blood, and may not therefore marry the heroine, a daughter of the ruler, the Inca Pachacuti. The part of the villain is played by the Villac Umu, and that of the " comic relief," by Ollantay's servant. After many troubles, including the imprisonment of the heroine, and the rebellion and capture, by a ruse, of the hero,

the lovers are united by Tupac Yupanqui, who has meanwhile succeeded to the throne on the death of his father.
This drama has been translated into English by Sir
Clements Markham, and includes many really poetical
passages.   It was originally written in Quichua.

The Quichua dialect was the official language throughout Peru, from Quito to Tucuman and Chile. Under the
Inca *régime* it was rendered obligatory for every individual in the empire to speak this tongue, and the task of
government was thereby considerably lightened. Originally it had been the dialect of the Quichua province and
the Cuzco valley, and since the other dialects in Peru
appear to have been akin, the subject peoples can have
had little difficulty in acquiring it.   The Inca nobility,
we are told, spoke among themselves a special dialect,
which no one else was allowed to learn.   This statement is supported by Garcilasso himself, who, as the
son of a princess of the royal blood, must have known.
He further remarks that at the time he wrote his history
it had become practically obsolete.   It is possible that
this language was the original tongue of the immigrant
conquerors from the south.

As regards science, the Inca, as true sons of the Sun,
had made some progress in astronomy.   Montesinos,
in dealing with the early rulers, gives various particulars
as to reforms in the calendar. Thus, according to him,
the thirty-first ruler changed the beginning of the year
to the winter solstice ; the thirty-fourth abolished the
old system of reckoning by lunar months, and established twelve months of thirty days, with a period of
five extra days at the end of the year ; while the fifty-
first discovered the necessity of intercalating a day every
four years.   At any rate the Inca calendar of later times
was arranged on this system. Probably the original
lunar year had been corrected by observation of the
solstices and equinoxes. For the observation of the
former, eight pillars arranged in two rows were set up

on each side of Cuzco, to the east and to the west, and the relative position of the sun at rising and setting was carefully marked ; these pillars were standing when Garcilasso left Peru in 1560. For the equinox, a sculptured stone pillar (or pillars) was set up in the space in front of the Sun-temple, and a line was drawn from east to west. When the shadow of the pillar fell along the line from sunrise to sunset, it was known that the equinox had arrived, and a festival followed. Various shrines called *Intihuatana*, for the observation of the equinox, existed in Peru, according to Garcilasso, and the Inca had observed that the nearer they were to Quito, the truer was the line traced by the shadow of the pillar, and Quito was regarded as a holy place in consequence. Certain reputed Intihuatana still exist, the most notable being at Pisac (Pl. XVII, 2). Here the surface of an outcropping rock has been levelled, and a short pillar left projecting in the centre, while round the rock is built a wall of typical Inca masonry in which is a doorway. (The pillar can be seen in the illustration a little to the right of the centre.) Short pillars, cut from the living rock surrounded by an artificially levelled area, also occur at other places, among them the sacred rock at Titicaca and at Ollantaitambo, and all of these have been identified with Intihuatana. Quite recently Uhle has attempted to prove that these pillars are in reality altars to the sun. His arguments are based on several grounds, that the pillars are too short for the purpose, that in many localities more than one occur close together, that the level area which surrounds them is sometimes partly overshadowed by a neighbouring rock. But tradition is too strong to be lightly set aside ; the pillars may merely have marked the site where the temporary gnomon was set up when the stated season approached, for Garcilasso implies that this was done at Cuzco, and its shadow watched until it coincided with certain marks. A longer gnomon would overtop the rocks, where such exist, that abut upon the area around it ; and one of the short pillars is furnished with a shallow depression, possibly for the reception of some such appliance. While as to the fact that more than one occur at certain localities, it must be remembered that Garcilasso uses the word in the plural in his account of the ceremony at Cuzco. Eclipses naturally attracted much attention, and, in the case of the sun, were supposed to portend disaster. An eclipse of the moon was regarded with hardly less horror, since it was believed that the satellite was dying and would fall from the sky, bringing about the end of the world. Like many other peoples the Peruvians tried to avert the evil by making a tremendous noise with all sorts of instruments, and they also tied up the dogs and beat them, hoping that the Moon, which was supposed to be particularly fond of dogs, would be moved at their howls and throw off her sickness.

The Inca were also acquainted with surveying to the extent that they made relief-maps of the provinces in clay, as an aid to administration. Sarmiento states that these maps were first made under Pachacuti ; and Garcilasso saw a similar plan, made to scale, of Cuzco, on which every house and street could be distinguished. It is obvious that they had made some progress in mathematics, since they could hardly otherwise have administered the empire, or attained such skill in architecture. And the presence of balances with finely carved beams of bone and pans of wood or net (Fig. 11, *k*), proves that some system of weights must have existed. Various professors, termed Amauta, presided over the different arts and sciences, and gave instruction to such as were qualified by permission to receive it ; but, as has been mentioned in a previous chapter, all knowledge, except of handicrafts, was reserved for the ruling class, and the lower orders were excluded from any sort of higher education.

CHAPTER X—THE SOUTHERN PROVINCES OF THE PERUVIAN EMPIRE

THE area now to be discussed stands in continuous relation to Peru, and traces of Inca influence are found throughout; but here that influence had not gained so strong a hold at the time of the Spanish conquest as in the region immediately to the north, and the natives had preserved much of their original culture. The reason for this is geographical. Beyond Arica lies the waterless waste of Tarapaca, and, south of the Bolivian frontier, the barren and desolate tablelands of the Puna de Atacama and the Puna de Jujuy formed barriers between the peoples of what is now Chile and the northwest Argentine on the one hand and Peru and Bolivia on the other. The main physical features of this district are exactly similar to those of Peru ; the twin chains of the Andes continue unbroken, and are bounded on the west by a narrow strip of coast which is quite barren except in the neighbourhood of the rivers ; between the two cordilleras is the same succession of lofty plateau-land and valleys. Speaking archæologically, the area falls into three main regions, the coast, the highland deserts, and the valleys south and east of the latter, but there had been considerable intercommunication, and all had fallen under the influence of the Inca. In terms of modern geography, therefore, this area consists of northern Chile as far as the river Maule, the southern boundary of the Inca empire, and the Argentine provinces of Jujuy, Los Andes, Salta, Catamarca, Tucuman, La Rioja and Cordoba (except the low-lying plains).

The chief physical feature of the country is the scarcity

of water, especially on the coast, but also throughout large tracts of the interior ; and certain facts seem to point to the conclusion that the supply has been diminishing for centuries. At one time the desert of Tarapaca must have been covered with forest, since the bones of ant-eaters are discovered in quantities in the ravines, and the more extensive desert of Atacama to the south must have been fairly well populated, to judge from the innumerable graves which are found everywhere along the coast. Other changes have taken place in more recent times, such as the gradual disappearance of the llama from the highlands. At the present time this animal is hardly to be found except in the Puna de Atacama and the highest valleys around Tinogasta, but the remains in graves prove that it ranged formerly as far south as Cordoba.

It has been said above that this region falls, archæologically, into three districts, of which one, and the most important, consists of the Argentine portion exclusive of the Punas of Atacama and Jujuy. Here are found the remains of a culture which in general is known as Calchaqui from the fact that the tribe of this name sprang into prominence owing to their determined resistance to the Spaniards.[1] Another and lower culture is found in the highland deserts, and this may be connected with one class of remains found on the coast. On the coast are traces of considerable admixture. Undoubtedly the whole fringe was in very early times occupied by an extremely primitive people, who were displaced later by immigrants slightly more advanced in culture, possibly from the inland desert region already mentioned. But beyond Copiapo an entirely different stock was found at the conquest, a people of Araucanian affinities, who had, however, been much modified by contact with the Peru-

[1] Some have thought that the true significance of this term is too local to warrant its application to the whole area, and the name " Diaguite " has recently been suggested.

vians. As the earliest remains of the coast appear to be also the earliest of the whole area, it will be well to consider the complicated ethnology of this district before proceeding to the more homogeneous culture of the interior.

Along the whole seaboard, and even inland to a distance of 250 feet above the sea-level, are found mounds of shells containing the bones of fish, birds and mammals, pottery of varied character, and implements of bone, stone and copper. But all these mounds cannot be referred to the same people, since the burials in them and in their neighbourhood reveal three types of man. The earliest of these was the long-headed type, who buried his dead in an extended position, sometimes one above the other, the men apart from the women. This people made pottery of a very rude description, but were apparently unacquainted with the use of metal, and, possibly, even of the bow. They were followed by a round-headed folk, who buried their dead in a squatting position, like the Peruvians, and whose culture stood altogether on a higher plane. They worked stone with some facility (flutes, mortars and large quantities of finely-flaked arrow-heads bear witness to the fact), made fish-hooks, harpoon-heads, spoons and needles of bone, manufactured good pottery and were acquainted with weaving and the use of copper. The long-heads appear to have retired southward before them, and their last representatives are probably the Alacaluf of Tierra del Fuego, but it is possible that some intermixture between the two took place, since the latest remains of the coast, as well as the population of the present day, are medium-headed. Who the round-heads were cannot be stated with certainty, but it is probable that they were related to the inhabitants of the upland Punas of Atacama and Jujuy. This probability rests not only on the geographical proximity of the latter, but also on archæological evidence, for remains have been found on the Loa river and in the bay of Antofagasta which are exactly similar to those of the desert uplands. Even traces of Diaguite or Calchaqui influence are not wanting on the coast, penetrating at least as far south as Coquimbo. In the southern part of this province urn-burials have been discovered, as well as walls built of rough stones (similar to those of the Diaguite region), which were already there when the conquering Inca passed through the country ; moreover it seems likely that the coast-dwellers imported their copper from the far interior, probably in exchange for fish and shells, since many of the latter have been found in the inland region.

Their pottery however is rather of the Peruvian type ; it is well made, often covered with a slip, and painted with designs in black on the red surface. The principal patterns are scrolls, meanders, lozenges and chequers, but figures of the llama also occur. At the time of the conquest the strip of coast between Arica and Atacama was peopled by the Uros, a primitive fishing and hunting tribe whose home was on the Desaguadero leading south from Titicaca, but of whom a number seem to have been settled on the shore as mitimaes by the Inca. In Tarapaca were the Charca, also a Colla people, who seem to have been there some time, since skulls with the typical Colla deformation are found in the graves (later than those of the round-heads) associated with llama-wool textiles, the bodies being buried contracted in the Peruvian fashion. To the south of them were the tribes called collectively Chango, who seem in former times to have extended further north, and who buried at full length. From the earliest age down to a period subsequent to the Spanish conquest, these coast people seem to have led much the same life. For their food they looked mostly to the sea ; they gathered large quantities of shell-fish which they broke open with stone hammers on flat slabs of rock, speared crabs and sea-urchins with bone harpoons (as is done at the present time, though the spear is now armed with telegraph-wire), caught fish with nets and hooks, and hunted larger game, such as birds (principally pelicans), seals and huanacos. To judge from the population at the conquest, they built small huts of *totora*-wood and seal-skins, and made use of balsas constructed from the same materials. Of their religion nothing is known, except that small chalk idols have been found in the graves of the round-heads. The last people probably used their stone mortars to grind seeds and roots, and may even have practised a little rude agriculture.

The Inca conquest, probably, had little effect upon these primitive coast-dwellers; objects of Inca type are certainly found in many of the later graves, and no doubt a tribute of fish was levied upon the inhabitants. But their country must have offered small scope for development, and the Inca appear to have concentrated their efforts upon the tracts south of Copiapo. From this point southward the country was occupied by a very different people, the Araucanian-speakers; who, at the time of the Spanish conquest, spread from Atacama to Chiloe. According to Montesinos friendly relations had been established between the Inca and the inhabitants of the northern section of this region, in the reign preceding that of Uiracocha, but the actual conquest of the country did not take place until the time of Pacha-cuti or his son Tupac. As will be seen in the next chapter, the ethnology of the Araucanians is complicated; south of the river Maule they were almost entirely nomad and were distinguished by an indomitable courage which defied both the Inca and the Spaniards. But their north-ern branch, the Picunche, extending roughly from Atacama to the Maule, were at most semi-nomadic, and, when the Spaniards arrived, lived in permanent huts and practised agriculture, being familiar both with irrigation and the properties of manure. Usually this more sedentary form of life has been attributed entirely to Inca influence, but it is far more probable that some rude form of agriculture was already in vogue at the time of the Inca conquest. To judge from the fact that the country had been subdued but a short time before the arrival of the Spaniards, it seems unlikely that the inhabitants could have made such progress had they not been acquainted beforehand with the rudiments of agriculture; and there is no reason why they should not have resisted the Inca arms with as much success as the tribes of kindred speech to the south, if their culture had been identical with that of the latter. It will be seen later that the southern Araucanians are obviously closely connected with the Pampas tribes, who immigrated into the country and conquered the original Araucanians, but adopted their speech. It may be concluded, therefore, that these original Araucanians were a people who practised some primitive form of agriculture, and that the Picunche, though forming a section of the later Araucanian nation, included so large an element of aborigines that their more sedentary form of culture persisted. The introduction of superior methods, especially irrigation, by the Inca, the establishment of security and the suppression of inter-tribal warfare, could thus produce, within a short period, results which had been otherwise almost incredible. That the conquest was complete we know from the fact that a large number of *mitimaes* were established in the country. At length, after disastrous attempts to subdue the nomadic Araucanians further south, the river Maule was fixed as the boundary of the Inca empire. Inca remains, however, are not found in any considerable numbers south of the Choapa, and it seems probable that the district between this river and the Maule was not so much effectively occupied, as placed under military control.

The people inhabiting the Punas (sterile plateaux) of Jujuy and Atacama, and at least part of the coast, from an irregular line drawn from Santa Catalina to the river Loa, are known as Atacama. Thanks to the labours of Ambrosetti and Boman a fair knowledge of their archæology has been obtained, but little is known of them from other sources. They constructed dwellings of rough stones piled together without mortar, similar to the slate walls seen in north Cornwall, a form of construction which is locally known as *pirca*. The more extensive of these habitations consist of an intricate system of walls, covering a considerable area, and forming enclosures unprovided with doorways, so that many of them cannot be reached except over the walls of the rest, a peculiarity recalling the buildings of the Peruvian coast. Many of these chambers contain a monolithic pillar, the meaning of which is unknown. The dead were deposited in caves, in a squatting position along the walls, or were buried in the ground in a contracted position. From the mortuary caverns and graves numbers of objects have been obtained which shed considerable light on the daily life of the people. Discoveries of maize, stone mortars, and spades prove that they were to some extent agriculturists, apart from the fact that traces of terrace-cultivation have been found locally. Some of the spades are of plain wood, but others are furnished with blades of schist of a type peculiar to this area ; certain knife-shaped objects of wood, also characteristic of the region, may possibly have been employed in agriculture. But the Atacama were also a pastoral people ; remains of the llama are frequent, as well as the wooden toggles belonging to their harness. Like the Peruvians they kept dogs, but of a different variety. Game of course was scarce in this desolate neighbourhood, but quantities of arrows, besides bows, have been found, which may have been used in hunting or in war. These arrows are of two types, wood-pointed and stone-headed ; the two are not usually found together, but the irregularity of their distribution has not yet been explained. The stone heads are well worked, better in fact than those of Patagonia (Fig. 32) ; in the uplands they are more usually furnished with a tang, while those on the coast are not. These heads are lashed to a wooden foreshaft, and the shaft itself is feathered, and sometimes furnished with a counterweight of resin.   Many of the skulls exhibit signs of artificial deformation, and the form of the teeth was occasionally modified by chipping.   Woven clothing of llama-wool was worn, in the form of tunics with or without sleeves, similar to those of Peru though rather longer ; these are well made, and often ornamented with stripes woven in the material.   Spindles, and wooden needles furnished with eyes, have also been found.   Over the tunic was worn a poncho, and a hide cuirass has been discovered on the coast. Wooden needle-cases, spoons, spatulæ, and "palettes" are among the carved objects, and are often ornamented with human figures rudely cut and, in some cases, with inlaid eyes.   The stone objects do not show great variety ; besides those already mentioned, flat axes of schist, similar to the spades, are characteristic of the region, and perforated stones like those found in far greater numbers in central Chile, also occur.   In the neighbourhood of Salinas Grandes, finds have been made of implements unlike any elsewhere in this area, consisting of rudely chipped axes, mainly ovate in form, and polished celts with a groove encircling the butt. This neighbourhood was the centre of a considerable trade in salt, and it is possible that these objects were in some way connected with the salt industry.   Metal objects are rare, but star-shaped pendants and knives of Peruvian type (similar to Fig. 27, c) have been found. Cobres, near Salinas Grandes, is the site of ancient copper-workings, but these must most probably be ascribed to the Diaguite or the Inca, since the remains of a *huaira* have been discovered on a neighbouring hill. Galleries were driven into the lode at an angle of 45 degrees, and the ore was crushed with large stone blocks. The pottery for the most part is rude and without ornament, but fragments with designs in black painted on a red slip—similar to the ware of the coast burials—is not uncommon, and occasional specimens show Peruvian influence. Inca influence is naturally more apparent near the coast, in the neighbourhood of the great road which ran from Cuzco to Copiapo, passing through San Pedro de Atacama. The Atacama culture appears to have extended beyond the plateau, notably along the Quebrada del Toro which stretches in a southerly direction from Salinas Grandes; but here it is modified by Diaguite influence, the exact character of which can be better understood after that interesting people have been described.

The area of the Diaguite culture seems to have comprised the southern portion of Jujuy, Salta, Catamarca, western Tucuman, Rioja and San Juan; the last two provinces, however, have been insufficiently investigated, and by far the largest proportion of remains comes from southern Salta, Catamarca and western Tucuman. One language, called Kakan, prevailed throughout. From the little information which has been preserved concerning the tribes of this region, it would seem that their religion was markedly similar to that of the Andean peoples further north. The Sun was worshipped as the most important power, and offerings were made to him in order that he might grant fertility to the fields and herds. One form of offering consisted of a deer's head in which were stuck a number of arrows. The Thunder ranked next in importance. But perhaps the most ancient form of worship was the cult of trees and of stones, of which the latter was connected with ancestor-worship, and survives to some extent at the present day. At the highest point of a pass a heap of stones is generally to be found, and the Indian traveller never fails to deposit an offering of coca at this primitive shrine. Small stone figures of llamas have been discovered which

PLATE XXIV

Photos. Dr. Schreiter

NORTH-WEST ARGENTINA

Sculptured Monolith : Tafi Valley

Diaguite Ruins : Yocavil Valley

THE SOUTHERN PROVINCES 225

almost certainly were fertility charms like those of the region to the north. Reverence was also paid to Pachamama, and a dance in which animal masks were worn (as on certain occasions in Peru) used to be held in honour of a divinity called Chiqui. It is impossible to say how far these practices were the result of later contact with the Inca, but it is probable that most of them date from the earliest times and are due rather to community of origin than to later intercourse. The dwellings (Pl. XXIV, 1) erected by the Diaguite tribes cannot be compared with the more important structures of Peru and Bolivia, but resemble the least imposing of the buildings of those countries. The walls, dry-built of well-chosen stones (*pirca*), are arranged in a rectangle or circle, and except in rare cases do not attain a height greater than about 1½ yds. Traces of roof-beams have been found, and it is probable that these were furnished with a covering of thatch as in Peru. The houses are arranged in villages, nearly always on some eminence, and very frequently contain one or more monolithic pillars (Pl. XXIV, 2), sometimes sculptured, of which the significance is unknown. In Catamarca circular constructions of *tapia* have been found. The remains from graves show that the Diaguite were expert weavers, manufacturing tunics of llama-wool, which were often ornamented with stripes. These tunics were rather longer than those of Peru, and the sleeves, when present, were very short; many spindle-whorls of engraved stone have been found, but no loom has at present come to light. From the pottery figurines and the pictographs, it may be gathered that plumed head-dresses were common, consisting of a woollen band fringed with feathers arranged regularly or in groups. Cylindrical beads of turquoise and other blue minerals were worn as ornaments, as well as embossed copper breast-plates (Pl. XXV, 3), and diadems of gold and copper. Hide sandals were in general use. Maize was cultivated, and in some

Q

places the hill-sides are terraced, but traces of terrace-cultivation are rare, and the practice is probably due to Peruvian influence. Stone mortars are common in the ruined dwellings (Pl. XXV, 1 and 2) ; the majority are of a very rude pattern, but a certain number of magnificent specimens, with lizards and frogs in relief, has been found ; such works of art may also be the result of contact with the Inca.

Graves are numerous throughout the country. We are told that, in later times, the dying were attended by their friends and relations, and that arrows were fixed in the ground in a ring around the patient. After death a period of mourning and feasting ensued, and the deceased was buried together with his dogs, arms and other possessions, his hut being burnt. Death, except by violence, was attributed to evil magic, and the souls of the dead were supposed to become stars. The graves vary considerably in type, but the body was always arranged in a contracted position, usually on its back or side, very rarely in a vertical position as among the Atacama. Frequently the head was removed and buried at a distance. The graves are found sometimes isolated, sometimes in groups. Occasionally natural caves have been utilized as mausolea, and in some cases the dead have been buried in their houses. Sometimes there is no indication to mark the presence of a burial, in others, alignments of stones in the form of rectangles, circles, semicircles and ovals, are arranged on the surface of the ground ; in rare cases a tumulus is raised above the grave. Sometimes again the body is enclosed in a ring of stones beneath the earth, or the grave may be lined with pirca or with great slabs. Urn-burial, in the case of adults, is very rare, and confined to a few localities in the ‚east of this area ; the urns are unornamented, and it has been conjectured with some reason that this custom may be due to Guarani influence intrusive from the east. But this brings us to one of the most peculiar and interesting features of the Diaguite culture. Whole cemeteries have been discovered, mainly in the Calchaqui and Yocavil valleys, devoted to very young infants, whose remains are deposited in large urns of excellent pottery covered with elaborate painted decoration. Two main types of urn can be distinguished, characteristic respectively of the

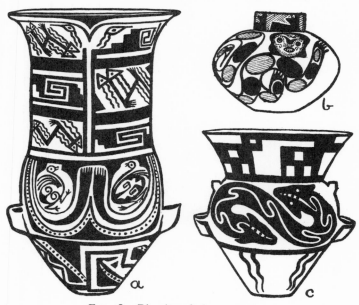

FIG. 28.—Diaguite polychrome pottery.
a Santa Maria (burial-urn).   *b* Andalgala.   *c* Tinogasta (burial-urn).
(Scale ⅛.)   [After Lafone-Quevedo.]

neighbourhoods of Santa Maria (Fig. 28, *a*) and of Tinogasta (Fig. 28, *c*); each type is found in both localities, but in general the Santa Maria urns are comparatively long and narrow, those of Tinogasta wide and depressed. In either case these urns consist of a globular body, with a handle on either side, surmounted by a neck with everted edge. Most of them, especially the Santa Maria type, have a human face painted on the neck, with a number of lines, possibly representing tears, leading from the eyes to the cheeks; the hands are also represented, placed together under the chin, and sometimes holding a cup as in Ecuador and Peru. In the Tinogasta type, human features are less common, and have in some cases been added in relief. The rest of the decoration consists of figures of birds and reptiles, and various geometrical patterns, some at least of which are derived from the former. On the Santa Maria type, birds are more common, on the Tinogasta type, snakes and frogs. These designs are painted in black and red on a cream or buff slip, or, in the Tinogasta area, in black on red; the pottery itself is good and reddish in colour. It has been suggested that the new-born infants whose remains are enclosed in these urns were the victims of sacrifice; and the fact that they are buried together apart from the adult population, and in special receptacles of so elaborate a nature, seems to support this view. Urn-burial of any sort is rare in the Andean region, and it is interesting to recall that the Puruha of Ecuador were accustomed to sacrifice the first-born and preserve the body in a vase of stone or metal (p. 66). The Diaguite urns are furnished with covers in the shape of pottery bowls similarly ornamented. As a whole the pottery of this region is well worthy of close study. Besides vases of coarse manufacture, some of which appear to be of earlier date than the finer ware, the pots fall into two main types, polychrome and black. In both types the clay is well mixed, though the paste is not so good as in Peru; powdered sherds or friable rock was mixed with it, and the vessels were built up by the coiling process, or, in rare cases, moulded in a basket. In the case of the polychrome ware, the vessel was then covered, sometimes on both surfaces, with a cream or buff slip, on which the designs were painted in black picked out with crimson. In the case of the black ware, thick plumbago slip was employed, and the designs incised with a graving-tool possessing one or more points (Fig. 29, *a* and *b*). The shapes of the vases are graceful and symmetrical; the bodies are usually globular with a small flat base, and are furnished with a short neck terminating in a rim, and, in many cases, a pair of handles. The Peruvian pattern shown in Pl. XXII, 5–7, is frequently found, and many of the specimens were, no doubt, imported, but the type was frequently copied on the spot and adorned with designs which are quite local in character (Fig. 29, *c*). Other Peruvian types are vases with

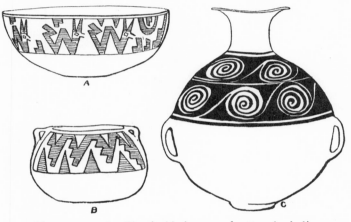

FIG. 29.—A and B Diaguite black engraved pottery (scale ⅛).
c Vase of Peruvian type but local manufacture ; Calchaqui valley (after
Boman : scale ¼).

globular bodies on an expanding foot (like Fig. 6, *c*), and jugs with a single handle. In general the ornament is much the same as that of the funerary urns, with the exception that the vases for ordinary use were not given the same anthropomorphic character. Birds, frogs and snakes, in all stages of conventionalization, are common, as well as geometrical designs, which in some cases recall the Yca style. The engraved pots bear designs even more closely akin to those of the Peruvian coast, grotesque monsters with multiple heads (Fig. 21, *c*) which bear a striking likeness to the oldest Nasca vases, and dragon-like creatures (Fig. 21, *e*) which must certainly belong to the same species as those of the red-white-black ware of Recuay and elsewhere (Fig. 21, *a* and *d*). Certain of the painted vases from the Tinogasta area, which bear figures of conventional pumas drawn in bold flowing lines (Fig. 28, *b*), also recall the Nasca pottery. It was once thought that the black ware, which is commoner in the neighbourhood of Tinogasta, might belong to a period different from that of the painted pottery, but the recent discovery of both types in a single grave would seem to prove that they were contemporary.[1] Pottery figurines made of both classes of pottery are common.

Few implements of wood and bone have been found, possibly owing to the fact that the climate is unfavourable to the preservation of these materials. Bone arrow-heads, however, are found in some numbers, as well as arrow-heads of silicious rock. The bow seems to have been the chief weapon of the Diaguite tribes, some of whom, we know, were good fighters, and offered considerable opposition to the Spaniards. We are told that the warriors were accompanied by their women, who, torch in hand, drove back those who would seek safety in flight, and, when the battle was lost, hurled themselves from a rock rather than fall into the hands of the conquerors. Axes both of stone and copper were also employed, the former perhaps rather in agriculture than in war. Characteristic of this region is a type of celt which is furnished with a transverse groove at the butt which does not quite encircle the implement. This type, though common in North America, is rare in the Southern Continent except in Ecuador (Fig. 4, *e*). A single stone mask

---

[1] I have just received from Prof. Lafone-Quevedo the following note on the quality of the pottery of the Tinogasta district :—" In the London district [i.e. around Tinogasta] especially, in the polychrome and black pottery ornamented with dragons and hydras, we have very beautiful specimens of the potter's art ; perfect material, carefully prepared and burnt almost to a glaze—some of the fragments might be modern stoneware, so very hard are they."

PLATE XXV

N.W. ARGENTINA

1, 2. STONE MORTARS: CATAMARCA
3. COPPER DISC: CATAMARCA
4. COPPER AXE-BLADE: CATAMARCA
(Scale: 1, 2, 1/8TH; 3, 4, 1/6TH)

has been discovered, and the occasional occurrence of more or less spherical stones, artificially ground, points to the fact that the sling was known here as well as in Atacama.

Copper objects are common, and this metal was probably smelted out locally, as in Peru. Many of the objects are quite Peruvian in type, knives (similar to Fig. 27, *c*), light tanged axes, small chisels, *topos* (cloak-pins, as Fig. 11, *e*), tweezers (as Fig. 11, *i*), and so forth ; but a certain number seem to be more or less peculiar to the district. These are certain types of axes, plaques, bells, and the so-called " knuckle-dusters." Besides the heavy axe-blades with one or more pairs of projections at the butt, a number of ornamental blades have been found which were probably used as insignia or for ceremonial purposes. The simplest of these have a curved projection issuing from the top edge of the blade (Fig. 30, *b*), the more elaborate have the butt modelled and engraved to form a monstrous head crowned with rays (Pl. XXV, 4) ; the most ornate represent in solid metal a blade of the latter form hafted in a flat handle. The plaques are of two types, large and solid, with rude faces and figures of snakes in relief (Pl. XXV, 3), or smaller, covered with far more elaborate designs partly cast and partly worked. The finest specimen which has yet been discovered represents a human or divine figure standing between jaguars or pumas (Fig. 30, *a*). The bells (Fig. 30, *d*), which are quite unlike anything else in South America, are oval or rectangular in section, and wider at the mouth than at the top, round the rim usually runs a band of ornament in relief, and the top is flat and pierced with two holes for suspension. Wooden bells of similar shape have been found in Atacama, together with copper pendants and other objects which are obviously of Diaguite origin. The so-called " knuckle-dusters " (Fig. 30, *c*) are also unique and consist of a semicircular band, large enough to admit the hand, with a more or less ornamental spur or knife-blade projecting from one end. The portion of the band which would pass over the knuckles is usually broader than the rest, and is sometimes ornamented with small figures in relief. The whole weapon recalls the ring-handled daggers which are characteristic of the western Sudan. Gold objects are rare, and con-

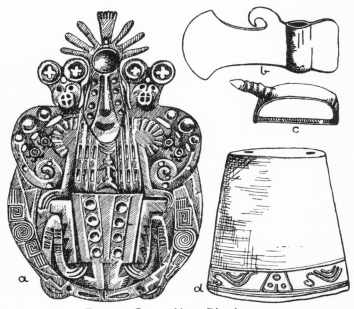

FIG. 30.—Copper objects, Diaguite area.
a copper plaque; Catamarca (½).   *b* copper axe; Belen (⅛).
c copper "knuckle-duster"; La Paya (¼).   *d* copper bell; Jujuy (¼).
[*b–d* after Ambrosetti.]

sist mainly of ornaments, such as diadems, which were probably worn by chiefs. The metal was probably imported from Peru, for though gold-workings are found near Santa Catalina, there is no proof that they belong to pre-Spanish times. Amongst other objects may be mentioned calabash bowls ornamented with designs in "poker-work," similar to those which have been found in the Atacama region and in Peru ; and a wooden beaker with inlaid designs in mastic, like specimens found in northern Bolivia.

As mentioned before, the region of the Quebrada del Toro, which runs from Salinas Grandes to the Lerma valley south of Salta, and the Lerma valley itself, are interesting as affording remains which show a mixture of cultures. In the Quebrada del Toro, at different sites, are found pirca ruins, on the one hand of isolated buildings like those of the Diaguite, on the other, of huge agglomerations of dwellings like some of those of the Atacama. Other points in common with the archæology of the Atacama are, the number of wooden implements, knives and llama-harness-toggles, very rude pottery, and (locally) perpendicular burials. Features bearing witness to Diaguite influence are: the presence of plumbago ware, large urns of the Santa Maria type, but undecorated, vases with painted ornament, and (locally) horizontal burials. The Lerma valley is interesting for two reasons, the presence of a remarkable series of tumuli, and a cemetery containing adults buried in large undecorated urns.

The tumuli are low mounds of reddish earth, nine or ten feet in diameter, each surrounded with a single or double row of stones ; they are disposed with perfect symmetry in long parallel lines, and number more than fifteen hundred. A group of them is surrounded with a rectangular rampart of earth, about three feet high and six feet wide, inside which runs a ditch. Excavations showed that the earth, of which these tumuli are composed, differs from the black soil on which they are raised, but revealed no remains of any sort, though a neighbouring " camp," also surrounded by a rampart, yielded many fragments of black engraved ware. The purpose of these tumuli is at present a mystery. Adult urn-burial, which is not characteristic of Andean culture, is also found in the Lerma valley, in San Pedro east of Jujuy, and at one or two other places in the east of the region with which we are now concerned. As stated before, it has been conjectured that this custom is due to Guarani influence emanating from Brazil, and to the same source may be attributed the few pipes, of wood and stone, which are also found here.

Of the eastern neighbours of the Atacama and Diaguite peoples little can be said ; in the north, around the Quebrada de Humahuaca, north of Jujuy, lived the warrior Omaguaca, who built pirca dwellings and fortifications, made rude pottery with the heads of men and birds in relief, and lined their graves with stone. South of them were wild tribes called Lule, Toba and Toconote, hunters in the main, but practising a little agriculture. Further south in the Sierra de Cordoba lived the Comechingon, linguistically different from the Diaguite, but with a culture more nearly approaching theirs. They inhabited small villages, one for each clan, composed of communal houses and surrounded with a cactus hedge ; they were agriculturists practising irrigation, and wove long tunics of llama-wool, which they decorated with shell buttons. Other ornaments were bracelets and frontlets of copper. Their area has not yet been archæologically explored.

Petroglyphs and pictographs are by no means uncommon in this part of South America ; those of Chile and that portion of north-west Argentine which lies west of the Diaguite area (Pl. XXVI, 9) are similar to those of Peru, and figures of llamas form a frequent feature of the designs. In the Diaguite region the patterns consist in the main of irregular interlaced curves and geometrical ornament ; they are found usually at the side of roads where the valley narrows. Some of them in the Humahuaca valley show horses, a fact which proves them to be of a date subsequent to the arrival of the Spaniards.

That the culture of this district is intimately related to that of Peru is obvious from its archæology. The

PLATE XXVI

ARGENTINA

ROCK WITH PICTOGRAPHS : ANTOFAGASTA DE LA SIERRA

(From Wright's " Chile," by permission of Messrs. Barry & Sons)

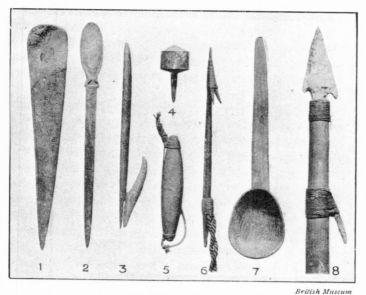

British Museum

SOUTHERN PERU AND CHILE

1. BONE AWL : HUASCO
2. BONE SPOON : HUASCO
3. BONE FISHHOOK : HUASCO
4. WOODEN ARROWHEAD : ARICA

5. STONE SINKER : ARICA
6. COPPER HARPOON : ARICA
7. WOODEN SPOON : ARICA
8. STONE-HEADED FISH-SPEAR WITH COPPER BARB : ARICA

evidence for the antiquity of that relation has already been discussed. It need only be mentioned that, besides the coast road through Atacama to Copiapo, traces of other Inca roads exist in the region of the Calchaqui valley, the Quebrada del Toro and the Lerma valley. It is probable that the Inca hold was strongest in Tucuman, since that province offered practically no resistance to the Spanish conquerors.

CHAPTER XI—THE SOUTHERN ANDES AND PLAINS

FROM the area last described we pass southwards to a region where all traces of Inca influence are lost, and a lower culture of different type prevails. This region is constituted by the southern section of Chile, the southern portions of the Argentine provinces of Mendoza, San Luis, Cordoba and Santa Fé, Buenos Aires and the rest of the Argentine Republic to the south. In the west the physical formation of the land is of the same character as in Peru. The Cordillera of the Andes stretches southward in an unbroken line until it falls gradually beneath the waters of the Antarctic, but the western cordillera fails to preserve its continuity to the same extent. The latter begins to break down in Valdivia, where a succession of lakes has been formed, and, after recovering itself, finally falls away in a series of islands off the coast. In the north, the high ground of the Andes stretches into the Argentine provinces of Mendoza and Neuquen, but falls rapidly eastward into a vast open plain, known as the Pampas, covered with herbaceous vegetation sloping gently to the Atlantic, and extending as far south as the Rio Negro. This plain is broken only by isolated series of hills in Buenos Aires. South of the Rio Negro is the Patagonian plateau, consisting of a succession of low chains, undulating plains, deep depressions and table-lands. The scenery here is extremely desolate, at the worst, wide expanses of sand or gravel, at best, extended plains of scrub, ringed round with barren mountainous country. Even in the western district, where a succession of large lakes is found, the country maintains the same

character. West of the Andes the rainfall is considerable, but in the Pampas and throughout Patagonia the
climate is both dry and invigorating.

The llama is not found in this part of America, but the
huanaco is common, and the rhea, or American ostrich,
is characteristic of the country east of the Andes. In
earlier times a more varied fauna roamed the country ;
remains of gigantic sloths have been discovered as far
south as southern Patagonia, the toxodon, a large hoofed
animal, wandered over the Pampas, where too existed
huge armadillos and the sabre-toothed cat. Even a primitive form of the horse was present, though it had long
been extinct when the first white men entered the continent. It is necessary to mention these animals, which,
at any rate in other parts of the world, are characteristic
of the quaternary or pleistocene era, because the remains
of man have been found associated with them. The jaw
of a sabre-toothed cat has been discovered with a flint
arrow-head fixed in it, the bones of great sloths and other
animals, broken and scratched by the primitive hunter,
have been found, and carapaces of the giant armadillo
have been unearthed in surroundings which suggest that
the men of this remote epoch used them as shelters. One
of the most interesting of such finds is the discovery, in
a cave at Ultima Esperanza (Last Hope) in Patagonia, of
the remains of one or more huge sloths (*mylodon*) together with abundant traces of the primitive hunters who
killed and ate them. Here the animal remains, some of
which may be seen at the Natural History Museum, appear so fresh that we are almost forced to conclude that
these, and perhaps other, extinct monsters lingered on in
South America until a period considerably later than
quaternary times.

However that may be, the discovery of actual human
remains in strata belonging to the pleistocene era, proves
the existence of quaternary man in this part of the New
World. Most of these finds have been made in the pro-

vince of Buenos Aires, and the fact that man's presence in South America at this early age is now universally recognized is due in the main to the labours of Ameghino. It was several years before the antiquity of his discoveries was generally accepted, no doubt partly because his dating of the geological formations, in which the remains were found, could not be endorsed by geologists at large. Most of them he attributed to the pliocene, or even the miocene, era, but it is now generally believed that they belong, with one possible exception, to the middle quaternary period. Even that exception is generally held to be no earlier than the first quaternary epoch.

In Europe the quaternary age is associated with a special type of rudely chipped stone implement, the succeeding era, with stone implements showing finer flaking (including arrow-heads, not found in quaternary times), and tools of polished stone. It is interesting to observe that both these types, known respectively as palæolithic and neolithic, are found in Patagonia. At present the palæolithic remains are few, and confined principally to the coast region between the rivers Chubut and Chico, but one of the sites is of importance since here alone both types have been found in superimposed strata. In Arroyo Observacion, a little to the north of Cape Blanco, implements of palæolithic type were discovered in a quaternary stratum, while in the ground at some distance above were imbedded others of neolithic character. The palæolithic implements of South America consist mainly of knives and scrapers (Fig. 32) of a type corresponding, not to the earliest class of such objects which are found in Europe, but rather to those characteristic of Saint Acheul and Le Moustier; nor are they entirely limited to Patagonia, since they have been found also in the province of Buenos Aires.

As to the physical characteristics of the race which manufactured and used them, a sufficient number of skulls has been discovered to establish the presence of

two types in South America even at this early date.
One of these is distinguished by a long and narrow
form of head, with retreating forehead, the other by a
broader skull of higher type ; both were short in
stature. The same elements, the broad-headed and
long-headed, can be distinguished among the population, of which we are now dealing with the area, though
by the time of the conquest they had become so mixed
as to render exact classification of the various peoples
extremely difficult. Along the southern Chilean coast
and archipelagos are found the remains of the same two
primitive populations as in the coastal districts of the
region last described, the earlier long-heads and later
broad-heads ; and right down in the south, in Tierra
del Fuego, there still exists a very primitive race of
hunters and fishers, of whom the northern section, the
Alacaluf, are probably the descendants of the early long-
heads whose remains can be traced so far to the north.
But the later ethnology of the coast has been further
modified by occasional intrusions from the Araucanian-
speaking peoples further inland.

The classification of the inlanders is a very difficult
task ; though speaking a common language, they exhibit considerable physical and cultural variety. The
strong probability that sedentary, agricultural habits
prevailed to some extent in Chile before the coming of
the Inca, has already been shown ; and it is also likely
that the sedentary tribes were the originators of the
Araucanian language, which, at the arrival of the
Spaniards, prevailed from Atacama to Chiloe. Upon
this population descended certain nomadic hordes from
the Pampas, displacing and fusing with the aborigines.
Where the adopted element was small, the invaders retained in the main their nomadic habits, though they
gradually borrowed certain features of their neighbours' culture ; where it was large, they seem to have
conformed to the more sedentary mode of life which

they found among the aborigines. The Picunche people, mentioned in the last chapter, seem to consist in the main of this early Araucanian element, with a slight admixture of invading blood ; their neighbours to the south however, the Moluche, between the Maule and the Tolten rivers, were nomads, and this section of the country was probably the point at which the invading tribes entered Chile, driving the former occupants to the south, where they became part of the Huilliche nation between the river Tolten and the north of the island of Chiloe. Here small agricultural communities were found by the explorers, scattered among the nomadic tribes, and these probably represented the remains of the old Araucanian stock. To the east of the tribes already mentioned, along the western brow of the Andes from Aconcagua to Valdivia, were the Puenche, in culture similar to the nomads of the Pampas, but speaking Araucanian. Beyond the Andes were the Pampas tribes proper. To the last-named, who extended as far east as Buenos Aires, the collective term Puelche is often given. These Puelche, whose original home seems to be north of the Rio Negro, also contributed an element to the population of Chilean territory, which they frequently raided between Villa Rica and Corcovado. Some of their tribes in this neighbourhood seem even to have adopted the Araucanian tongue.

The names mentioned are not racial, but national. Thus the term Huilliche merely means " Men of the south," and includes the very primitive fishing population of the coast (the relics of the ancient shell-fish eaters mixed with more modern elements), the inhabitants of the small agricultural oases, and the nomads of the highlands, who appear to have been a branch of the Puelche. So too the name Puelche means " Men of the east," and was applied generally to the nomads of the Pampas. To some extent however there is justification for grouping the Pampas tribes together, in so far as one form of culture prevailed throughout.

The physical characters of the people as investigated by Latcham seem to support the above classification of tribes. The more sedentary tribes of Chile have broad heads, but the Moluche type is less broad. The Puenche again is long-headed, and this fact agrees with the theory that the Moluche people had their origin in a Puenche invasion. In the Pampas itself, in historical times, only broad-headed people have been found, but on the Rio Negro long skulls have been discovered, the possessors of which were probably the ancestors of the Puenche. The Huilliche remains are very mixed, as well as those of the coast to the south as far as Fuegia. The fact that the invaders have abandoned their own language in favour of the Araucanian speech offers no difficulty; a body of raiders do not usually carry with them many of their own women, but on the other hand, if the invasion is successful, many female captives fall into their hands. In the matter of language it is the female element which counts, since the children naturally grow up speaking the tongue of their mothers. We know that in historical times the frequent wars between the Moluche, Huilliche, Puenche and others were almost invariably caused by their custom of seeking wives outside the tribe. For this reason it is probable that large numbers of the women of the original Araucanians were captured by the more warlike intruders, and thus their language spread, surviving the race which had given it birth.

South of the Rio Negro, in the Patagonian plateau, the ethnology is far more simple. Here, at the time of the discovery, wandered small groups of nomad hunters, a tall round-headed race, known as Tehuelche. This people may be related to the Pampas tribes, though in many respects they stood on a lower plane of culture. In fact one of their tribes which must have

R

crossed in early times to Fuegia, the Ona, were found living under conditions nearly as primitive as the Alacaluf. Some intermingling seems to have taken place between these Ona and the aborigines of Fuegia, since the former differ from the Tehuelche proper in being longer-headed.

Thus we find present among the population of this area at the time of the discovery the two elements, long- and broad-headed, which have been discovered in the prehistoric graves. The former of these is probably represented by the Fuegians, the vanished (earliest) population of the Chilean coast, and the more advanced Puenche, while the Tehuelche and the Puelche tribes may be the descendants of the early broad-heads, who amidst the healthy surroundings of the Patagonian plains and Pampas developed in stature far beyond their first ancestors. The comparatively short Araucanian may be an offshoot of the broad-headed Andean race with which we have hitherto been dealing.

The arrival of the white man, as usual, was the cause of considerable ethnic disturbance. In the province of Buenos Aires the Querandies, a people apparently allied to the tribes of the Pampas, rapidly became extinct ; various Puelche drifted across and occupied the region formerly occupied by them, and were followed later by Araucanians. The nomadic population was eventually driven across the Rio Negro, where it occupied a portion of Tehuelche territory, driving the Tehuelche further south. In the west a magnificent struggle for independence was made by the Araucanian-speaking nomads, who, we have seen, were for the most part of Pampean origin. For over a century a guerilla war was maintained, which proved very disastrous to the Spaniards, and which forms the theme of Ercilla's great epic. Even in the end they remained unconquered by force of arms, and their independence within the Moluche district was recognized by treaty. Since that time they have gradually become merged in the rest of the Chilean population. Thus the distinction of resisting with success the arms of the white man belongs alone to one of the less cultured peoples of America, and though they were Araucanian in speech, yet, it must be remembered, the spirit which animated them was the spirit of their Pampean ancestors.

The social system of the peoples of this region affords a remarkable contrast to that of the, almost, over-regulated country over which the Inca ruled. Though in the main patriarchal, as is usual among nomadic peoples, its leading features were individual freedom and equality. The Araucanians, at any rate in historical times, were led by four independent chiefs, whose authority was based upon the fact that they were the leaders in war. Each of these was supported by five Ulmen, or district chiefs, who acted as council and who regulated the affairs of the tribe, though their decisions had to be ratified by popular assent. In the case of injury to an individual the right of private revenge was recognized, and this fact limited the powers of the chiefs. It is highly probable that in former days a looser form of organization prevailed, and that in later times, owing to the protracted struggle with the Spaniards, the power of the leaders became consolidated by use. But it never in any way approached absolutism, custom was the real ruler, and what authority the Ulmen possessed was vested in them as the repositories of customary law. Chiefs were called *Toki*, and, as the word itself implies, carried a stone axe of particular shape. Stone objects (Fig. 31, *a*) of a remarkable type discovered within a comparatively small area, consisting of the Andean region of south Mendoza, Neuquen and the neighbouring part of Chile, have been thought to be the ceremonial axes of chiefs. This may be so, but it seems unlikely that they are to be connected with the Araucanian-speaking population found by the Spaniards; the form is so peculiar that some notice would probably have been taken of it by the early chroniclers. The inference is that they became obsolete in pre-Spanish times, but so few have been found, and in so small an area, that it seems at present unprofitable to discuss their origin.

Among the tribes of the Pampas and the Tehuelche, a similar social structure prevailed, and, though here too the heads of family groups exercised little power, they possessed nevertheless more authority than among the Araucanians. This was especially the case among the Tehuelche, of whose leading characteristics that of filial affection is particularly noticed by early travellers. The families of this people were grouped in clans, and some have suspected the presence of totemism from the existence of a legend that one clan once made war upon another because the latter had eaten a rhea. However, the cause of offence may have been simply an infringement of hunting-rights, or trespass. The rank of clan-chief was hereditary, one of the sons of the deceased chief being chosen to fill his father's post. Among the Araucanians marriage by capture, real or simulated, was the rule, among the Tehuelche and Pampas tribes, marriage by purchase. Among the second at least no man was allowed to marry until he had given proof of his prowess in war and the chase. The Araucanians sought their wives outside the tribe, but among the Tehuelche this practice was rather the exception than the rule except in the case of the chief.

Comparatively little is known of the religion of this area, but the information which exists appears to point to a worship of the powers of nature. The Araucanians adored a god named Pillan, who had his dwelling in the Andes and manifested himself in the fire and smoke of volcanoes, in lightning and thunder ; to him they made supplication in times of war and rejoicing, performing ceremonies of an elaborate nature. They also believed in a variety of subordinate spirits good and evil. The

Tehuelche seem to have reverenced a supreme god whom they invoked on hill-tops, but they also practised a cult of certain animal-shaped deities, who were supposed to inhabit caverns near particular lakes and mountains. These lesser deities were believed to have created and instructed men, and were probably clan-gods. Both Araucaniansand Tehuelcheemployed the servicesof professional shamanistic priests, whose duties were principally medical. Their method of treatment was more vigorous than scientific, and consisted in continual singing of charms and sounding of rattles, varied by suction applied to the seat of pain. The Tehuelche do not seem to have regarded them with very great awe, and a shaman who was believed to have caused the death of a tribesman was immediately killed. Priests in Patagonia might be of either sex, but were generally women.

Throughout the whole region, simple burial seems to have been the universal method of disposing of the dead, but, especially in Patagonia, a considerable variety of graves has been observed. The most common is a simple excavation in which the body is laid in a contracted position, and a cairn of stones piled on the top ; such cairns are both circular, and elliptical with a stone set on end at either extremity, and sometimes show signs of having been coloured red. Around lakes Colhué and Musters these cairns are common ; the stones have been heaped over the body, and hardly any excavation has been made in the ground for the reception of the latter. Here the corpse was usually arranged in a contracted position, lying on its side facing the east. In this locality no manufactured objects have been found associated with the burials, except one stone pipe, which was discovered in a grave surrounded by four others, placed one at each corner. Bones of the Patagonian hare have been found in the cairns, and may be the remains of funeral feasts. All these graves occur in spots affording a good view of one of the lakes, and some have interpreted this fact as an indication that these sheets of water were regarded as sacred. No remains of the horse have been found in these graves. In the Gallegos basin natural caverns have been utilized as burial-places, while advantage has been taken of natural crevices in the soil in the neighbourhoods respectively of Cape Blanco and Lake Colhué. On the coast the body is simply laid in the sand. The most elaborate form occurs on the upper Deseado, where the remains of several individuals are found within a circle of stones. Except in the case of the graves around lakes Colhué and Musters the implements of the dead were always laid with him among the nomadic tribes, and, in later times of course, his horse was sacrificed above his grave ; in Patagonia traces of what may be child-sacrifice have been found. The Tehuelche believed that the souls of the dead were born again. The primitive tribes which fringed the coast buried their dead extended at full length, the men apart from the women : provisions and the various possessions of the deceased were placed in the grave.

As before indicated, the population of this region derived its sustenance principally from hunting. The primitive coastal tribes collected shell-fish, caught fish and other marine animals by the aid of rude canoes, and shot sea-birds with bows and arrows. The Araucanians, the tribes of the Pampas and the Patagonians, pursued the huanaco and rhea, but though bows, and arrows with stone heads, were common to all, the Puelche tribes were distinguished by the use of the bolas. This weapon consisted of a stone fastened to one end of a cord of twisted hide, to the other end of which was attached a smaller stone ; the latter was held in the hand, while the first was whirled around the head, and the whole launched at the quarry so as to entangle it and prevent escape. The bola-stones, of which numbers have been found, are well-made and beautifully symmetrical ; the larger, or bola proper, may be one of several types, spherical or

ovoid with an encircling groove round which was fastened the cord (Fig. 31, *c*), or furnished with rounded
bosses separated by grooves which give the implement
a somewhat cubical outline (Fig. 31, *b*). The smaller
stones for holding in the hand are also of more than
one pattern—both bi-conical and spherical examples
have been found — but their method of attachment
was different, since they were enclosed in a small hide

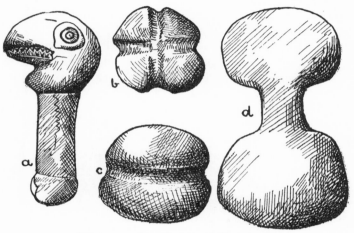

FIG. 31.—*a* stone "axe"; Chillan, Chile.
b and *c* bola-stones; lower Chubut R.   *d* stone axe, Chubut.
(*a*, ⅓, after Lehmann-Nitsche; *b*, ⅖; *c*, ½; *d*, ⅙; after Outes.)

bag to which the cord was fastened. They are also frequently furnished with a small depression in which
the knot of the cord fitted. The appliance was one
which, owing to its utility, was bound to be borrowed
by the peoples who came in contact with the Puelche,
and isolated finds of bola-stones have been made as
far north as Jujuy, as far south as the Chubut, and
also in Chile ; but it is known that the Chileans
were not using it at the time of the Spanish conquest,
and there is no mention of it among the Tehuelche
before 1776 ; in both cases therefore its presence must

be due to late Puelche influence. As regards the types of arrow-heads an elaborate study has been made of these and other stone implements by Outes, with the result that he has established the existence of a close similarity throughout the Tehuelche and Puelche areas; the remains of the Chubut valley, the lower Negro basin and the southern portion of Mendoza and the neighbouring provinces being especially closely akin. A difference exists between the arrow-heads of this area and those of Chile; by far the larger proportion of the former are furnished with a tang by which to secure them to the shaft (Fig. 32, *a*), whereas the latter have no tang (Fig. 32, *b* and *c*). The triangular form is the most common, and, at least in Patagonia, arrow-heads of bone were also in common use. As remarked above there is reason to believe that the original Araucanians practised a rude form of agriculture, whereas the tribes of the Pampas were purely hunters; the use of maize however was known to the Araucanian-speaking nomads, and meal and *chicha* were prepared from it. Agriculture was also practised in isolated parts of the island of Chiloe, where sharpened stakes were used for digging. The Querandies of Buenos Aires province indulged in a little cultivation, and also the Tehuelche, though to a very slight extent. The Patagonians usually ground their grain on a flat stone, with the aid of a rude pestle, but regular mortars have been found in Chile, on the Rio Negro, in Buenos Aires and on the Chubut. Whether the perforated stones which are so characteristic of Chile were used as the weights for digging-sticks is uncertain, since many of them seem too light for the purpose. A few of these objects have been discovered in Patagonia, and in the Andean region of Santa Cruz, but they were almost certainly brought from Chile. It is quite possible that they were club-heads, similar to the more elaborate specimens from Peru and Ecuador.

Besides hunting, the pursuit which was the mainstay of their existence, the nomad Puenche also played the part of traders in salt and textiles. Their wanderings took them far afield, and, at any rate in later times, bodies of them penetrated to the Atlantic shore and the Straits of Magellan. In their trading operations they played, of course, the part of middlemen, obtaining their wares from their more settled Araucanian neighbours ; it seems likely that this commerce is of comparatively late origin. Fire was produced by all the tribes north of Fuegia by the friction of two pieces of wood, one of which was used as a drill upon the other. In the treeless parts of Tierra del Fuego sparks were struck from two lumps of pyrites.

The Araucanian nomads were a very warlike people, as the Spaniards found to their cost, and it is safe to infer that, before they were forced to combine against a common foe, inter-tribal combats were very frequent. War was decided by the council of Ulmen, and the chief summoned the warriors by sending round an arrow dipped in blood, or, according to some, a blood-stained axe and arrow. The Tehuelche were a less quarrelsome and revengeful people, and though their habit of abandoning the aged and useless members when the tribe changed its residence seems cruel, yet in circumstances such as theirs the presence of the unfit was a public danger, and their reputation for hospitality would seem to prove that such a custom was imposed upon them by necessity. Yet wars between the clans were not infrequent, if we may judge from the numerous traces of battlefields which are found in their country. The arms of the chase were used in war, the bow and the bolas, and also spears ; though among the Tehuelche the last-named appear to have been borne by chiefs rather as *insignia* than as weapons. This people carried their arrows arranged in a sort of crest in their head-bands, and also used defensive armour in the shape of hide cuirasses, but the latter practice is not earlier than the eighteenth century. The Querandies of Buenos Aires, at any rate in their wars with the Spaniards, employed arrows armed with burning grass. Textile garments were manufactured in Araucanian territory, and also by the Querandies, but the true nomads clad themselves in skins, though the Patagonians wove narrow head-bands. In the north their clothing was of a limited description, but the Tehuelche, especially the women, were more fully clad in apron and cloak. Bone necklets and shell beads were worn as ornaments ; the Tehuelche used ostrich feathers for personal embellishment, and, locally, nose-pins and lip-ornaments. Silver pins and ear-ornaments, so common in later times, appear to have been introduced among the Tehuelche by the Puelche. A stone ring, found in a Tehuelche grave, appears to have been a breast-ornament. Foot-gear of sewn hide was worn in Patagonia, and paint was applied to the body as ornament both here and in Chile. A distinction is seen in the character of the habitations constructed respectively by the more sedentary and by the nomadic peoples. Where agriculture was practised in Chile, small huts were built ; elsewhere hide tents were erected. Those of the Tehuelche were large, of huanaco-skins stretched on a wooden framework ; they were divided into compartments by means of screens, and one such dwelling sheltered a number of families. Caves also were inhabited in the region of the Gallegos valley and the upper Deseado.

As might be expected in an area inhabited for the most part by nomadic tribes, there are few manufactures to chronicle. The weaving of the Araucanians has already been mentioned ; very rude pottery was made in Chile and also in Patagonia, but not in Fuegia or, apparently, by the Puelche, though fragments of coarse vases with impressed geometrical ornament (such as Fig. 34) have been found in the territory of the extinct Querandies.

By far the largest and most important class of remains is constituted by the stone implements, concerning which a few words must now be said. The implements of palæolithic type have already been mentioned ; these consist of knives of various shapes, oval, lanceolate and asymmetrical (Fig. 32, *i*), furnished with an edge all round, which in some cases shows traces of secondary

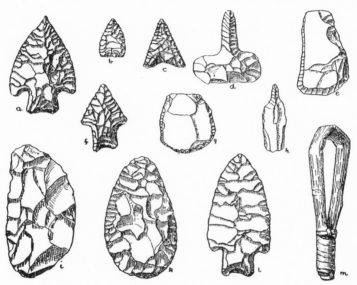

FIG. 32.—*a, d–l*, Patagonia ; *b* and *c*, Taltal (Chilean coast, about 25° S.) ; *m*, modern glass scraper, mounted ; Punta Arenas, Patagonia. (Scale, *a–l*, $\frac{4}{11}$; *m*, $\frac{1}{6}$; *d, e, g, h*, after Outes ; rest British Museum.)

flaking. Nearly all are surface finds except at Observacion, near cape Blanco, where they occur at some depth. Finds of similar implements have been made at Tandil, Lobos and Bahia Blanca in the province of Buenos Aires. The implements of neolithic type are all found on the surface, and were in use at the time of the discovery. As regards material the primitive stone-worker seems to have shown a preference for silicious rocks ; obsidian implements are found but are not common.

"Factories" have been discovered in the Sierras Colora-
das, a range of hills near and parallel to the coast between
the Rio Seco and the Rio Deseado, and it would seem,
from a study of the remains here, that the implements
were rough-hewn on the spot and taken away to be
finished at leisure. The ruder, and probably earlier,
specimens were shaped by direct percussion, the finer by
indirect percussion or pressure with some primitive tool,
just as the Fuegians at the present time fashion delicate
arrow-heads of glass by pressure with a bone. Thanks
to the labours of Outes, more can be said of the implements of Patagonia than of any other part of this area,
but even in Patagonia there are large tracts of which very
little is known, such as the region between the valley of
the Rio Negro and that of the Chubut, and again south
of the Santa Cruz. Up to the present, the richest sites
have been discovered in the valleys of these two rivers
and in the neighbourhood of lakes Colhué and Musters.
A certain amount of research has also been carried on in
the provinces of Buenos Aires and Mendoza.

The finds in general consist of objects of a type
familiar to students of prehistoric archæology. Small
"scrapers" (Fig. 32, *e* and *g*), worked along the edges,
were probably used in the preparation of hides; they
were no doubt fixed in a haft in the same manner as in
historical times (Fig. 32, *m*). "Perforators" of various
patterns (Fig. 32, *d* and *h*) are not very common, though
they have been found in Patagonia and in southern
Mendoza and were probably employed for making holes
in hides through which to pass thongs—a primitive form
of sewing. Knives (Fig. 32, *k*), varying in quality from
simple flakes with retouched edges to shapely blades
worked all over, are found in considerable quantities
from the Santa Cruz to Mendoza ; arrow-heads have
already been mentioned above, as well as the bola-stones,
characteristic of the Puelche region, and the perforated
stones which are in the main confined to Chile. Axes

seem to be characteristic of Chile and Patagonia, though in the latter region they are rare. The Chilean type is oval in section, narrowing towards the butt, sometimes regularly, sometimes somewhat abruptly. The most interesting of the Patagonian forms is an implement with a curious abrupt constriction at the centre (Fig. 31, *d*). Like all Patagonian axes,[1] the majority come from the lower Chubut valley, the rest from the lower Negro. Some of them are ornamented with shallow engraving, and they were probably hafted by bending a pliant branch round the "waist" of the implement and securing the ends with a lashing. In spite of the fact that this type is confined to a comparatively small region of Patagonia, its peculiarity has led some students to suppose that it must be referred to some intrusive influence; if this be so, that influence would probably be Puelche. In any case none of the specimens show signs of wear and were probably carried as *insignia* or reserved for ceremonial use. The remarkable bird-headed axes from south Mendoza and the neighbouring region of Chile have been described above. Other objects which may be mentioned are stone pipes of Puelche pattern from the lower Chubut; spindle-whorls from the Rio Negro, Chubut and Santa Cruz, and peculiar engraved stone tablets which are found over a more extended area from the Rio Negro to the Santa Cruz, and from the great lakes to the sea. An engraved pebble has been found at San Blas near Viedma in the province of Buenos Aires. In the same province, it may be noted, close to Corrientes implements of a very rude class have been found. These are plain oval pebbles from one end of which a few flakes have been removed so as to give them a rough edge. From their appearance they might date from the very earliest times, but they

---

[1] An aberrant type of axe has been found near lake Nahuel-Huapé on a tributary of the upper Negro; this has two projections at the butt similar to the axes found in the Andean region from the Calchaqui area to Ecuador (e.g. Fig. 4, *k*).

have been found only in the most recent stratum on the surface and cannot therefore be of any antiquity. We may summarize shortly as follows. Flaked implements of palæolithic type have been discovered in Patagonia and Buenos Aires ; while those of neolithic type are common to the whole area. The remains of the region between the Santa Cruz and the southern plains of Mendoza, including the southern corner of Buenos Aires, show remarkable similarity. Implements of polished stone seem to be of late introduction into Patagonia and in many cases show Puelche influence ; a close connection seems to exist between the lower Negro and lower Chubut in this respect, and from this fact Outes supposes that the latter region was occupied, at least temporarily, by a group of nomads who made a *razzia* from the north and became isolated there.

Brazilian Nuts.

From the Los Angeles Times.

South American connections are the Joneses, father and son. Recently Jones, jr., who had just returned from Brazil, was relating some rather tall stories of life down there, when he asked:

"Now, during that awful heat, what do you suppose it was, aside from the temperature, that made it impossible for us to take our after dinner siesta?"

"Why, what?" asked the gullible sister

"The peculiar noises," continued Jones, jr. "You see, the coffee was popping on the trees. The sun was so hot the grains just roasted before they were picked."

Whereupon dad yawned.

"Rather warm down there," he admitted. "But when I was in Brazil you couldn't sleep at night. Every once in a while there would sound the most extraordinary cracking noise that ever fell upon human ear."

"What were the sounds, dad?" asked Jones, jr., with a grin.

"The rubber trees stretching themselves," answered dad.

CHAPTER XII—EAST AND CENTRAL
SOUTH AMERICA

IT may appear absurd to attempt to deal comprehensively with this vast area, comprising Brazil, Uruguay, Paraguay and the provinces of Argentina confined between the rivers Uruguay and Parana, an area equal in extent to one-half the South American continent, but there are several reasons why such a course is advisable. Though very little is known of the archæology of the region in proportion to its enormous size, yet the researches made seem to point to a culture which is fairly homogeneous, belonging to a low evolutionary stage, and of no great antiquity. This homogeneity extends also to the geography of the area in question. That area consists of the highlands of the south and east of Brazil, which extend also into Paraguay and Uruguay, and the low plains which surround them, and which formed in very early times the bed of the great inland sea separating these highlands from the Andes (including at a later date the Patagonian plateau) and the highlands of Guiana. Nowhere were the physical conditions favourable to the development of an advanced culture ; the low-lying country to the north and north-west, drained by the Amazon and its tributaries, is covered with a vast forest so luxuriant as to exclude both light and air ; while that to the south-east is liable to periodical floods, when the rise of the Parana and Uruguay transform the country for miles into the semblance of a vast lake. The northern forest extends down the eastern coast, and even the higher ground of the coastal provinces of Brazil, at any rate in former times, was thickly wooded, with the exception of Ceara, which is subject to long-continued periods of drought. In the central uplands grassy country exists, but the soil is not very fertile. Except for the llama and its congeners, found only in the Andes, South America possessed no animal the care of which could give rise to a pastoral population, and the llama is not found in Brazil. In Uruguay, where the high country gradually loses itself in the plain, rolling grass-country is found, and here the early explorers discovered a nomad population of hunters, similar in mode of life and in character to the inhabitants of the Pampas.

The classification of the primitive tribes which peopled this region is not, and can hardly be, complete ; many of them disappeared soon after their discovery ; and very little is known of the rest. In any case no attempt to group them according to physical characters has yet been successful, and ethnologists have been compelled to fall back upon language as a determining factor. According to this criterion, four main groups of tribes can be distinguished : the Carib, whose original home appears to have been the upper Xingu, and who have spread thence over Guiana and the lesser Antilles ; the Arawak, who appear to have originated in the north, and to have occupied gradually the Orinoco and Amazon basins ; the Tupi-Guarani, who, starting probably from some point in the west or southern centre of this area, seem to have gradually worked down to the estuary of La Plata, and thence up the coast to the Amazon and even beyond ; and finally the Ges, who were the aborigines of the plateau district. The various and extended migrations of these peoples have rendered the distribution of their various tribes extremely complex, and it is difficult to point out an area of any size which is inhabited by one of them alone. In the main, the Carib and Arawak occupy the Amazon and Orinoco plains, the Tupi-Guarani and Ges the rest of the region.

It is to some extent doubtful how far the remains which are scattered over this huge area should be included in the purview of archæology proper. In so far as they represent a form of culture which has for the most part disappeared before the advance of white settlers, they stand on the same footing as those of the Andean region ; but the process of extinction has not proceeded so far, and there exist still many tribes living under conditions very similar to those of early times. Even in the localities from which the aborigines have vanished there are indications that their old habits were not abandoned so hurriedly, and there is little or no evidence to show that their remains are of any degree of antiquity, except in one case. The exception occurs in the province of Minas Geraes, where, at Lagoa Santa, a number of human remains were discovered which were associated with the bones of extinct mammalia usually regarded as typical of the pleistocene period. The human skulls which were there found have been shown to stand in relation both to those of the more primitive tribes of the Ges family, and to those found buried in some of the shell-mounds of the coast. The question of these shell-mounds, usually known as *sambaqui*, has afforded some difficulty, and the question of their origin, and that of the remains found in them, cannot yet be regarded as absolutely settled. Investigations, except in a few cases, have not been carried out with sufficient exactness, and details as to the exact position of the various finds are for the most part wanting. These shell-mounds are found scattered along the coast from the mouth of the Amazon to the most southern province of Brazil, as well as on the banks of the lower Amazon and Tocantins. It has now been proved that by no means all of them are due to human agency, such as the well-known kitchen-middens of the Danish coast. The larger mounds, amounting in some cases to over one hundred thousand cubic yards in volume, show many strata

s

each composed of a different variety of shell, and it cannot be supposed that the inhabitants of the shore confined themselves to a diet of one species of mollusc for many years together; it has also been shown that some of them occupy ground which was still under water in times prior to the advent of the white man. But other less enormous mounds undoubtedly occur, the composition of which proves their artificial origin. These consist of shells mixed with earth, bones of fish and mammals, charcoal, and stone implements, as well as remains of human skeletons. The human remains are buried simply and not enclosed in pots, a practice to which frequent allusion will be made later, and no traces of cannibalism have been found. The question as to how far pottery can be associated with the primitive tribes of the shell-mounds is not easy to settle. As regards the mounds of the southern provinces, competent observers have stated that pottery has never been discovered in their undisturbed interior; for the northern provinces exact information is lacking, and a further difficulty has been added by the fact that the mounds had been much disturbed, by those in search of shells from which to manufacture lime, before attention was called to their archæological importance. The mere discovery of pottery fragments on the surface of a mound is not sufficient to prove that the tribes responsible for the presence of the latter were acquainted with the art of working in clay, for the pottery may be due to latercomers. In fact it is probable that an invading people of higher culture would select convenient eminences in the low country on which to establish temporary settlements, or in which to bury their dead. The discovery at Laguna in Santa Catharina, on the sea-level, of remains of all periods, including a fragment of telegraph insulator, is sufficient to prove this. Fragments have been found in the surface earth of shell-mounds on the Amazon and Tocantins, and these may be placed in a similar category. They are few and of coarse manufacture and in any case could only be associated with the latest generations of mound-builders who might have learnt the art from more advanced neighbours. But if the

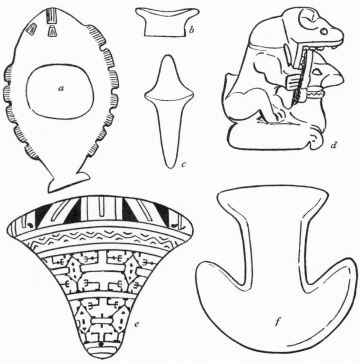

FIG. 33.—Brazil: *a* stone "palette"; Santa Catharina.
b stone lip-stud; Pernambuco.   *d* steatite carving; lower Amazon.
c stone arrow-head; San Paulo.   *e* pottery "tanga," island of Marajo.
     f stone axe, Minas Geraes.   (Scale, about ⅔; *a–e* after Netto.)

mound-builders were ignorant of the fictile art they were admirable workers in stone. In the mounds of Santa Catharina have been found numbers of small diorite mortars probably for grinding pigment, in the shape of fish or birds (Fig. 33, *a*), extremely well finished, and unlike any other objects discovered in the area under discussion. In San Paulo, finds have been made of peculiar bi-conical objects (Fig. 33, *c*), probably arrowheads, of syenite and serpentine, which show equal skill in manufacture. Besides these more striking objects, stone axes are common, and in the neighbourhood of many of the mounds are grooved rocks where they were polished. From such indications, then, as may be gathered from the method of burial, the nature of the human remains, the absence of pottery and the excellence of the stone implements, the conclusion is not unwarranted that the people, to whose presence these remains bear silent testimony, belonged to the Ges family, whose best-known representatives of the present day, the Botocudo, are good workers in stone, are ignorant of pottery, and do not practise urn-burial.

The shell-mounds must be distinguished from the many settlements of which traces are found along the shore, and inland on the banks of the rivers where exploration has been most active, and also from the artificial mounds of earth unmixed with shells in which native burials and remains have so often been discovered.

It is difficult to summarize results of investigations made throughout the rest of this huge area and assign the various shades of culture to their proper authors, without becoming tedious. Arguments based upon the quality and ornament of potsherds, or the pattern of stone implements, are apt to make extremely dull reading except to the enthusiast. Still, some picture must be drawn of the culture of the eastern portion of the continent if only to point the contrast between the conditions prevailing there and, on the other hand, in the Andes.

By far the largest proportion of remains consists of pottery, and it will be well to start with that of ruder type and more simple decoration, which occurs in the south, and proceed northwards to where, at the mouth of the Amazon, the art had risen to a considerably higher plane.

In Entre Rios and Corrientes, especially along the banks of the Parana, in the open country between Buenos Aires and Rosario, and in the more thickly wooded district from Rosario northward, many traces of aboriginal settlements have been discovered in the shape of pottery, stone arrow-heads and mortars, implements of

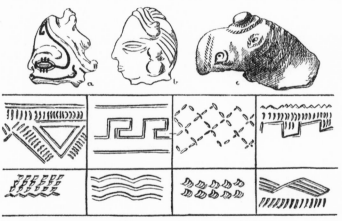

FIG. 34.—*a* head of pottery figurine ; island of Marajo.
b   „   „   „   ; Santarem.
c fragment of pottery vase ; Parana delta.
Below, impressed designs on pottery characteristic of Buenos Aires, Entre Rios and Corrientes.
(Scale, *a–c* about ¼.   *a* and *b* after Netto ; *c* after Torres.)

bone and antler, and human remains. The pottery shows considerable homogeneity, and from two localities as far apart as Campana, a little to the south-east of Zarate, and Goya, fragments which may be taken as typical of the district have been found. These are portions of small vases, of rather thick ware, mixed with sand and well baked, with the heads, chiefly of birds, in bold relief (Fig. 34, *c*). The modelling, if somewhat coarse, is vigorous, and the details are emphasized by impressed " string-patterns." Traces of a red slip are found on some of these. Fragments of other vases, with similar incised designs, mainly rectilinear, of dots, meanders, key-patterns, zigzags and series of diagonal lines (see Fig. 34), are also common. No great age can be attributed to these, since the mound at Campana, in which objects of this description are found, rests upon alluvial soil of quite recent date, belonging to the same formation as the islands of the delta.

Further north, on both banks of the Parana, in Missiones and Paraguay, pots with similar impressed ornament have been found; and, though the bird and animal forms peculiar to the last district do not occur, a finer class of pottery appears, with impressed designs of a like nature or patterns in red and black on a white slip. That there is no difference in age between the two styles is evident from the fact that representatives of both have been found enclosed in a large funerary urn. Similar painted and engraved pottery has been discovered in the islands of the Parana delta. We shall see that the ware of south-eastern Brazil also resembles that of Missiones, and it must be mentioned that the vases from cemeteries on the right bank of the Paraguay, right up in the Brazilian province of Matto Grosso, and even from two burial-places discovered by Boman in the Argentine provinces of Jujuy and Salta, display a similarity to the funerary pots of the upper Parana. Engraved ware was also manufactured by the semi-nomadic Charrua, now extinct, of the southern coast of Uruguay.

With regard to the forms in which the early potters of these districts made their vases, one feature is constant, a rounded base. The commonest types are globular or pyriform, the upper portion of the wall often inclining inwards more or less abruptly to form a shoulder, which is sometimes surmounted by an everted lip. As a rule the burial-urns are ornamented with rude impressed patterns.

In the southern provinces of Brazil, pots with designs, still of a similar character, painted in red, or less often black, on a white slip, become more common, though the engraved ware is still the more frequent; and in San Paulo painted decoration was sometimes applied to funerary urns also. The shapes are much the

FIG. 35.—Brazil: pottery urn; island of Marajo. (After Netto.)

same as those already described, with a rounded base, though in Rio Grande do Sul a more elaborate type, the outline of which suggests two or more bowls superimposed, has been found. In this region more information can be gathered concerning the method of manufacture. In the last-mentioned province the vases appear to have been formed by coiling long strips of clay around a suitably shaped stone, the coils being welded together subsequently, and the exterior and interior surfaces carefully smoothed with some primitive appliance. The Tapes, an extinct tribe living near the Lagoa dos Patos, amongst others, employed this process, and, further, fired their pots in a hole in the ground surrounded with stones. These Tapes produced vases, both of the painted and engraved types found elsewhere in the southern provinces.

But for the finest ware we must proceed further north, to the island of Marajo at the mouth of the Amazon. Here in the islet of Pacoval, which is apparently of artificial origin, situated in a lake, numbers of vases and funerary urns have been discovered, while similar finds have been made on the same island in certain artificial mounds to the south-west. Besides the superior quality of the pottery, the following are the features which distinguish it from that already described. The urns and vases (such as Fig. 35) are often made in human shape or are furnished with human features on the short necks ; applied and moulded ornament in relief is common; most vases are provided with a flat base; designs are frequently engraved in the white slip and filled with pigment ; the painted and engraved patterns are in the main conventionalized representations of the human face (Fig. 36). The pots appear to have been made by the coiling process, but are so carefully finished that no trace of the coils is seen ; in the case of the numerous figurines, however, they have been observed. After the vase had been allowed to dry, moulded ornaments in the form of grotesque lizards, human figures and faces, and the like were added, and a cream-coloured slip was applied in which delicate designs were engraved. A painted design was usually added, following the engraving or applied details, if such were present, and the pot was fired probably by the same process as that mentioned above. Some of the larger vases appear to have been made in more than one piece. Other types not found in the localities hitherto described are bowls with everted foot, and unornamented water bottles with narrow mouths (one somewhat similar, however, has been discovered in Missiones). The figurines are all very similar, being represented in a seated position with the legs apart, and the hands on the hips, under the knees, or clasped beneath the chin; the features are applied in

FIG. 36.—Engraved designs, derived from the human face, from pottery vases; island of Marajo. (After Netto.)

relief, and the nose and eyebrows are conjoined. The conical shape of the heads (Fig. 34, *a*) almost suggests that the inhabitants practised some form of deformation, but it may represent the method of dressing the hair.

A peculiar class of object, not found elsewhere, is constituted by the so-called *tangas* (Fig. 33, *e*), triangular in shape, and convex in section, which are found in the burial-urns of women. These are furnished with three small holes, as if for suspension, and it has been suggested that they are the " translations " into pottery of the small triangular leaf coverings worn by many of the women of primitive Brazilian tribes in historical times. They are ornamented with especial care in the same style as the vases. Other objects of pottery are engraved discs, sometimes with a cylindrical handle at the back, sometimes with a groove encircling the rim. The former may have been stamps, somewhat similar to those of the Chibcha, and the latter ear-ornaments.

Evidently allied to the inhabitants of Marajo were the people on the Ilha do Para, also in the Amazon delta, and on the opposite northern bank, on the river Maraca. Here are found natural grottos, artificially enlarged, which have been used as primitive mausolea, and contain burial-urns in human and animal shapes. An urn of the former type, found at Maraca, represents a man sitting on a stool (a more elaborate piece of modelling than occurs on Marajo), whose head forms the cover to the urn. Others, on Para, are furnished only with conventional human features on the neck. These are painted, the face in yellow, surrounded with a broad red border, the body of the vase with white meanders on a dark ground. A new type consists in a simple clay cylinder furnished with a cover; but this class of urn is evidently of late date, since one of them was found to contain Venetian beads of the sixteenth century. On the coast of Brazilian Guiana are found remains which may be related to those last mentioned, though the form of burial, in L-shaped pits, differs from anything else reported of this area. In these graves were found pots with similar patterns in red on a buff ground.

More closely allied to Marajo are some of the remains found further up the Amazon, in the neighbourhood of Santarem. Here heads of figurines have been found (Fig. 34, *b*), similar to those of Marajo, though more naturalistic. Still further off, near Atures on the Venezuelan bank of the Orinoco, a cave was discovered, containing ovoid burial-urns with lugs in the form of snakes and lizards, and ornamented with painted meanders and labyrinths. In this locality, however, many of the bones were deposited in leaf baskets, but the description of the pottery seems to point to some connection with Marajo. Near Santarem, in the neighbourhood of Itaituba on the Tapajos and on the banks of the Rio Negro, quantities of fragments have been found, which appear, however, to show greater affinities with the pottery of southern Brazil in some respects than that of Marajo. At the first locality the vases were

FIG. 37.—Brazil: funerary urn, Para.   (Scale, ¼.   British Museum.)

ornamented with thumb-impressions round the rim, or with designs painted on a white slip, but none with painted and engraved decoration. Applied ornament, in the form of spirals and meanders or the figures of men and animals, occurs, and must be attributed to influence emanating from Marajo. Similar finds have also been made on the lower Trombetas, and again in the plains of Erere, though in the latter locality the style of decoration is far more simple. Finally in Para burial-urns (Fig. 37) have been found with rudimentary human features in relief, and with flat bases.

The question of the manner of burial next arises. Some form of urn-burial is common over the whole area, from the river Plate to the Orinoco valley, but the method is not invariably the same. In some cases the body is placed in the urn entire, as in the Parana delta, Rio Grande do Sul, and Rio de Janeiro. Elsewhere the skeleton has evidently been disarticulated first, as in Uruguay, Para, Maraca and other parts of the Amazon basin, and Atures. In San Paulo and Marajo both methods appear to have been followed, though in the last locality the dismembered burials are far the more numerous. Urn-burial of the first class also occurs in Matto Grosso, on the upper Parana, and in the Bolivian Chaco. Simple interments without urns have been found on the lower Parana, and in the sambaqui of Santa Catharina, and this method was practised also by the Charrua in Uruguay.

Before attempting to draw conclusions from the variation in types of pottery and methods of interment, it will be as well shortly to summarize the other remains found throughout the area.

Stone axes of various types have been found everywhere, the most common being plain celts with pointed or rounded butts, some polished all over, others with the polishing confined mainly to the edges. In the present state of our knowledge no significance can be attached to this difference in type. More elaborate celts with semilunar blades and a projecting tang (Fig. 33, *f*) have been found in some numbers in north Brazil, in Para, on the Tocantins and in Maranhao ; a few have been discovered in Minas Geraes and San Paulo, and one in Rio Grande do Sul. Grooved celts, again, are rare in the south, though more common in the north, while slotted celts (such as Fig. 4, *i*) are confined to the Amazon valley and Guiana. These are the principal types, though a few other forms have been found locally. Chipped stone arrow - and spear-heads are confined to the most southerly provinces of Brazil, and the former have been found in Uruguay, Entre Rios, Corrientes, and Paraguay. Such objects are usually found in association with bolas-stones and sling-stones, which are characteristic of the same region. Stone pestles and rings (probably club-heads), again, appear to be more common in the south, and also discoid hammer-stones with a depression on either surface for the fingers.

To judge from finds of pottery and steatite pipes, the use of such utensils for smoking tobacco must have been more common among the southern tribes, though these pipes have been found as far north as Alagoas. The practice of piercing the lip, and wearing an ornament of resin or stone, was far more general, since these articles of adornment (called *tembetas*, 33, *b*), occur from Missiones to Marajo; and, though it is doubtful whether they were employed by the inhabitants of Rio Grande do Sul, they were observed by the early colonist among the Charrua of Uruguay. Finely-carved "amulets" have been found in the Amazon valley, especially on the lower Trombetas, representing animals in combat (Fig. 33, *d*) or men seized by jaguars.

To summarize this, perhaps rather wearisome, catalogue of finds ; we have, in the north of Brazil, an area characterized by vases in human form with flat bases, a white slip, and engraved, moulded, applied and painted ornament. The finest examples are found at Marajo, but the art seems to extend some distance up the Amazon, and even southward to Para. In the south, we have vases with rounded bases only, with impressed decoration of a rude character as a rule, and a lesser proportion of painted ware, the latter becoming less frequent as we proceed south ; human forms are absent. In the Corrientes and Entre Rios region of the Parana, painted designs are not found, but moulded decoration of a peculiar type occurs.

The natural inference is that these two styles, representing roughly the lower Amazon valley on the one hand, and the country further south on the other, must be attributed respectively to tribes of different stock; and that the peculiar style of pottery found in the neighbourhood of the Parana between Campana and Goya implies the presence of yet a third element in the extreme south.

When we come to consider the evidence from methods of burial, we find that secondary interment in urns is almost universal in the Amazon basin,[1] but that in the south both primary and secondary urn-burial is found, as well as simple interment on the lower Parana and in Uruguay. Now it is accepted that primary urn-burial (where the body is interred entire) is characteristic in the main of the Tupi-Guarani family, and that secondary urn-burial (where the skeleton is disarticulated) is characteristic of the Arawak, Carib and Ges. The distinction is not absolute, since it is known that Tupi-Guarani tribes used to preserve the bones of warriors who had fallen fighting outside the borders of their own district and bring them home for burial; it is known also that the Cayua, a Guarani tribe of the Rio Paranapanema, a tributary of the Parana, even abandoned urn-burial altogether in favour of simple interment, a fact which proves that changes in the mode of sepulture are not unknown among tribes of the Tupi-Guarani family.

So far indications seem to point to the hypothesis that the southern tribes belonged in the main to the Tupi-Guarani stock, with, possibly, an intrusive element in the most southerly part of the area. It seems as if the Ges must be left out of account until more is known of Brazilian archæology. There are reasons for believing that they were, for the most part, unacquainted with pottery, though some tribes must have acquired a knowledge of it from their neighbours, in which case their

[1] The evidence of primary interments on Marajo is not quite conclusive.

ware would hardly be distinguishable from the ruder pots of their tutors. Even the stone implements, until a more accurate classification is possible, can shed no light upon this question.

It would seem to follow that the remains in the more northern parts must be attributed to the Arawak and Carib. It is dangerous perhaps to attempt to disentangle the component elements of the archæology of this district until a more thorough survey has been made, but there are indications that two styles exist. Many of the remains on the uplands, e.g. on the lower Negro, at Cafezal on the left bank of the Trombetas, at Taperinha near Santarem, and in the plains of Erere, differ considerably from the pottery typical of Marajo. Even in Marajo itself a considerable variation in the quality of the ware has been observed, though for the most part only the finest pots and fragments have been brought away by collectors. But, at any rate at the time of the conquest, the most numerous and valiant of the inhabitants of the island were the Aruan, an Arawak tribe. Again the patterns on the Marajo pots are by no means unlike the painted decoration of those of the Cocama of the upper Ucayale, also Arawak. We may therefore, at any rate provisionally, set down the Marajo style as Arawak, the other as Carib.

Turning now to the extreme south, we have found indications of an intrusive element in the region which we have allotted in the main to the Tupi-Guarani. Though, as has been shown, at least one Guarani tribe has been known to abandon urn-burial in favour of simple interment, yet the peculiar pottery of the Parana between Campana and Goya gains an added significance when it is found associated with a form of burial which is at least extremely uncommon among tribes of the Tupi-Guarani stock ; and the suggestion of an intrusive element from the south becomes almost a certainty when the evidence obtained from the distribution of chipped arrow-heads and the bolas is considered. These two classes of object are associated with the form of pottery and the style of burial just mentioned. That their range is greater in a northerly direction is not surprising, since their utility is obvious, and stone implements pass readily from hand to hand. In witness to the latter fact it need only be mentioned that a score of diorite axes have been found on Marajo, no diorite being known in the Amazon valley below the first falls of the Xingu or the Trombetas. However, the presence of the bolas far north could not be expected ; it is a weapon which would be of no use in the forest, and, until the introduction of cattle, there was no animal on the open tablelands of Brazil which could well be hunted by this means ; nevertheless stone arrow-heads are not open to the same objection. In any case it is a fact that both these and the bolas are characteristic of the tribes of the Pampas.

Fortunately something is known of the extinct primitive peoples of Uruguay, and of the Tapes of Rio Grande do Sul.

The Charrua, already mentioned, were almost a typical Pampas tribe ; they were half-nomad, turbulent and taciturn ; individual freedom was a great feature of their social system, and their temporary chiefs, men of personal ability whom they consented to follow, had only a limited authority over them. The social system was patriarchal, the heads of families met in council to discuss tribal affairs, and the sons lived with their fathers until they married. They buried dead tribesmen in cemeteries on small hills, together with their weapons, and piled stones over the graves. Their huts were made of skins or branches, and their garments of hide. In all these features they resembled the tribes of the Argentine Pampas ; but they also made pottery, which they ornamented with engraved patterns, and their women wore lip-ornaments, habits which they had probably learnt from their neighbours. Other similar peoples existed in Uruguay, but others again were found whose customs suggest a Tupi-Guarani origin. Such were the Chana, northern neighbours of the Charrua, a peaceable folk who made good pottery and practised secondary urn-burial.

The Tapes, west of the Lagoa dos Patos in Rio Grande do Sul, also made pottery resembling that already described as typical of southern Brazil; but they used the bolas, and their social system seems similar rather to that of the Charrua. We are told that they spoke a language which did not belong to the Tupi-Guarani stock, and they have been set down as a Ges tribe in consequence, but it seems more likely that they were originally immigrants from the Pampas, though their migration probably took place at a date earlier than that of the Charrua. A further indication of influence exerted from the south is seen in the distribution of pipes of a pattern similar to those used on the Pampas. That they have spread further to the north is only natural, since geographical conditions, short of the absence of tobacco, would not set a limit to their range, and no customs are so readily borrowed as those connected with eating and drinking, under which head the smoking of tobacco must be included. Tobacco was of course known to the tribes in the north, but it was smoked in the form of cigars. We may conclude, therefore, that an intrusive element from the Pampas exists in the south, the original culture of which has become more or less modified by contact with the Tupi-Guarani.

Petroglyphs and pictographs, engraved or painted on rocks, have been discovered in nearly every state in Brazil, as well as in the Guianas. Many of them are situated at the falls of rivers, and some, in the northern portion of the region, bear a certain resemblance to those in Venezuela. In the north engraved designs are more common, in the south, painted ; but sufficient material

T

has not yet been published to render any classification possible. Most of them resemble childish scribblings, except in the Amazon valley, where more recognizable figures have been observed.

As indicated at the beginning of the chapter, none of these remains carry with them any indication of date, except that evidences of contact with Europeans have been found in a few cases. To these must be added the chevron beads found in a burial-urn at Linha in Rio Grande do Sul. Of the same province it has been stated that pottery fragments have been found in ancient settlements in such a position as to give rise to the belief that a plain unornamented type preceded one with a white slip and painted designs, and that rude impressed ornamentation was older than either. But this, though in itself probable, requires confirmation.

A few traces of Andean influence have been discovered, consisting of silver discs pierced in the middle, found in Rio Grande do Sul, and a copper axe of Peruvian type, exhumed on an island in the river Ribeira in San Paulo. Furthermore, Cabeça de Vaca observed small copper axes in use among certain Guarani, and it is probable that these also came originally from the Andes. Speaking generally, the tribes of this area were living in an age of stone, but the facility with which they worked it, and the quality of their pottery, show that many of them at least had made considerable progress in cultural evolution.

APPENDIX

FROM the sketch of South American archæology
given in the foregoing chapters the gaps in our
knowledge are only too apparent ; but it may serve a
useful purpose if they are shortly summarized, and some
indication given as to the localities where archæological
investigation is especially required. In Colombia, points
of particular interest are : firstly the north-west of the
province of Antioquia and the Darien portion of the
Isthmus, since they form geographically the connecting
link between Central and South America ; and secondly
the remarkable ruins of San Agustin, which have never
been properly investigated, and which might prove to
be connected with the early megalithic remains of Peru
and Bolivia, or with the coast of Ecuador. But as a
matter of fact the whole of Colombia is practically virgin
ground as far as the scientific explorer is concerned, and
it is earnestly to be hoped that the leaders of the G. G.
Heye Expedition, at present at work in Ecuador, may
ultimately carry out their intention of extending their
operations to this country. Venezuela, again, is practically untouched, and the highlands may yet yield remains of the greatest archæological value in determining
how far this region may be connected with Colombia.
Quite recently a number of remarkable black pottery
vessels, mostly in the form of animals, has been said
to have been found in the Santander province of Colombia, near the Venezuelan border. These are very rough,
and their appearance does not suggest any great age,
but the question might be worth investigation. In
Ecuador good work has already been performed on the

coast by the expedition already mentioned, but the highlands still require careful exploration, especially in the
province of Cuenca, where the remains may show some
connection with the north coast of Peru. In Peru itself, including Bolivia, much irreparable damage has been done
(as also in Colombia) by treasure-seekers; but the admirable work of Uhle has proved that, by means of careful
excavation carried out on proper lines, we may yet be
able to reconstruct the outlines of pre-Inca civilization.
Truxillo and its neighbourhood especially should be
the next sphere of research.[1] Of the inland parts, the
vicinities of the various Inca fortresses should be carefully searched for traces of the earlier population, beginning with the site of Chavin de Huantar, which has
never yet been adequately described. At Tiahuanaco
the work begun by Stübel and Uhle, and continued by
the Créqui-Montfort Expedition, should be completed,
and investigations inaugurated in the neighbourhoods
of Hatun-Colla and Chucuito. In any case the field is still
extremely rich, but the explorer must concentrate his
attention on a single area and be content to deal
thoroughly with a small neighbourhood before proceeding elsewhere. It is only by the patient collection
of detailed information that a firm basis for theories can
be prepared, and if the investigator can confine his attention to the details, and leave the theories for a later
stage, so much the better for his final results. In the
Argentine, archæological research is being carried out
on the proper lines by a small but extremely efficient
body of men, and it would be well if their enthusiasm
could be emulated in Peru, where the lifelong labours

---

[1] Since the above was written, Dr. Hrdlička has published a short
preliminary account of investigations in this neighbourhood (Smithsonian
Miscellaneous Collections, vol. 56, No. 16. *Some Results of Recent
Anthropological Exploration in Peru*), from which it appears that when his
collections have been studied in detail it may be possible to evolve for the
Truxillo district a more complete system of sequence-dating.

of Uhle have gained little encouragement and no local imitators. Thanks to local enterprise, assisted by expeditions from France and Sweden, a very good picture can be formed of the archæology of the Argentine highlands, and work of a sound scientific nature has been and is being carried on in Buenos Aires and Patagonia. Owing to the vast extent of the area to be covered much remains to be done ; in the north-west, the provinces of La Rioja and San Juan are still imperfectly explored, and the region between the Rio Negro and Rio Chubut, and again south of the Rio Santa Cruz, require investigation, which no doubt will soon be forthcoming. Of the great region occupied by Brazil very little is known, and the dense forest which covers so large a proportion of the territory renders archæological work almost impossible at present. Still an organized series of excavations in the shell-mounds on the coast, and along the banks of the Amazon and its tributaries, would be of the greatest value provided that the relative positions of the various finds were properly noted.

It may perhaps be useful to include in this appendix a short bibliography of works dealing in greater detail with the different regions of South America. To put forward a list of this kind is to invite criticism, since perhaps no two individuals would compile an exactly similar list. Let it be said at once that the following bibliography cannot claim to be more than some slight guide to those who wish to go more deeply into the subject of South American archæology.

Literature dealing with Venezuela from this point of view is remarkably scarce, but a very fair account of the remains found in certain limited areas, together with a history of the conquest, is given by G. Marcano in *Ethnologie Précolumbienne de Venezuela* (Paris 1899).

Colombia is more fortunate, in the *Historia General* of L. F. de Piedrahita (1688) and the *Noticias Historiales* of Pedro Simon (1627), of which the sixth book has been published in translation by the Hakluyt Society. Cieza de Leon, mentioned below under Peru, also gives much valuable information concerning Colombia. Of more modern authors, E. Restrepo Tirado and Vincente Restrepo have written admirable treatises on the natives. To the former is due *Estudios sobre los Aborigines de Colombia*, and *Provincia de los Quimbayas* (Bogota 1892); to the latter, *Los Chibchas* (Bogota 1895). A. Stübel and M. Uhle's large work, *Kultur und Industrie der sud-Amerikanische Völker* (Berlin 1889–90), illustrates a number of Colombian objects in gold and pottery.

For Ecuador, besides the writings of Cieza de Leon, we have the *History of the Kingdom of Quito*, published in 1789, by Juan de Velasco, and also passages in Zarate and Oviedo which are quoted in full in M. H. Saville's *Antiquities of Manabi* (New York 1907–10), a work dealing fully with the coastal districts. G. Dorsey's *Archæological Investigations on the Island of La Plata* (Field Columbian Museum, Chicago 1901) is also a valuable publication, and Gonzalez Suarez' *Los Aborigines de Imbabura e de Carchi* gives an extremely useful account of the northern provinces, though everyone will not agree with his theories. His *Atlas Arqueologico* should also be mentioned. The work of Stübel and Uhle mentioned above also figures a number of Ecuadorian antiquities.

In dealing with Peru we find a great mass of literature of which only a few books and articles can be mentioned here, notably a valuable bibliography of works dealing with Peru compiled by G. Dorsey (Field Columbian Museum, publication 23, 1898). Of the older authors many of the most important have been translated and edited by Sir Clements Markham, and published by the Hakluyt Society. These include the *Travels* of Pedro Cieza de Leon, a first-hand authority, and the *Royal Commentaries* of Garcilasso de la Vega, himself a great-grandson of Tupac Yupanqui, and perhaps the most readable of all the early historians. Besides these, the " official "

History of the Incas by Sarmiento de Gamboa, Acosta's *History of the Indies*, and the *Report* of Paolo de Ondegardo have appeared under the same auspices, together with works valuable for the study of Peruvian religion, as those of Salcamayhua, Avila, and Molina. Other authors of importance from the same point of view are J. de Arriaga, *Extirpacion de la Idolatria del Peru* (Lima 1621), A. R. Gavilan, *Historia de Copacabana* (Lima 1621, a book of great rarity, of which, however, a copy exists in the British Museum), and Calancha, *Chronica Moralizada* (Barcelona 1638), while the works of still other early writers will be found in the *Memoires sur l'Amérique* of Ternaux-Compans (including Montesinos, Balboa and Xeres), and the *Collecion de libros raros o curiosos* of Jimenez de la Espada. Before turning to more modern authors, mention may be made of A. A. Barba's *Arte de los Metales* (Madrid 1640), which gives details as to the indigenous method of smelting in Peru. Of later works, the *Peru* of E. G. Squier (London, 2nd ed. 1878) must be mentioned first, which is still the best general account of the ruins throughout the country. C. Wiener's *Pérou et Bolivie* (Paris 1880) is also interesting but not altogether reliable. From the historical side Sir Clements Markham's *The Incas of Peru* (London 1910) is the most valuable, since it contains the most modern theories, and is based upon an unique knowledge of the early literary sources ; in this book will be found an admirable summary of the early authors together with remarks upon their respective credibility, and also a translation of the drama of Ollantay. Of purely archæological works the *Pachacamac* of Max Uhle (University of Pennsylvania 1903) is the most important, especially when supplemented by the two papers published by the same author, in the *Report* of the Americanist Congress of 1904 (Stuttgart), on his subsequent researches at Moche and Nasca. It is greatly to be hoped that this author will soon have the opportunity of giving to the world the extensive material which yet awaits publication. Another important work dealing with the coast is Reiss and Stübel's *Necropolis of Ancon* (Berlin 1880–87), in three large volumes. Regarding the Peruvian highlands, an admirable account of Tiahuanaco is contained in Stübel and Uhle's *Der Ruinen-stätte von Tiahuanaco* (Berlin 1892), while the most recent researches are sketched by the Comte de Créqui-Montfort in the *Report* of the Americanist Congress mentioned above. The ruins on the island of Titicaca have been treated in detail by R. E. Bandelier, *The Islands of Titicaca and Coati* (New York 1910), and the same author has also published a description of the peninsula of Sillustani in Vol. VII of the *American Anthropologist*. This publication contains many useful papers both by Bandelier and by Uhle dealing with Peruvian archæology, while the Reports of the Americanist Congresses, and of the Société des Américanistes de Paris, include a variety of papers of great importance. Of books dealing in general with certain sides of Peruvian culture, may be mentioned the three works of A. Baessler, *Peruanische Mumien*, *Alt-Peruanische Metallgeräte* (both Berlin 1906) and the imposing four volumes of *Peruvian Art* (Berlin 1902–3) of which a translation by the late Prof. A. H. Keane exists. Stübel and Uhle's *Kultur und Industrie* must also be mentioned in this connection ; while the treatise on weaving by Max Schmidt, *Alt-peruanische Gewebe* (Baessler-Archiv I, 1, Berlin 1910), and Max Steffen's *Die Landwirtschaft bei den Altamerikanischen Kulturvölker* (Leipzig 1883), are worthy of special mention. From the religious side a paper by S. A. Lafone-Quevedo, *El Culto de Tonapa* (Revista del Museo de La Plata, III, 321), is suggestive, though the conclusions are liable to dispute ; but the book on the religion of Peru yet remains to be written.

As regards the Argentine Republic the literature is also extensive ; but a very good idea of the archæology can be gathered from a small book by F. F. Outes and C. Bruch, *Los Aborigines de la Republica Argentina* (Buenos Aires 1910), which contains a well-chosen bibliography. Another book furnished with a still more extensive bibliography, including also many works on Peru, is E. Boman's *Antiquités de la Région Andine de la République Argentine* (Paris 1908), which is an excellent work in every respect; while for other literature, all of it of great importance, the names of J. B. Ambrosetti, S. A. Lafone-Quevedo, and F. F. Outes may be sought in the British Museum Catalogue. In particular may be mentioned *El Bronce en el Region Calchaqui* (Buenos Aires 1904), and *Los Cemeterios prehistoricos del Alto Parana* (Buenos Aires 1895) by the first of these authors, *Tipos de Alfareria en la Region Calchaqui* (Rev. Mus. Plat. XV, 295) by the second, and *Alfarerias del Nordoeste Argentino* (Ann. Mus. Plat. I, 5) by the third. Other papers which may be consulted with advantage are R. M. Torres, *La Cuenca ael Rio Parana* (Rev. Mus. Plat. XIV, 53) and J. H. Figueira, *Los Primitivos Habitantes del Uruguay*, while the *Revista* of the La Plata Museum, so often cited, is a veritable storehouse of knowledge concerning this region.

For Chile the literature is far less abundant. The works of J. T. Medina, including his *Aborigines de Chile* (Santiago 1888), contain a great deal of information, and the paper by R. E. Latcham, *Anthropologia Chilena* (Rev. Mus. Plat. XVI, 241), gives the latest theories regarding this region. Two papers by O. H. Evans (Man 1906, 12, and 1907, 41) give a good idea of the coastal district of Atacama, while the work of Boman, mentioned above, deals in part with the inland region.

Of Patagonian archæology, as far as the remains of early man are concerned, a treatise edited by R. Lehmann-Nitsche called *Nouvelles Récherches sur la Formation Pampéenne* (Rev. Mus. Plat. XIV, 143) not only sums up the excavatory and geological evidence in masterly fashion, but gives references to the works of others, principally of Ameghino, who have laboured to elucidate the problems presented by Patagonian archæology. This paper, taken in conjunction with the admirable work of F. F. Outes, *El Edad de la Piedra en Patagonia* (Buenos Aires 1905), gives practically a complete picture of our knowledge of ancient Patagonia.

Brazil cannot boast of a literature commensurate with its great size. The most important treatises are perhaps C. F. Hartt's *Contribucões para a Ethnologia do Valle do Amazonas*, and L. Netto's *Investigacões sobre a Archæologia Brazileira* (both in the Archivos do Museu Nacional do Rio de Janeiro, VI), and H. von Ihering's *A Civilisacão prehistorica do Brazil Meridional* (Revista do Museu Paulista, I). To these may be added two papers by E. A. Göldi in the *Report* of the fourteenth Americanist Congress (Stuttgart) and a number of papers, by Ehrenreich, von den Steinen, Kunert and others, published at intervals in the *Zeitschrift für Ethnologie* (Berlin).

The works given above, as before stated, constitute in no sense a complete list, but they will at least form a nucleus, or a series of nuclei, around which students may construct their own bibliographies if they desire to become more closely acquainted with the fascinating problems of South American archæology.

INDEX

Manabi, 63–65, 67, 70, 72–74, 81, 181, 184, 189
Manco, 78–80, 86, 100, 112, 153, 157, 175
Manizales, 35, 42–44
Manta, 52, 59, 67
manure, 120, 121, 220
Maori, 116, 190
maps, 215
Maraca, 266, 268
Marajo Id., 188, 264, 266–272
Maranhao, 268
Marcano, G., 277
Markham, Sir C., 48, 75, 77, 98, 119, 134, 160, 205, 212, 213, 278, 279
marriage, 22, 23, 101, 105, 110, 117, 159, 208, 245
Matto Grosso, 262, 268
Maule R., 48, 75, 97, 101, 216, 220, 221, 240
Maya, 177, 191
Mayta Ccapac, 78, 88
Medina, J. T., 281
Mendoza, 236, 243, 248, 252, 253, 254
metallurgy, 40–42, 70, 103, 140, 208, 212, 223, 231, 232
Mexicans, 7, 12, 29, 134, 207 (See also Maya)
Michua, 15, 16
migrations, 10, 50, 52, 221, 241, 242, 254, 256, 273
Minas Geraes, 257, 268
mining, 103, 208
Missiones, 262, 265, 266
mitimaes, 75, 105, 197, 219, 221
Moche, 179, 181
mojos, 2
Mojos L., 2
Molina, C. de, 160, 162
Moluche, 240–242
Montesinos, F., 77, 78, 80, 81, 83–86, 88, 90, 91, 94, 100,

102, 116, 168, 186, 187, 189, 213, 220, 279
moon-worship, 11, 25, 27, 66, 153, 154
Mortillet, A. de, 210
Moxo, 76
mummies, 26, 34, 35, 64, 144–146, 148, 149, 153, 154, 156, 157, 159, 167
musical instruments, 21, 31, 32, 46
Musters L., 245, 246, 252
Muzo, 10, 12, 15, 24, 26, 33, 42, 43

Nahua (See Mexicans), 7, 12, 29, 279
Nahuel-huapé L., 253
Nasca, 95, 106, 108, 119, 148, 177, 179–186, 191, 196, 229
Naymlap, 50, 51, 54
Negro R. (Brazil), 267, 271
Negro R. (Patagonia), 236, 240–242, 248, 252–254, 277
Nemequene, 16, 17
Nencatacoa, 27, 28
Netto, L., 282
Neuquen, 236, 243
Nompanem, 14, 21
nose-ornaments, 18, 24, 25, 30, 32, 35, 36, 61, 130, 250
Nutabi, 9

Observacion, 238, 251
Oliva, D. de, 11
Ollantaitambo, 133, 136–138, 185–187, 214
Ollantay, 212, 279
Omaguaca, 234
Ona, 242
Ondegardo, P. de, 148, 279
Orinoco R., 2, 256, 266, 268
ornaments, 18, 20, 24, 25, 36, 45, 61, 62, 110, 129–132, 225, 234, 250. (See ear-ornaments, lip-ornaments, nose-ornaments)